NORTHERN TIGERS

NORTHERN TIGERS

BUILDING ETHICAL CANADIAN CORPORATE CHAMPIONS

A MEMOIR AND A MANIFESTO

DICK HASKAYNE

WITH PAUL GRESCOE

KEY PORTER BOOKS

To my parents and my brother who taught me the fundamentals of business and the importance of ethics to the sucess of our free-enterprise system.

Library and Archives Canada Cataloguing in Publication

Haskayne, Richard F
    Northern tigers : building ethical Canadian corporate champions / Richard Haskayne, Paul Grescoe.

ISBN-13: 978-1-55263-876-7, ISBN-10: 1-55263-876-6

1. Haskayne, Richard F. 2. Success in business—Canada. 3. Business ethics—Canada. 4. Businessmen—Canada—Biography. 1. Grescoe, Paul, 1939– 11. Title.

HC112.5.H38A3 2007   338.092   C2006-906433-4

The publisher gratefully acknowledges the support of the Canada Council for the Arts and the Ontario Arts Council for its publishing program. We acknowledge the support of the Government of Ontario through the Ontario Media Development Corporation's Ontario Book Initiative.

We acknowledge the financial support of the Government of Canada through the Book Publishing Industry Development Program (BPIDP) for our publishing activities.

Key Porter Books Limited
Six Adelaide Street East, Tenth Floor
Toronto, Ontario
Canada M5C 1H6

www.keyporter.com

Text design: Marijke Friesen
Electronic formatting: Jean Lightfoot Peters

Printed and bound in Canada

07 08 09 10 11 5 4 3 2 1

CONTENTS

INTRODUCTION

IT WAS LIKE BEING ALIVE and well at a big, cheerful wake following my own funeral. The nearly nine hundred people gathered at the Hyatt Regency in Calgary that evening had come not to bury me, Richard Francis Haskayne, but to praise me. If it was all a bit embarrassing, it was also wonderfully heartening to hear myself eulogized, and occasionally roasted with good humour, to learn what my friends and colleagues really thought of me.

There was some irony, however, in the fact that the institution organizing this tribute was American and even named after the twenty-eighth president of the United States. I was receiving the Woodrow Wilson Award for Corporate Citizenship from the Woodrow Wilson International Center for Scholars at the Smithsonian Institution. I was one of only five Canadians so honoured. Yet whatever reputation I had with my peers rested in part on my belief that Canada must have many more homegrown, domestically based companies of ambitious scale and scope—the kind of corporations that some people, me included, describe as Northern Tigers.

In nature, according to *The Tiger Handbook*, "Northern tigers live in a colder climate and need a larger body to stay warm." In the jungle of business and industry, size is only one attribute that corporations must have to survive and flourish, both in Canada and the world. I've always felt that Canadians should be not only creating but also controlling their own business enterprises, keeping them headquartered in this country, and building them to be strong and nimble enough to withstand takeover attempts from foreign interests seeking control.

I'd been at the centre of one such takeover not long before, as the last chairman of the lumber giant MacMillan Bloedel of Vancouver. And at the time of my tribute, I was on the board of the American company that had acquired it, Weyerhaeuser of Washington State. Given the circumstances, I was glad to be a director, an insider who might continue to favourably affect the fortunes of the thousands of men and women in Canada who still earned their livelihoods working in our Canadian forests and mills and offices.

I'd been a director of seven other Canadian companies: EnCana Corporation, Canadian Imperial Bank of Commerce, Manulife Financial, Hiram Walker Resources, Crestar Energy, Husky Energy, and Royal LePage. As chair or president, I'd also helped run eight other major domestic companies: Hudson's Bay Oil and Gas, Home Oil, Interprovincial Pipe Line, Interhome Energy, NOVA Corporation, TransAlta Corporation, TransCanada Corporation, and Fording Inc. In the chapters that follow, through the lens of my long career, I show how some companies I've been involved with have created sound strategies and executed them wisely to become true corporate champions—Tigers—and how others have failed.

This book is both a memoir and a manifesto—a capitalist manifesto. One of its three major themes is my long-standing plea to raise the bar on ethical behaviour in business. As I said in accepting the Woodrow Wilson Award, "We have entered a time of extreme cynicism that naturally results from a great many widely publicized corporate scandals. Some people are so critical that they suggest the term 'corporate ethics' has become an oxymoron."

Another theme is what I view as the enormous need for private philanthropy—not simply the largesse of corporations and governments, but *personal* contributions of time and energy as well as welcome cash to charitable, social, cultural, and educational institutions.

But the overarching theme is that, in a ruthless global economy, Canadians increasingly need to develop our companies into powerful, influential Northern Tigers that make all the major decisions at home, not in some far-off foreign head office. If we don't, we'll continue to lose a lot more MacMillan Bloedels. I still vividly—and painfully—recall that day in the spring of 1999 when I received a phone call from MacBlo's president, Tom Stephens. I was in no shape to field any unsettling news. My wife, Lois, was trying to shield me from all potentially disturbing communication with the outside world as I recovered at home in Calgary from an emergency heart bypass operation.

I took the call because Tom had recently been brought in to restructure and resurrect the failing west-coast forest giant. It had been rudderless for too many decades and failed to grow through consolidation in a fiercely competitive industry. Now Tom was telling me that an American giant was coveting MacBlo, a widely held Canadian public company. And I was soon sadly aware that even in my three-year role as chairman, I found it difficult to oppose the takeover because of the company's poor stock performance. It was unsettling to preside over the demise of a corporation that had once helped define British Columbia and might one day have evolved into a possible Tiger in the world of forestry.

During my career, I've been front and centre as an unwilling witness to other corporate deaths. But fortunately, I was also involved in many more successes among Canadian companies that exhibit the qualities of the natural world's tigers: strength, nimbleness, single-mindedness, and, perhaps most important of all, a deep respect for their habitat, their home ground.

As for me, my roots are in the nurturing rural community of Gleichen, Alberta, where I was the son of an entrepreneurial couple, met and married my first wife, Lee—and long ago learned the importance of honouring where you come from.

Chapter One

A BUTCHER'S SON
Gleichen and Beyond

HIGHWAY I EAST OF CALGARY runs straight as a ruler across the level Alberta prairie for much of the hour's drive to the hamlet of Gleichen, Wheatland County. The Trans-Canada cuts through countryside that is lush with grain and, here and there, heavy with loose herds of cattle. It's all as familiar to me as my own skin. On this mellow late-August morning, I was aware only now and then of its touchstones and waymarks, the odd long curve and the occasional low rise of farmland. Immersed in my memories of all the decades I'd driven this road, I was heading to Gleichen for a homecoming during Alberta's centennial. Gleichen is the community that helped shape me, with people whose integrity and example combined to create an ethical foundation on which to build my own career. They inspired, instructed, and then actively prodded me to look well beyond its borders to a wider universe of education and opportunity. One teacher was a little more direct than others: "If you don't go on to university, you deserve a swift kick in the ass." That was language I understood. Everything important I know about life and business today, I learned in Gleichen.

Three-quarters of the way there, you pass through much-larger Strathmore, one of the original sidings along the Canadian Pacific Railway that knit this country together in the late nineteenth century. The land starts to roll in gentle gold and green hills. Far off on the horizon looms the spindly legged water tower that was once the tallest structure on the southern Alberta landscape. It still locates

Gleichen, which is another CPR stop that began as a ranching centre and a jumping-off point for settlers. These days the old tower, like the hamlet itself, is in need of work, and maybe I could help out. A road sign marks the neighbouring Siksika Nation, the Blackfoot Reserve with the Bow River running through the middle. A few kilometres further, after a long incline, is the buffalo jump where Blackfoot hunters once herded bison over an escarpment to their deaths. When I was growing up here, Native kids—Kenny Bigsnake, George Manyshots—were some of the best hockey players on our local teams. As a defenceman on the Bassano Damsiters, I learned how to be a team player, collaborating with tough guys like Larry Plante (who ate glass as a party trick).

Turning off the highway, I passed the sign announcing Gleichen with its ambitious motto—"Glorious Past/Greater Future"—and stopped at the water tower. A couple of old friends, the Hnatiuks, were driving by and pulled over. I used to date Gwen's sister, Ann, in high school. "Thanks for getting Fording up there," remarked John, a happy shareholder in Fording Canadian Coal Trust of Calgary. Not long ago, I'd been chairman of the original company, helping fashion a merger that turned it into the world's second-largest shipper of metallurgical coal as well as an attractive stock. "Fording's now 20 percent of the total metallurgical exports in the world," I told him. In any account of what I describe as Northern Tigers—corporations with head offices in Canada that are big and strong enough to fend off foreign takeovers without government protection—Fording ranks high.

After we chatted awhile, I continued on down Sixth Avenue into town. What I didn't notice for a few minutes, until a friend with me pointed it out, was that the signs along the road all read "Haskayne Avenue." My parents would have been so damn proud to see the family name up there. And proud to know that their son, who'd learned ethical behaviour from watching them become part of the heart and soul of their community, was being honoured in this way. It was an overwhelming moment for me. I realized that my friends back home still considered me to be one of their own, decades after I'd left for university and life in the big-city corporate arena—rather than taking over my folks' butcher shop or going into a bigger business with my brother, Stan.

Main Street, which used to be a gravel road with wooden sidewalks, is paved today. But there's just an empty lot on the former site of the Pioneer Meat Market (R.S. Haskayne, Proprietor), which looked like the flat storefront of a western movie. We all lived there in the house behind the shop during the Depression and war years, often taking in relatives and out-of-town teachers. In the shop, during those tough years, Bob and Bertha Haskayne dispensed overweight cuts of meat to impoverished customers. They were the definitive small-town entrepreneurs. Dad used to say, "The only thing you have in the world is your independence, and you have to have the money that allows you to be independent." But what I knew from watching him and Mom at work was that true independence means not just having the money, but also making sure you earn it in honestly. As a teenager, after the three dairies closed down in a declining Gleichen, I used to sell tokens to townspeople that they traded for bottles of milk that I collected off a train each day. Between that entrepreneurial venture and working for my folks in the shop, I'd earned enough money to put myself through the University of Alberta, the first of the Haskaynes to go beyond high school.

My memory lane led me to the end of Main, where the local library inhabits one of two remaining classic red-brick buildings. The sign below the eaves still identifies it as a branch of the Canadian Bank of Commerce. As a high school student in nearby Cluny, I deposited the paycheques of my trusting teachers in their accounts there. Many years later, I was to sit as a director on the board of the amalgamated Canadian Imperial Bank of Commerce, which, like our other big domestic banks, has many of the qualities of a Northern Tiger. But it's hard to get a swelled head in your hometown: I recalled that just down the street from the bank, Doc Farquharson, a doctor and pharmacist, had run a drugstore and soda fountain where I bought milk bottles with nipples that I was still enjoying as a late-blooming five-year-old. I didn't give up the habit until my parents convinced me to hand over the bottle to

Santa Claus to pass on to some poor kid. What I didn't know was that the Santa who accepted my reluctant offering was my father in a fake beard. He was the same determined individualist who had scheduled a chilly bicycle race with two buddies for Christmas morning only a week after I was born. "It will start at the nuisance ground and end up in town," the *Gleichen Call* had announced with mock solemnity.

MY PARENTS WERE IMMIGRANTS from Liverpool, who still spoke with the round Liverpudlian accent when I was growing up. My grandfather was a butcher, so it was no surprise that his son got into the business. In 1913, my father came to settle in Calgary first, working for the fabled Pat Burns just a few months after a fire had destroyed Burns's cold-storage plant and warehouses, the biggest meat-packing business in the West. Bertha, a publican's daughter, followed Bob to Canada that year and married him in a double wedding with her brother Jack and his Marion—and Jack also became a butcher. Dad then went to work as a meat-cutter and Mom as a feed-yard cook in Gleichen for the Pacific Cold Storage chain of slaughterhouses and butcher shops. The area had been a hub of the Blackfoot and buffalo trails leading to Calgary and Montana. It was the site of the historic Treaty #7, where five Native tribes surrendered their land rights and became wards of the nation in 1877. Six years later, Gleichen was a logical locale for a station when the CPR came through. (The town, named for a German count who'd invested in the railway, should have been pronounced *Glai*-khen, instead of the *Glee*-shen its residents have always called it.)

In 1913, Gleichen's population was at its peak, home to two thousand people and the livery barns, barrooms, and shops that served ranchers raising mixed breeds of cattle and homesteaders farming wheat and oats on the rich, deep-brown soil. My brother, Stanley, was born the following year. In 1920, my folks bought a meat market in nearby Carseland, where the sleeping quarters upstairs were so cold that Stan said the water pipes froze and the walls were white with frost. Nine years later, they sold it to take over another one in Gleichen: Pioneer Meat Market, which they ran with spotless coolers and sawdust on the floor.

My parents were all-around butchers; they bought the local animals and birds, killed and processed them, and then sold the beef, veal, lamb, pork, and poultry, often with a marketing flair ("A set of carvers will be given away as a Prize to the person guessing the weight or nearest correct weight of a carcass of beef we will have on display," one Christmastime newspaper ad read). The Haskaynes quickly became indispensable strands in the fabric of the community. Mom—the Missus—was a stout, short woman with jet-black hair who loved the world and everyone in it. Dad— the Old Man—was slim, nearly six feet tall, and sandy-haired. He was much more reserved than Mom, but had a dry sense of humour that emerged in surprising and sometimes ribald ways. When customers asked him why he saved the wood bungs from the ends of wrapping-paper rolls, he said he sold them: "They're wooden assholes for hobbyhorses" (he's probably the reason I still swear too much).

While his wife was a teetotaller, my dad sometimes drank a little more than he should, sneaking shots of rye from the bottle reserved for houseguests, and replacing them with tea. Walter Hayes was one of our boarders, the son of family friends, and he remembers Bob coming home from a pub and telling his buddy the town blacksmith, "C'mon, the Missus will cook you a steak."

Bertha, looking down from a window, said, "Go get your own damn steak where you got your beer."

When he drank, Dad became argumentative. During one session, he took a bet that became a Gleichen legend. The challenge was to set a record time for collecting a live cow and then dressing its whole carcass into marketable cuts of beef. He had a friend drive him the mile to the slaughterhouse, where he butchered the animal, and then back to the shop—all in twenty-one minutes, forty seconds. As much as making bets, my dad liked singing and playing the accordion, talents I didn't inherit. He also loved telling stories, like the one about the woman who came into the shop one day and asked the price of lamb chops.

"Ninety-nine cents a pound."

"Oh, they're expensive," she said. "Across the street, they're only eighty-nine cents a pound."

"In that case, why don't you go across and buy them?"

"They don't have any today."

"Well," my father replied, "when we don't have any, we sell ours for seventy-nine cents a pound."

My brother was twenty and my mother forty-three when I arrived on the scene during an Indian summer–like December 18, 1934. I was a surprise package: At first Mom thought the swelling in her belly was a tumour ("and it was just that damn Dick"). The week before my birth in a Calgary hospital, the *Gleichen Call* coyly made reference to my parents' living quarters with a two-line item: "Bob Haskayne now calls his apartment block Cupid's Retreat." The *Calgary Daily Herald* optimistically reported more momentous news of the day: "Peace and Goodwill Spread in Europe: Gen. Goering Calls for Friendship with Britain" and "Relief Situation Brighter: For every month of 1934, with the exception of August, reductions are shown in the number of persons on relief in Canada."

But the Depression still had a chokehold on the country, and, while we were no poorer than anyone else in town, some Canadians were suffering a lot more than others. The *Call* reported that a well-educated, local Blackfoot farmer, who was ill and grieving the death of a son, shot himself in the heart with a rifle. And, a few days after I was born, an old man on the reserve at Gleichen was found frozen to death in the snow. My folks were always kind to the Natives who came to shop wearing moccasins and carrying papooses, and who sometimes, with their government-subsidized meat rations, were better customers than struggling farmers. In fact, the Haskaynes were noted for being nice to everyone, as Ralphene Hayes (Walter's sister) recalled years later. Her parents supplied the butcher shop with four-hundred-pound blocks of ice from a frozen coulee to keep the meat chilled through the hot prairie summers (Gleichen hit a Canadian record the summer of 1903 when the temperature registered 115 degrees

Fahrenheit). Ralphene was an observant young girl who roomed with us while attending high school in town and even changed my diapers. "To a growing child, Bertha was special—a kindred spirit," she said. "Her generous heart was all-encompassing (her teapot was never cold), and she always found the best in everyone from young to old."

Dad gave kids who visited the shop a raw wiener to chew on, and his favourites got an ice cream cone from the house. Both he and Mom looked after their poorer customers like a couple of Robin Hoods. She might ask how much cash someone with a big family had to spend that day, and if the reply was $2, she'd plunk a roast worth $4 on the scale and say it cost $1.90 (and I wouldn't be surprised if she charged well-off customers double). Ralphene's son, Stu Bolinger, who now runs one of the largest farming operations in the area, has his own memories of my mother's generosity: "There were some seedy old bachelors who Bertha would get into shape. It just wasn't in her genes to turn anybody away."

I was always impressed by my dad's integrity. When farmers brought their animals to him for carving up for their family dinners, he insisted (unlike many butchers) on saving the surplus bones for his clients. The idea was that they could weigh the bones and the cuts of meat together to see if they added up to the animal's original weight—and be assured that he hadn't slipped a few of their steaks and roasts into his own cooler.

Mom belonged to every club in town and cooked turkeys to support the causes of any denomination. My parents went to the Anglican church every Sunday, and the ministers came to our house after the service for a lunch of lamb chops. Among them was Reverend Douglas Ford, who later became the bishop in Calgary—he used to slip off his jacket at our house and sing popular songs like "Elmer's Tune." My folks sent me to Sunday school, which, like most organized religions, didn't capture my imagination. Dad was a Mason, and Mom was an active member of the Order of the Eastern Star, but when I got older and was invited to join the Masonic Lodge, I declined.

I liked the idea of regular school, though—so much so that Betty Bolinger, Stu's aunt, said that as a five-year-old, I sat longingly on the steps of the Gleichen elementary school day after September day. Because I was born late in the year, I couldn't start classes till the following term. I kept bugging Doc Farquharson, the druggist and school-board chairman, who finally said, "Oh, hell, let him go." He gave me a pencil and paper, and I ran to school without bothering to tell my mom. She sent the whole town out to look for me.

There's no question my parents doted on me. The only spanking I ever got was Mom swatting me on the behind with a cloth when I was bothering her in the shop. For a small-town boy, I was dressed pretty well, too. Ed Plante, my friend Larry's brother, tells his buddies: "I got Dick's hand-me-downs. He used to be dressed up like an English boy—breeks and long socks." Larry, who also wore some of my cast-offs, says: "Dick the Englishman looked a helluva lot better than Larry the Frenchman." Stu Bolinger insists the whole town doted on little Dick. "In the era you were born," he reminded me, "there was still a lot of strength in western communities—in mentorship and the skills these people brought. People would care for each other. You were raised during the war years when Canada had a job to do. Watching you grow up, I know you had a wonderful sense of support and love. The crucible that shaped you was the community." I have to agree with Stu's comment: In a caring small town, you have all these constituencies observing you—parents, teachers, neighbours—and if you do anything wrong, everybody knows about it.

We did get involved in some hijinks, of course. Larry, the class clown who was raised as a Catholic, had the job of lighting a fire Saturday nights at the United Church. He got a bunch of us boys together more than once to perform make-believe services, complete with his attempt at speaking in mock Latin while we knelt and stood and counted the rosary beads—until an amused Reverend Morrison witnessed the indiscretion and then Larry's less-forgiving dad put a stop to it. Jeanne Sauvé, who went to school with me as a Corbiell, reminisces about how my brother had just bought several calves fresh from a 4-H show when a group of tipsy teenaged boys and girls, me included, rode them bareback. The next day, my dad was wondering why the hell all the animals were so badly bruised.

My brother, two decades older, was like a second father to me. I missed Stan badly when he volunteered for the Canadian Army during the Second World War and went to fight in Europe. What I realize now was that he didn't have to go—as a thirtyish husband and father with his own butcher shop in neighbouring Bassano— but his sense of integrity made him lease his business and sign up. Luckily, he came back unscathed, and we became even closer as I entered my teens.

Right from the start, I took to school with abandon. Mrs. Sherbach, a calm disciplinarian, taught three of the upper elementary grades together. A marvellous teacher who commanded respect without using the strap, she had a big impact on my deep desire to learn. For high school, Gleichen students had to go to Cluny by bus, and later, my dad let me drive his half-tonne truck to Bow Valley Central, which made me popular with the other local kids. We were a mixed bag: the offspring of farmers, town merchants, and Native families (my classmates included Alice Owlchild and John Yellow Old Woman). Though I got up up before six o'clock in the morning to do all my homework, beginning a lifetime habit of rising early, I was never quite at the top of my class. That spot was reserved for Adele Corbiell, an auburn-haired beauty whom I dated for a long time and might have married. She not only had the highest marks but also sang like a bird, played the piano, and was the student social convenor and the social editor of our school annual, *Footprints*. Not surprisingly, I was the yearbook's business manager as well as the student council's treasurer. My class write-up in grade twelve noted, "We believe his main source of income at present is winnings from the frequent bets he calls."

Actually, I had other sources. Stu thinks I absorbed a propensity for business almost by osmosis from my entrepreneurial folks. He likes to tell the story of how as a little kid I loved ketchup and would eat it with anything. "You're going to have to start buying your own ketchup," he claims my parents told me. Apparently I went next door to Brown's grocery store and asked, "If I buy a case, can I get it cheaper?" I began working in our meat market early on, learning to butcher and serving customers even as a kid. When I was in my mid-teens all the dairies in town closed, and Betty Bolinger kept pushing my father to bring in milk from a plant in Bassano for her baby. Our shop was the only one that could refrigerate it—with ice in our new cooler—but Dad didn't want the bother of picking up all the bottles off the train every day and returning the empties. I volunteered to take on the job. Because my dad also didn't want to carry milk on credit, he started a pre-purchase system using black plastic tokens that read "Dick's Milk." We bought a quart of milk for about fifty cents, which I resold for a ten-cent profit.

Meet a need, price the product or service fairly, and deliver it efficiently—it works whether you're distributing milk, oil, coal, or financial services.

Bob Haskayne was also a good accounting teacher. Every night he tallied customers' accounts with double-entry bookkeeping in a matrix form. I was intrigued by a table that showed the cost of a whole carcass of beef, how much of each cut of meat it would yield, and a listing of various profit margins that helped him calculate the final per-pound prices. Then he taught me about pricing to market conditions: Ranchers in Bassano had more money and bought more steak than our Gleichen customers, but we sold ten times as many homemade sausages, especially to Native people.

For all my fascination with business, my real love was sports—baseball, curling, and most of all, hockey. We lived at the outdoor rinks, even in thirty-below weather. Our local juvenile team was the Gleichen Gunners, launched in 1921, and among its graduates was defenceman Doug Young of the NHL's Toronto Maple Leafs and Detroit Red Wings. The rural population had shrunk so much that by the time I was in my teens, the Gunners were absorbed into the Bassano Damsiters. I became captain of that team, playing defence with Larry (Deeke) Plante. He was six-foot-three and 215 pounds, and I was built like a fireplug at five-nine and 175. Though I wore hard-lens glasses and had poor peripheral vision, my short legs were strong and I could skate fast and score goals. Together, we made a great pair, knowing each other's moves and often playing for almost the full sixty minutes—he scared the hell out of most opponents, so all I had to do was steer them into him. In the fall, we trained by running along the railway tracks to the slaughterhouse and back.

Just how far I could have gone in the game, I'll never know. One of my early mentors was Matt Murray, the stepfather of a pretty and down-to-earth Irish-born girl named Lee who I'd noticed in a class a couple of grades behind me. Matt played Junior A hockey before the war, where he rose to the rank of major but came back home from England to drive the school bus and help coach local hockey along with the hard-swearing Buster Stott. Matt once told Stu Bolinger that I was the best young player he had ever coached. Then I got an impartial confirmation of whatever skills I had from Wild Bill Hunter, who owned the Medicine Hat Tigers, where Young and later NHL leftwinger Brian Carlin had played. He invited Larry and me to try out for the Junior A club. And Larry did sign with them and went on to play for the Spokane Flyers of the Western International League where, as "the Beast," he competed for the senior Allan Cup. (CBC TV once showed up to film my glass-chewing buddy eating the bulb from a goal light.) The Boston Bruins then asked him to sign a C-form, the standard way the NHL acquired young players in that era of a six-team league. Larry got married to Peggy instead and returned to Medicine Hat, where he played for a workingman's league for the next fifteen years.

Larry and I had been at the Tigers' summer training camp together, but when we broke for a couple of weeks, I came home—my family and teachers pressured me to get through grade twelve and go on to university. I was seventeen, taking two courses in the morning and working in the butcher shop afternoons, with a blood-streaked white apron and all. It was boring during the week, and so I was tempted when the Tigers' coach came by one day and said they'd had a lot of injuries and could use me on the team.

My dad wasn't keen on the idea, and neither was a high school teacher named Lester Inman. A crusty military type, straight from the Army, Mr. Inman and I had a good relationship. (Every Monday, I'd bring meat for the teachers, and once when I forgot, he said, "Judas priest, what are we going to eat?" I said, "You can have my lunch, if that will help.") Now he was telling me, in plain language, that I deserved a rapid boot in the behind if I passed up university for hockey or the family business. There was talk of my brother and me starting a chain of small-town stores specializing in meat and groceries. But in the end, Mr. Inman was more persuasive in suggesting that I knew a lot about business and should take commerce at the University of Alberta. I'd made enough money selling milk and meat to support myself, with a little help from all the government baby-bonus cheques my folks had saved. They were probably disappointed about my leaving, though my mother, when asked what Dick would do with a degree, replied, "Be an educated butcher."

By that time, Adele and I had broken up. She was a good Catholic and wanted to get married and have kids, which she did soon after high school. I had another, more casual girlfriend, Ann Koefoed, who was heading to the U of A. She filled out my application forms to make sure I followed through on my decision to study at the School of Commerce. (Ann—the sister of Gwen Hnatiuk, whom I'd chat with decades later at the Gleichen water tower during Homecoming weekend—remained a close friend until her premature death in 2003.) On a warm Sunday afternoon in September 1953, my brother and sister-in-law, Norah, drove me to Edmonton and dropped me off on a quiet campus. I looked around and thought, *Jeez, this is the first time in my life I don't know a soul.*

The situation soon resolved itself. In residence, I met Don Campbell from Calgary, another first-year commerce student. We went out on the grassy quadrangle to play touch football with other guys, most of them city slickers like him—and the shy, lanky

Don became my best, lifelong friend. He was impressed that while the urban boys hung back at socials during Frosh Week, a small-town kid like me just waded in and asked girls to dance. By second year, I'd joined Don's fraternity, Kappa Sigma, which was strong on academic achievement. By third year, we lived together in the frat house where he was treasurer (we called him "Harris" after the federal finance minister) and I was house manager, responsible for providing food, including pork hocks and other good cuts of meat I'd learned to butcher working in the family business. After visits to Gleichen, I'd bring back roasts that would be cooked by Maxine, the wife of a decade-older commerce classmate, Jack Culbert. To this day, I still get together with the Culberts and Don and his lovely wife, Marlene.

From my $10,000 savings selling milk and doing other work, I made two early investments. I bought a new, no-frills 1956 Dodge for $1,900 cash. And in the summer after my first year, I gave $1,000 to Pete, a sophisticated fellow from Gleichen who played the market when he wasn't working as a cook in bush camps. When my dad heard about my speculation, he said, "That's very silly. It's one thing to invest money, but you shouldn't just give it to somebody like that." I spent the next few months worrying as Pete disappeared from view till the following spring. While eventually doubling my money on my flyer, I learned a good lesson about giving up control of your funds and not keeping watch on them yourself.

It turned out that I liked the commerce program as much as Mr. Inman thought I would, winding up third in the class. Our accounting profs those years were J.D. Campbell, a strong-willed fellow with an air of confidence—whom Don and I admired so much that we visited him years later—and Dennis Goodale, who still keeps in touch with me because he invested in all the companies I've been involved with. By my final term, I was pretty well convinced that being a butcher was not my career of choice. My brother and I, discussing my future after college, considered the concept of starting a chain of mini-supermarkets in rural Alberta communities. I even had the design for a stand-alone vending machine to dispense snacks at service stations. But small towns were losing their attraction for me, and bigger business was beckoning. Don and I decided to article for three years to become chartered accountants. There had been only twenty-seven of us Depression babies in our class, and we were among the few going on to get our CAS. Juggling several offers, we made a pact to join the same firm, so I turned down a $180-a-month salary with Clarkson, Gordon & Co., the best in Canada, to go with Riddell, Stead, Graham, and Hutchison in Calgary for $5 less.

By then, I was pumped up about the value of post-secondary education and my own place in the world. Working toward my CA, I wrote a rousing challenge to high school grads in the Bow Valley Central yearbook, urging them to attend university if at all possible and trumpeting the virtues of the chartered accountant (of the male gender, you'll note):

> He is a member of a profession whose job is to analyze honestly and accurately statements of businesses and to provide guidance in their financial dealings.... Furthermore, in 1956 Chartered Accountants were included in the top five income brackets in Canada. Although this should not influence your decision in choosing a career, it is interesting to note if you have this type of ability...the fact still remains, that no matter what career you choose, you will never make a success of it unless you are prepared to WORK.

Riddell, Stead (which became KPMG) proved to be a good choice in at least one sense. Based in Montreal with regional affiliates, it did all the audits in Canada for Arthur Andersen, one of the Big Five American accounting firms. This fact meant that I was auditing large and small companies in a variety of industries, mining them like an archeological dig, soaking up their cultures and ethics as well as their profit-and-loss figures. An early lesson was that in business, as in battle, strategy is one thing, but execution is another. As Sir Winston Churchill once said, "However beautiful the strategy, you should occasionally look at the results." Too often, executives come up with a terrific-sounding strategic plan and then execute it ineptly—as I'd come to realize even more forcefully in the years ahead as a president, chairman, and director myself.

One of our clients then was Dominion Bridge of Montreal, which since 1882 had been making iron and steel and building bridges across Canada. I learned that it wasn't a bad place to work, but it couldn't hold a candle to the oil companies—with their well-educated and entrepreneurial people as well as their better pay scales and opportunities. I saw economically run ventures like Great Plains Development, a unit of Britain's Burmah Oil, and high-spending enterprises like domestically owned Home Oil in Calgary.

The most successful player in the petroleum game at the time was the Canadian subsidiary of Texaco in the U.S. What I learned in auditing its books and observing its ways of doing business—along with those of other subs of American multinationals—was that I wanted no part of any branch-plant operation. Texaco Exploration, which had found the big Golden Spike field after the Leduc discovery, was a well-managed and highly successful model of how to control a global mega-company. But the truth was that the Canadians couldn't even abandon a well without a Telex of approval from head office in New York. I'd come in as an external auditor at Texaco, and then the tough internal auditors would arrive from the States and terrify everyone. At one point, they offered me a job at their headquarters in New York, but I wasn't tempted for a second to join them down south.

Another major realization was that while auditing is a necessary evil, it was not one that I wanted to perpetrate. There's an old joke that says an auditor is a guy who arrives after the battle and then bayonets all the wounded. A typical situation involved showing a Texaco client a voucher related to an invoice the company had received and asking him if he'd pay it—and when he said he would, I'd reply that, in fact, it had already been paid. They were failing to follow the system for handling such vouchers that was

laid out in their own internal control system. Fascinated as I was
with business—and the oil business in particular—I didn't enjoy
simply checking numbers and trying to uncover people's mistakes
(again, even though I'd have to do my share of this later as an
executive). I knew that others were on the frontlines making decisions about where to drill a well and who the suppliers should be
and how the accounting for all that should be done. That's the
arena I wanted to play in, rather than being the behind-the-scenes
auditor second-guessing the real players in the game.

By then, my ties with my parents' and brother's butcher shops
were pretty loose. The last real link was an unusual arrangement
to supply them with what was considered waste meat from beef
flanks. I had two cousins working as butchers for Safeway in
Calgary who told me the leftovers from their flank steaks were just
discarded for rendering. It was quite edible—and in fact, our
Native customers liked to cut it in strips and dry it as a delicacy.
I'd get it for two cents a pound, drive a trunkful down to Gleichen
and Bassano on weekends, and sell it at the market price of ten
cents a pound. The profits contributed more to my income than a
whole week's wages as a trainee accountant.

I now had another link with the old hometown, but in
Calgary. My college social life had been hectic—I dated several
girls in my first two years on campus. None of those relationships
turned serious. And then I really got to know Matt Murray's step-
daughter, Lee. Her widowed mother, an O'Riordon from near
Cork, had brought her and her brother to Canada just after the
war to join Matt on his farm near Gleichen. Lee was a couple of
years younger than me, a bubbly, good-looking girl, auburn-haired
and a swell singer like Adele, and petite—almost doll-like. As
teenagers, we'd gone to the same dances in the surrounding towns,
especially Meadowbrook Hall out in the country, where a five-
piece orchestra played square dances and foxtrots and we all had
a midnight lunch the farm women made. As Jeanne Sauvé tells
people now, "We were always chasing the boys—Lee was chasing
Dick at the same time I was chasing Harvey. And we both caught
them." While I was articling, Lee moved to Calgary from Gleichen

to work at a law firm. We started dating, and one Wednesday afternoon in June 1958—a Wednesday because all the stores in Gleichen were closed—Lee and I were wed. Stan was my best man, and Don Campbell my attendant, as I'd been for him a couple of weeks earlier when he married Marlene.

Soon after, Don was surprised when I decided to leave Riddell, Stead. He'd stay with them for a few years before joining his family's insurance firm. I wanted more action. It was time to really get down to business.

Chapter Two

THE SHOULD-HAVE-BEEN
Hudson's Bay Oil and Gas

CANADIANS HAVE ALWAYS had soft spots in their nationalistic hearts for our two major department store chains. While Wal-Mart, the giant retailer that's as American as apple pie, has transformed our shopping habits with its low prices and extra-wide selection, earlier generations were raised on Eaton's and the Bay, two of our most recognizable institutions. The year I was born, 1934, the T. Eaton Company was advertising its mail-order catalogue to western farmers in *The Country Guide*, claiming with some justification that "family budgets are set by this handbook of the West." Yet after 130 years, Eaton's went bankrupt in 1999, a victim of its own failure to adapt to a rapidly changing retail environment. The Hudson's Bay Company (HBC) has an even more impressive pedigree, being older by two centuries than Canada itself. Founded as the Company of Adventurers of England trading into Hudson Bay in 1670, it once owned a third of what would become the Dominion of Canada. It's still the oldest such enterprise in the English-speaking world. So in early 2006, while going through four daily newspapers in my morning ritual, I was interested to read that the board of the troubled chain had recommended shareholders accept a sweetened $1.1-billion takeover offer from Jerry Zucker, a secretive South Carolinian industrialist. I felt badly because a former president and governor of the company was Don McGiverin, a friend who'd served with me on the board of Manulife Financial and who'd helped build

HBC between 1972 and 1994. Beyond that, I was sorry to see another national icon surrender Canadian financial control. But the hard truth is that since its fur trading days, the company had long since lost any sense of adventure and hadn't kept up with the times. Perhaps, I thought, it should have stayed in the petroleum game—where I once worked for a company partly owned by HBC: the late, lamented Hudson's Bay Oil and Gas.

HBOG, as people in the Oil Patch called it (pronouncing it *Aitch*-bog), survived for fifty-five years before it was swallowed by a more aggressive and much-overvalued competitor, Dome Petroleum. At the time, I was president of HBOG. Its demise was a dirty shame because, if left to its own devices, this respected company might have become a real Northern Tiger and supported the retailing empire through its thinnest times. The only bright spot in this cautionary tale of a misbegotten takeover is that many other Canadian oil and gas companies have seen the mess that was Dome and avoided some of the same missteps.

In 1960, I was a chartered accountant full of piss and vinegar, newly married and fresh from three years of articling, when I began poring over the calendar of the University of Western Ontario's commerce program. With all due respect to MBAS, I knew that CA programs generally are equal to master's programs in business administration, if not more valuable, because they allow you to tunnel deep inside the heart of a corporation in a hands-on way. But feeling there was still a stigma to being simply an accountant, I did consider taking an MBA. That's when one of the financial guys I'd worked with while doing my audits gave me some good advice. Graham Bennett, the chief accountant at Home Oil, had spent three months at Harvard studying for his master's in business administration—and had disliked the episode intensely enough to come back to Calgary with no advanced degree in hand. He advised me to get a year or two of experience before heading off to any graduate school.

Commerce grads with CA qualifications, like Don Campbell and I, were in a seller's market. I'd already had an offer from Home, which was a widely held Canadian independent, but—

surprisingly—Graham suggested I consider applying instead to Hudson's Bay Oil and Gas, where he'd been the internal auditor. "Hudson's Bay are tough bastards and they don't pay as much—and while Home may be a more exciting place to work, HBOG is a better-run company," he said. Not only that, the executive vice-president was Howard Blauvelt, a smart, iron-fisted CPA and MBA from New York. Blauvelt would later run Conoco, the U.S.–based global resource giant that owned a large chunk of the Canadian company. When HBOG asked me to come in for an interview, I spoke to Blauvelt and the controller, Frank Mair, and learned that I'd be reporting to Howard through Frank. That pleased me because Frank was a well-respected and widely recognized chartered accountant.

It was an easy decision to come on as the corporate accounting supervisor of six people who consolidated the accounts and issued all financial statements. What I found right away was that the company had an intriguing combination of American technical know-how and Canadian land holdings. The most extraordinary thing about HBOG was its asset base. In 1869, the Hudson's Bay Company sold to the new nation of Canada much of the enormous territory that England's King Charles II had granted HBC. But the company shrewdly kept the title to 7.5 million acres—1.75 sections of freehold land (meaning no rentals to pay) in every unoccupied township between Winnipeg and the Rockies, with waterways flowing into the immense inland sea of Hudson Bay. As Peter C. Newman, who wrote a four-volume history of the company, remarked recently, "The most obvious dereliction of opportunity was the failure to capitalize on the company's potential oil and gas reserves." In 1926, HBC formed Hudson's Bay Oil and Gas in partnership with Ernest Marland, a flamboyant English-bred, U.S.–based wildcatter—with HBC holding a one-third share, and the rest in the hands of Marland. The new company began to exploit the oil fields below the legacy of land that HBC hadn't known what to do with for 250 years. But it was soon forced to merge with the Continental Oil Company—Conoco—controlled by the legendary American financier J.P. Morgan, Jr.

HBOG just sputtered along until Imperial Oil's great gusher at Leduc, Alberta, set off the domestic oil boom in 1947, and then all the expertise that Conoco had developed down south came into play. Whenever a competitor found some good wells in an area, chances were HBOG would have land nearby to do its own drilling. The year after I came on board, the company had a net income of $7 million, based on very conservative accounting practices that prescribed immediately writing off all the dry holes we drilled— unlike most companies today that amortize the costs from non-producing wells. Before the end of the decade, the book value of HBOG's assets was larger than HBC's, and its net earnings were double. In later years, the interests of the two founding companies were diluted by public share offerings and acquisitions.

The other remarkable fact about HBOG was the corporate culture (which wasn't a phrase we used much in those days). So tight was the sense of camaraderie that former "HBOG-ers" meet to this day for an annual party in Calgary. Among them is my former administrative assistant, the remarkable Diane Reid, who recalls, "We were called conservative, but right from the get-go, it was a caring company—not only for the employees but the community, as well. We contributed to all the communities where we had offices. The company had a fantastic reputation, and everybody was so proud to have worked for HBOG." Not long ago, business journalist and author Peter Foster wrote that "Hudson's Bay Oil and Gas was an important and well-run oil and gas producer...a proud corporation with an admirable culture."

Note the past tense in his statement.

FATE CAN BE SO BLOODY UNKIND. My mother died of a stroke in 1961, just after she and my father had retired and moved to the gentler climate of Victoria, into the first new house they'd ever owned. Dad lasted for only a couple of years longer. He was heart-broken; his life was at loose ends. I'd learned so much from both of them, and seeing Bob Haskayne deteriorate was one of the worst periods of my life. Naturally, I didn't always agree with everything my dad believed. For instance, as a small-town entrepreneur, he'd distrusted all big corporations.

On the other hand, I had a feeling early on at HBOG that I'd enjoy not only being part of a big corporation but also, maybe, being able to shape its fortunes and even its philosophy of doing business. In the early 1960s, when the major players included the likes of Imperial, Gulf, and Shell, we ranked in the next highest level of senior producers, as opposed to marketers. Among the others in our class were Pacific Petroleums (controlled by Phillips Petroleum in the U.S.) and Canadian Superior Oil (partly owned by another American giant, Superior Oil). HBOG, being so sizable and holding such an extensive land base, needed good systems. And we had them: Our accounting department was highly disciplined, and when computers came in with a vengeance, ours were among the best in the business.

This administrative success was in large part thanks to my boss, the controller Frank Mair. A crack RCAF pilot during the war, he was one of the first BComms with a CA qualification working in our industry. In the Institute of Chartered Accountants, Frank was an activist in promoting sound accounting principles, and in his job, he was good with people—a smart, sensitive man. Too sensitive and nice, at times. I learned from watching him that you can be too kind to some people, when they'd be better off working somewhere else. I soon discovered that my auditing background helped me to analyze the problems and promise of the company, but—perhaps because of my rural roots—I also seemed to have a natural ability to network with others and create consensuses. Without realizing it at the time, I began practising basic psychology, trying to figure out why the hell people do what they do. If folks liked Frank, they also appeared to like me, and I, in turn, generally admired them—though not to the point of missing their flaws. And years later, while reading Jim Collins' now-classic business book *Good to Great*, I understood the instinctive feeling I had at HBOG that the best leaders are those who try to blend personal humility with professional will and who are ambitious for the company rather than simply for themselves.

I barely got to know Gerry Pearson, who'd come from Conoco and was president for only a year or so before another American colleague from the parent company succeeded him. Wayne Glenn was a character, a true Texas entrepreneur and a hulk of a guy, who knew the business as a petroleum engineer but was more of a hand-shaking, bear-hugging promoter. The company's own official history described his energy as "restless, dynamic and even frantic." We called him "Horsefly" because he was always hippity-hopping from one thing to another. But it was during his tenure that I became assistant treasury manager, overseeing all the corporate banking and acquisitions. And I fell in love with the complexities of financing deals.

Frankly, Wayne didn't know a whole lot about high finance. In 1963, we acquired Consolidated Mic Mac Oils and Security Freehold Petroleum for a total of $21.8 million and shares worth $8.6 million (which boosted public ownership of HBOG to more than 12 percent and reduced Conoco's interest to less than two-thirds and HBC's to a shade over one-fifth). Mic Mac, which had found its first good oil field near Leduc, was the creation of Bill McGregor, who, like me, had a youthful connection with milk— in his case, hauling the stuff from his father's dairy farm in Alberta's oil-rich Turner Valley. He'd already farmed out one hundred thousand acres to Union Oil and us in the Sturgeon Valley, where we discovered a rich Devonian-age oil field. While tidying up our acquisition of Mic Mac and checking the list of its shareholders, we found that we were missing a fair chunk of shares. It turned out that Wayne had acquired the stock to gain access to the shareholder list so that we could make an offer.

When I reminded him about his stake in the company, he asked, "What the hell did I do with those shares?" and then recalled that he may have put them in a safe beneath his desk, which he opened with the help of his secretary. Sure enough, that's where they were.

"How did you pay for them?" I asked.

"Goddam if I know."

So he asked his secretary, and that's how we learned our president had put the shares on his expense account.

Meanwhile, we'd bought Security Freehold, controlled by the Winnipeg brokerage and investment firm Osler, Hammond &

Nanton, which had no exploration acreage but did have a nice revenue stream. A year later, as became our practice, we held a post-audit review of how we were doing on the two deals. Drilling on the Mic Mac lands was coming up dry. At our management committee meeting, the irreverent Bert Hamilton, who later became vice-president of exploration, quipped, "Mic Mac, paddy whack, try to get your money back." But as it turned out, within a year, the fields were producing a reassuring seven thousand barrels a day and we all felt good about the first couple of major deals (in which we were ultimately successful).

As president, Wayne was interested in things financial, but they were neither his forte nor his successor's, Linden Jay Richards. In other ways, the two presidents were as different as oil and water. A geophysicist who'd been with HBOG for eighteen years, Lindy was a short, outgoing man who spoke with a gentle Oklahoma drawl and had a passion for exploration. In 1965, when he became president, I was chief accountant. That's when Frank Mair filled in a flattering personal-development form about me, rating my performance and prospects. Among my strengths, he noted, "mature analytical thinking, pleasant engaging personality, firm convictions based on logical reasoning, self-starter and leader, assumes responsibility." Supposedly, my only weakness: "Sometimes impatient"—which was true. Under the heading "Present opinion as to most responsible position he will be capable of filling (throughout the Company)," Frank wrote, "President of HBOG/Vice-president of Conoco." That forecast might have gone to my head if I'd known about it at the time. He did add that the experience I'd need to qualify for such positions would be fifteen to twenty years in various jobs with the company. He was dead right about that.

In retrospect, such evaluations reflect one of HBOG's strengths: the importance of succession planning. Many people in the Oil Patch today are direct products of the discipline of that system. And the lack of succession planning is a major weakness in many contemporary corporations in many industries.

I was soon to follow Frank in the controller's position. Working with Lindy Richards, my department introduced budgeting systems that sometimes baffled him, especially on the revolutionary subject of deferred taxes. Put most simply, it's when a company reserves some of its current year's profits—equal to the future tax liability on such transactions—to be drawn down in later years. In practice, the theory becomes more complicated. I practically wrote a PhD thesis on the concept, which was just coming into the Canadian petroleum industry. And when we were doing a financing in the U.S. with the investment bankers at Morgan Stanley, American lawyers and auditors suggested our system didn't comply with best accounting principles. In fact, we needed to prove to them that the Standards Council of Canada accepted our way of doing things before the Americans grudgingly granted us an exception.

We implemented another crucial budgeting change when we revealed the profit-and-loss projections for each department on a regular, quarterly basis to the key managers of the company. It sounds astonishing today, but HBOG's CEO and controller were the only two people at that time who knew what these consolidated figures were—and they would adjust the projections without consulting with their colleagues who were running the various departments

As the new controller, I was something of an anomaly in the industry because I sat on the small management committee, a long-held practice because the company believed it was critical that financial people understand the needs of the company's scientific and technical people. I told Lindy we had to give our managers projection figures for the entire company, and these figures would become their earnings targets: "We have to let people know, every quarter, where they stand."

"We can't do that," I remember him arguing. "We can't trust people to know those numbers."

"You don't trust Bert Hamilton, your vice-president of exploration?"

"Oh, I trust him implicitly. But he doesn't need to know those numbers. He runs the exploration department."

After Lindy reluctantly agreed to bring the managers into the loop on a trial basis, we faced a fourth quarter when the company was not likely going to meet its earnings targets, particularly because we'd been coming up dry at Alberta's promising Zama Lake oil and gas fields just south of the Northwest Territories' border. He was beside himself with concern until it was suggested that we ask every manager around the table what they could do to make their numbers more positive for the next quarter.

Stan Olson, the VP of production, piped up, "Well, hell, Lindy, you should've told me. I've got sulphur I've been holding back." HBOG was one of the largest sulphur producers in Canada. "I could sell sulphur, for Chrissake. If we need some more money to keep the wells drilling in Zama, I can do that for you." And Bert Hamilton added that he could delay some seismic drilling until the new year, if that would help the bottom line.

This meeting proved to be a breakthrough for Lindy, who, from then on, swore by the open discussion that arose during quarterly reviews of each department's projected earnings.

My job put me in contact with fascinating folks outside the company, like Mike Wilson. Canadians know him best as the finance minister in Brian Mulroney's government who introduced the GST and helped negotiate the Canada-U.S. Free Trade Agreement—and who, in 2006, was named by Stephen Harper's government as Canada's ambassador to the U.S. When I got to know him, he was a junior employee in the investment business in Toronto with Harris & Partners, who were among the first in the country to do commercial paper financing (short-term unsecured debt trading as a security and issued by large banks and corporations). "Jesus, Haskayne," he reminisces now, "do you remember when we did those four halves of '84?"—meaning a 4.5 percent rate on a twenty-year bond maturing in 1984. We worked with another bright young guy, Jim Pitblado—later, the chair of RBC Dominion Securities—and became personal friends.

I worked internally with one of my great mentors Ken Burgis, who was treasurer and, later, senior vice-president. Ken, from small-town Ontario, had little formal education, but he outworked everyone on his way up through the Canadian Imperial Bank of Commerce (CIBC). He brought his banking skills to the oil business—and to me.

My position at HBOG kept me in close contact with people of vastly different disciplines, from exploration to human resources, and one of them—Ken McNeill—became a lifelong friend and confidant. Diane Reid, looking at lanky Ken and me, used to call us Mutt and Jeff.

Ken was probably the only ex-homicide detective in the Oil Patch. He grew up on Canadian air bases where his dad's construction company built training facilities for the RCAF. After a year at a technology institute, he saw his teenaged hope to be an aeronautical engineer dashed by a downturn in the airplane industry (though today he still flies his own Cessna 177B Cardinal). His high school football coach, a police detective, urged Ken to join the Calgary force, instead. Starting as a patrol officer, the nineteen-year-old worked his way into the homicide division. He and his three partners were among the first polygraph examiners in Canada, and they started the department's first canine division. If they played the good-cop/bad-cop game with suspects, Ken—with his kindly, open face and relaxed manner—would definitely fill the role of the personable, sympathetic-sounding good cop.

After fifteen years, facing the prospect of a promotion to a desk job, he heeded the call of a former neighbour, Henry Thiel, who was head of HBOG's human resources. In 1969, when Henry told me he wanted to hire this flat foot to work in HR, I allegedly said, "You want to do what? You are out of your bloody mind. But if that's what you want to do, Henry..."

Ken tells the rest of the story with his usual wicked wit: "Hudson's Bay were trying to start up all these gas plants, and of course, being typical engineers, they built the plants and then thought they might need someone to run them. They had all these contractors up from the south—Texas Rangers, we called them—trying to run these very complicated gas operations and then went looking for staff. The Oil Chemical Atomic Workers [OCAW] union were having a field day, running every organizer they could into the lineup for these jobs. Hudson's Bay wanted to stay non-union, and Henry was pulling his hair out. The plant superintendents could not recognize an OCAW organizer from a hole in the ground, and Henry didn't have anybody in his human resources group that he trusted to shepherd the staff of the gas plants around. He made me an offer to join the employee-relations department and be in charge of recruitment. So I spent a lot of time on airplanes, going back and forth to the plants, holding hands with these guys.

"We always had better labour relations than anybody else in the business because we spent a lot of time in the field, talking to people about their bitches and gripes. Instead of a third-party union intervention, we had people in the plants or the field get their own little groups together. We'd meet with them and just simply say, 'You guys, sit down around this table and get together what you think your hot spots are, what's bothering you and what's going right and what's going wrong, and then we'll bring in the production or exploration manager so he hears it.' At the end of the day, we would either agree that they were sucking up a hosepipe or they had a good point and then generally got the management to have things changed. I don't know of any of the other companies in the industry that did it quite that way. None of them took the same face-to-face approach. Petro-Canada, Gulf, all of those were OCAW. Hudson's Bay Oil and Gas was never union— no worker's association, no nothing—and we worked hard at keeping it that way."

In 1970, Carl Jones became HBOG's first Canadian CEO. Another veteran of the company, a talented gas engineer, he proved to be a sophisticated, if conservative and somewhat withdrawn, chief executive. It was under his regime that we finally sold Blue Flame Propane Ltd., a wholly owned subsidiary cobbled together from three companies acquired a few years earlier. This was our attempt to get into the gas distribution business, and it was a disaster—a good example of a big company involving itself in a nickel-and-dime business. Blue Flame retailed propane from various outlets around the province. The fellow who'd built it stayed on to run the operation for us from the back of an envelope, like my own little low-overhead milk distribution venture in Gleichen. When I asked Old Bill all the typical accountant's questions about how he kept track of his costs, he finally replied,

"Dick, any guy with one eye and an asshole could figure that out."
Well, he'd made money, but with all the overhead and capital
expenditures on things like the new propane trucks that Hudson's
Bay Oil and Gas brought to the business, Blue Flame sputtered
into the red. The lesson was that some businesses should just be
left to small entrepreneurs.

The gentlemanly Carl Jones had come to the presidency late in
his career and didn't want to make any mistakes. His caution con-
trasted at times with the views held by both me and my friend and
ally at HBOG, Gerald James Maier. Gerry had six years on me in
age and seven in experience with the company. Like me, he was a
country-bred boy, growing up on a Saskatchewan family farm
before discovering a wider universe. For him, this journey started
with staying in his home province and attending senior high at
Notre Dame College in the town of Wilcox. Founded during the
Depression by Father Athol Murray, a legendary Roman Catholic
priest, the non-denominational, residential liberal-arts college
built on a foundation of classical Greek literature and philosophy—and classical Canadian hockey (at least fifty graduates of his
Hounds of Notre Dame went on to the NHL). Like me, Gerry loved
the game, playing left wing for the college while soaking up the
thoughts of great minds through the centuries.

Most intrigued by science, he took two years' engineering at
the University of Manitoba and then became a roughneck on an
oil rig near Edmonton to support his petroleum engineering studies at the U of A. Graduating, he worked briefly on rigs and
construction projects for Sun Oil before investing his life's savings
of $5,000 in an initially successful consulting/engineering firm that
went broke when the senior partners fell out. In 1953, Gerry left
entrepreneurialism behind to join HBOG as an engineer.

Though he worked from the Calgary office, he was mostly out
in the field when I first started there. Unlike me, he had a broad
international background with the company's American co-owner,
which gave him a much better world view than many of his compatriots. A former production vice-president at HBOG hired him to
play a similar role in Conoco's Australian operation for a few

years. Gerry also did stints at the U.S. headquarters in Connecticut—which at one point took him to the troubled African republic of Chad, where insurgents' bullets later killed the chief corporate pilot and the nation's president.

We didn't get to really know one another until the mid-1960s. Because Gerry and I were about the same size and came to work closely together and socialize as couples with our wives, people called us the Gold Dust Twins. Not identical twins—like the skills of my hockey buddy Larry Plante, Gerry's were complementary to mine. We learned to play to each other's strengths. For instance, he was a builder and was bored by the financing and accounting challenges that turned me on. I had more knowledge of the Canadian industry, while he knew the global situation better. And while tremendously articulate at times, Gerry was a tough negotiator, choosing his words carefully, playing his cards as tight to his vest as a riverboat gambler. Some people said he didn't talk enough and Haskayne talked too much—but either way, it worked.

But we did share a mutual passion for running an independent Canadian company. As Gerry says now, "We used to joke that our field foreman had more authority than some of the presidents of other oil companies in Calgary that were subsidiaries of the international majors."

We relished this empowering corporate culture. Of any company I've known, HBOG did the best job of the in-house education of its staff. Unlike many other Canadian oil companies, for instance, ours trained its own seismic crews. We did it for security reasons—so outsiders wouldn't learn where and how we were exploring—but the result was that HBOG trained a lot of good geophysicists who went on to develop distinctive technology. Another prime example: Even in the early 1960s, an elderly professor from Oklahoma taught in-house programs on management by objectives to a group of us from different disciplines. Though Peter Drucker had helped introduce the idea in *The Practice of Management* in 1954, I'd never heard of the concept of defining a company's goals, ideally in writing, so both managers and employees understand and buy into them and then setting timelines to monitor their progress. (I remember him saying that in one company, an efficiency expert tried to reduce the amount of toilet paper being used and kept setting up new objectives every week— from ten to eight to six sheets at a time—until it went down to four and never got any lower. The expert couldn't figure out why there were no further reductions until he found a sign on the inside of the door of one bathroom cubicle that read, "Tell me what the par is on this hole.")

Despite our fondness for HBOG, Gerry and I decided independently of one another to leave the company in 1973. He went to London to run Conoco North Sea Inc. I stayed home to help run a consortium that would bring natural gas from the High Arctic down to southern consumers. Or so I thought.

SOMEONE ONCE WROTE THAT it's the most unhappy people who most fear change. As the financial VP and treasurer, I wasn't unhappy at Hudson's Bay Oil and Gas by any means. There was a problem, though: Despite a strong balance sheet and surplus cash, we weren't pursuing any exciting new ventures under the cautious stewardship of Carl Jones. So I was probably looking for a change—and certainly not fearing it—when a fellow named Vern Horte approached me to get involved with a group known as the Canadian Arctic Gas Pipeline Ltd. It was, in spite of its official name, a consortium of twenty-eight oil, gas, pipeline, gas distribution and natural resource companies—half Canadian, half American. In 1968, Atlantic Richfield had struck oil at Prudhoe Bay along the coast of the Beaufort Sea on Alaska's North Slope. The largest American oil field in history, it also had some of the continent's largest deposits of natural gas. The gas consortium's scheme was to lay four-foot-diameter pipe from Prudhoe Bay east across Canada's Yukon to the Mackenzie Valley in the Northwest Territories and then south to the Alberta–Saskatchewan border.

A certain urgency soon overtook the project. Since 1950, American oil consumption had doubled as the United States, with 6 percent of the global population, was consuming a third of the world's energy. Then in October 1973, the Organization of Arab Petroleum Exporting Countries (OPEC) declared an embargo on oil shipments to nations that had supported Israel in its recent conflict with Egypt. Although Canada and Venezuela supplied the bulk of imported oil to the U.S., OPEC's action began crippling economies around the globe. Oil prices soared as the supply slowed to a relative trickle. The Americans' desperate push for a secure internal source of energy propelled the proposed Arctic Gas pipeline.

The consortium had an all-star cast. Vernon Horte, a chemical engineer, was a former president of TransCanada Pipelines, founded in the early 1950s to transport natural gas from Alberta to eastern Canada and parts of the U.S. Now he was president and CEO of Arctic Gas, and he invited me to come on as the controller, offering me double my HBOG salary, a car, and most of all, the chance to work on an exciting project with some of the most senior executives of some of the largest companies in the world. Vern's chairman was W.P. Wilder, a Harvard MBA who for a quarter-century had honed his reputation for financial brilliance at Wood Gundy, the major Canadian investment house. Bill had left there as CEO only because of the lure of this $5.5-billion project. An observer has noted that he was so cool under fire that he must have had ice water in his veins—the colour of Arctic blue. I'd known him for years in my role at HBOG. How could I reject such an offer?

Well, maybe I should have turned it down. Even then, in the earliest days of the organization, signals of forthcoming crises were sounding. Financing proved to be a huge problem. The American investment bankers Morgan Stanley pointed out that the pipe was to be buried in the permafrost over two or three winters and that financial disaster would follow if we failed to grasp that window of opportunity: A pipeline only 90 percent complete is inoperable— and unfinanceable. Key investors were simply refusing to underwrite such a risky scheme. And we were far from being the only game in town. NOVA and two American partners were among the four competing proposals that surfaced to move the gas south. Inevitably, politics intruded, too, as Native groups and environmentalists questioned the need for the pipeline and speculated about the potential damage it might do. The government of Pierre Trudeau, which at first seemed anxious to fast-track the project, began pointing out its flaws. Indian Affairs and Northern Development Minister Jean Chrétien eventually found that the project did not meet the social and environmental strictures laid down in contemporary guidelines. In 1974, Ottawa appointed Justice Tom Berger of the B.C. Supreme Court to head a royal commission, the Mackenzie Valley Pipeline Inquiry, to evaluate the pipeline's environmental, economic, and social impacts.

For me, Arctic Gas was both wonderful and awful. Wonderful because a lot of the people I've known in the global petroleum industry were those I met back then. I travelled widely, to our offices in Toronto and Alaska, and to conclaves in Houston and New Orleans. And though it was a typical consortium with more bloody committees—finance, tariff, engineering, environmental, you name it—I had the opportunity to sit in on what they called "management meetings." Here, however, the managers were the presidents of companies like Imperial Oil and Gulf Canada. Gulf's Jerry McAfee, for one, ranked among the gentle statesmen of the Oil Patch. As Timothy Pritchard of the *Globe and Mail* recalls, "[A]long came Jerry McAfee, an Oklahoman and the new president of Gulf Canada. Not only was Mr. McAfee more open, in the manner of an increasing number of U.S. executives, he was also determined that Gulf Canada not remain an also-ran in the oil business." Jerry was eventually called back to his home country to chair the scandal-ridden Gulf Oil Corporation in Pittsburgh, which was seeking a leader with his sense of integrity. In our sessions, he had always taken the high road while remaining a rock-solid businessman.

But mostly what I learned from my sojourn with Arctic Gas was how *not* to do things. Running the company too religiously by committee, for example, was an exercise in inefficiency and frustration. Because each of the partners paid only one-twenty-eighth of the share of any expenditure—and we were spending money like drunken oilmen—they tended to approve expensive initiatives, whatever their merits. An environmental specialist working for a partner company would think, *God, I'm never going to have access to more information than I can get out of the consortium, and we're only paying a twenty-eighth of the cost.* And then his company would say, in an almost threatening way, "If we don't pursue these environmental studies, we'll never get through the regulatory process."

Questions of ethics arose, too. There were executives in the bowels of some major American companies who would cut your throat to reach their objectives, regardless of what impact their actions had on the consortium. Of course, getting their own way was often why they were successful, but their winning-is-everything philosophy soured me on them. In one case, we were deciding how to calculate pipeline tariffs—the multi-million dollars' worth of charges each member would pay for transporting the gas from its origin to its destination. As administrators, we agreed with our consultants that the consortium should treat all the parties equally, but there were widely divergent views between American and Canadian companies.

Determining these tariffs was crucial to the overall financing of the pipeline deal. At a final crunch meeting in Houston to decide the issue, I was asked to arrive a couple of days early. Knowing our point of view, one major corporate group—whose designated executives were at a fairly low level—threatened to boycott my presentation and, if I went ahead with it, suggested I was in danger of losing my job. I'd never had anyone attempt to intimidate me like that before. In a tense confrontation where I told them this was a bullshit way of operating, I refused to back off from our position. In the end, they backed off, and my presentation proceeded.

Another example of mixed morality: We signed contracts before I came on board that allowed member companies to withdraw from the project with three months' notice. This provision was ridiculous because an undertaking like the pipeline demanded long-term commitments. Meanwhile, people in certain companies who voted for huge expenditures had spoken to me privately and gave me the impression that they would be getting out of the project before long. How could they approve these costs, knowing they likely wouldn't be saddled with them? I stayed with Arctic Gas two and a half years. By then, disappointed by the jockeying for power and the lack of progress in financing, I was ready and willing when Hudson's Bay Oil and Gas came calling. Because Carl Jones was nearing retirement as president, the board wanted him to have a succession plan in place. "Well, my two top guys— Gerry and Dick—have gone," he pointed out.

"Go and hire them back," the directors said.

Carl approached both of us, making it clear that the company would do whatever it took to have us back. My wife, Lee, and I talked about my returning, as we always discussed major decisions. A sensitive sounding board, she would be intimately involved in all my personal decision-making over the thirty-five years of our marriage. She was keenly intuitive about people, and I was often sorry on those occasions when I ignored her advice about personnel matters. For example, Lee advised me against hiring a high-potential engineer whom all of us at HBOG considered to be an all-star: "I'm telling you, he's not going to work out." She saw a different side of him than we did, and it took me five years to realize that her instincts about the guy had been right all along.

On the same November day in 1975, Gerry and I returned to HBOG as senior vice-presidents. We were assured that the board was not identifying either Gerry or me as the eventual top dog. In fact, neither of us would inherit Carl's mantle directly.

After I left Arctic Gas, the consortium continued to stagger along. In 1977, Judge Berger's royal commission, citing issues of the environment and Native land claims, effectively killed the project by recommending that the federal government place a ten-year moratorium on it.

The most unhappy people most fear change? Well, I was making another change—returning to a company with little, if any, political infighting—and couldn't be happier making it.

Chapter Three

THE DEATH OF HBOG
Dome Petroleum

IF THE COMMUNITY OF GLEICHEN was the melting pot that helped shape my moral centre and basic business skills, Hudson's Bay Oil and Gas was the crucible that first tested my ethical instincts and management talents in the context of a big company. The in-house training combined with a culture that minimized internal strife helped to produce outstanding employees. It's astonishing how many of them, like Gerry Maier, later became leaders—sometimes at the pinnacle—of major corporations.

There was Dave Powell, for one, who would someday be chairman of Talisman Energy, Canada's leading deep-sea gas explorer. And Charlie Fischer, who joined HBOG in 1972 with chemical engineering degree in hand, worked in gas processing, production operations, and corporate planning. He moved on to run TransCanada Pipelines' upstream oil and gas subsidiaries—the companies that explore for, develop, and produce resources—and then joined Nexen Inc., Canada's fourth-largest independent petroleum producer, where he's now president and CEO.

Pat Daniel joined a year after Charlie as a process engineer to design gas plants, and then he transferred to the emerging computer field to manage our information systems, a field where the company was a pioneer. Because computers came under my purview, I got to know Pat and was impressed by his technical expertise and managerial acumen. Today, he's president and CEO of Enbridge Inc. of Calgary, operator of the longest crude oil and liquids pipeline system on the planet and the largest natural-gas distribution company in Canada. He first worked in New York State for Hooker Chemical, which was later found to have buried toxic waste in the Love Canal neighbourhood of Niagara Falls, NY, causing severe health problems in the community. In contrast, reflecting on his later career with Hudson's Bay Oil and Gas, Pat says, "We knew we were working with an honest company and senior managers with a high degree of integrity. They were very hard-working, very high achievers, and that environment attracted good people."

Allen Hagerman was a chartered accountant and had an MBA from Harvard when I hired him in 1977 as an analyst in corporate planning. The son of a chief financial officer I knew at Husky Oil and NOVA, Allen was practical, dependable, and honest. He eventually became planning director and treasury manager. HBOG was a team operation with little politicking, he remembers: "There was a community feeling, and we were very proud of our assets and what we'd accomplished." He went on to Home Oil and Interhome Energy before becoming CFO at Fording Coal and, lately, at Canadian Oil Sands, the largest partner in northern Alberta's enormous Syncrude oil-sands venture. (I value Allen so highly that he's one of two executors of my estate.)

Diane Reid was my administrative assistant (or "executive secretary," as we called it back then), and she remembers HBOG as being "like a big, people-oriented family." A native Calgarian, she joined the company as her first job out of business college and was soon working in employee relations, where she drank up the caring culture. And this bright young woman, who always looked so much younger than her age, was one of the most caring. As Ken McNeill reminds me, "Diane was a perfect foil for you—a consummate professional. She knew you well, knew what you needed when you needed it. And she could tell people where to go in such a manner that they looked forward to the trip." We were always fiercely loyal to one another (she went on to work with me at Home Oil, and I'm delighted to know that she works today with Gerry Maier).

So when Gerry and I arrived back at HBOG, people of high calibre were well in place. Stan Olson was executive VP, second-in-command to Carl Jones. Stan—a tall, almost austere-looking man until he smiled—was another headstrong production guy, like Gerry, and though highly articulate, still took the time to select each word with care. He'd been with the company for a quarter-century and, within a couple of years, would succeed Carl as president and then CEO. But because Stan was approaching sixty-five, his growth strategy for the company was (like Carl's) less assertive than Gerry and I would have liked. By then, we'd become executive VPs: Gerry ran the guts of our business—conventional exploration and production, worldwide—while I handled finance, administration, computers, and our involvement in pipelines and Syncrude.

In 1976, when HBOG celebrated its fiftieth anniversary, we settled into our own forty-two-storey tower on Seventh Avenue. The company was the largest non-integrated oil company in Canada (meaning that we had no marketing, transportation, or refining operations) and the ninth-largest oil company in sales, with net earnings of $78.7 million. During the last half of the decade, we explored the Dutch and British sectors of the North Sea as well as in Greenland, Turkey, Egypt, and Australia. By 1980, our net earnings were $145 million, we were Canada's third-largest producer of natural gas, and, outside the country, had oil and gas plays producing in the U.S., offshore Norway, and especially Indonesia. Management had the confidence of our board. Five of the directors were nominated by Conoco, and three by Hudson's Bay, and the rest were independents. Among the board members were Walter Light of Northern Telecom, George Bleumenauer of Otis Elevator, and Ian Barclay of B.C. Forest Products. As Peter Foster remarked in his book *Other People's Money*, the company was then a Cadillac—"one of the largest and soundest in the Alberta oilpatch...a rock-solid corporate empire of huge landholdings and high quality oil and gas production."

One of the key contributors to the success of our international holdings was Dave Powell, a wiry Welshman—about my size and a year older than me—with a global background in the petroleum industry. He had his countrymen's typical coal-black hair, gift of the gab, and tendency to launch into song in social situations. A coal-miner's son, he'd been inspired by geologists working in West Africa where he was doing his national service with the British Army. Afterward, he took an honours degree in geology and then joined Burmah Oil of London, which had him do a master's in petroleum-reserve engineering and sent him to Burma as a field geologist. The oil company was one of the biggest and best of its day, owning pieces of British Petroleum and Shell. His career took him to India, Pakistan, Ecuador, and Australia before Burmah Oil made some unwise investments in oil tankers and became laden with debt.

In Australia, Dave had met Gerry Maier, now HBOG's second-in-command, who in 1978 had urged him to join the company as manager of geology for a new international arm. With a passion that could excite the people who worked for him, he zoomed up the ladder in little more than a year to become president of the division, HudBay Minerals. His knowledge of Indonesia brought us major holdings in the narrow channels and shallow reefs of the Malacca Straits, which link the Indian and Pacific Oceans. Our discoveries there would produce about 100 million barrels of recoverable oil.

In the spring of 1980, Stan Olson retired. Our board chose Gerry as the first Canadian chairman and CEO, replacing John Kircher, who was also Conoco's deputy chairman. And I was named president. Here, finally, was our chance to propel HBOG into more aggressive growth. Gerry always says he returned to HBOG out of a sense of nationalism, with the vision that it could truly be what we've come to call a Northern Tiger. It was an ambition I shared.

OUR TIMING, AS IT HAPPENED, was bloody terrible. Only half a year later, the Liberal government of Pierre Trudeau, demanding more control over energy resources, enacted the much-loathed National Energy Program (NEP). The rationale was to increase

Canadian ownership of the industry and protect Canadians from rapidly rising oil prices. Predictably, Albertans protested this federal intrusion into provincial rights and the accompanying tax grab to share the province's wealth with the rest of the country. The fallout from the NEP still has resonance today, as *Globe and Mail* business columnist Eric Reguly reported in the spring of 2006:

> The NEP was a disaster (I lived there at the time). Among other horrors, it created the petroleum and gas revenue tax, or PGRT. Note the word "revenue." This was a tax on sales, not profits. The NEP's timing was equally disastrous. It coincided with the fall in energy prices, doubling the pain and plunging Alberta into a tailspin that wouldn't end for more than a decade.

Albertans were not the only victims. Within the first nine months alone, Canada suffered from more than a $10-billion outflow of capital. The Canadian dollar slumped drastically, and the official bank lending rate topped 21 percent, the highest in any major industrial nation. My memory is that we figured the NEP would cost Hudson's Bay Oil and Gas alone about $90 million a year in PGRT, a significant chunk of our cash flow. Even worse, we'd been deemed a foreign company because of Conoco's ownership stake, despite the fact that it was held in a voting trust that didn't give the American company control. The irony is that just before Energy Minister Marc Lalonde announced the new rules, Gerry convinced our board to buy an airplane, a Gulfstream jet from the Ivory Coast—used, but with gold taps and all the trimmings. And it was on that fancy Gulfstream that we flew to see our directors, such as George Richardson in Winnipeg, the governor of the Hudson's Bay Company, who could view the expensive plane from his office while we told him about the financial crisis the NEP would wreak on HBOG.

Within weeks, we began considering how we could merge with an all-Canadian company to avoid the crippling taxes and take advantage of new grants that encouraged domestically controlled enterprises. Behind closed doors, we secretly fashioned a deal to merge with Inco Limited of Toronto, the world's second-largest nickel producer, and at the same time, Conoco agreed to reduce its interest in HBOG to as little as 30 percent. Nobody knew about the pact until Gerry and I went to Ottawa to give Marc Lalonde the details behind this proposed Canadian giant that would combine petroleum and mining—a Northern Tiger in the making.

Lalonde, fresh from the 1980 election that had returned the Liberals to power, sat in his office on Parliament Hill, dining on a full breakfast in front of us. Looking on was his executive assistant, the lawyer Michael Phelps (later the CEO of Westcoast Energy). Once we'd outlined our proposal, the minister said, in effect, our scheme was simply not acceptable: "I have a list on my desk of a number of people who want to buy your fine company, which will be much better for both of us." As far as he was concerned, that was the end of it.

After the meeting, we were just bristling with anger. Our mood wasn't improved when we encountered Roy Maclaren in the hall. A business-magazine publisher and a member of Parliament from Toronto, he was Lalonde's Parliamentary Secretary. "How did it go, boys?" he asked.

"Not very well."

"Well, it would have gone much better if it wasn't for your South African content."

South African content? Oh, he was referring to Hudson Bay Mining and Smelting, a Canadian-based company controlled by South Africa's Anglo American Corporation, long considered a pillar of apartheid in that country. Unaccountably, Maclaren—who tabled reports and answered questions in the House on behalf of his minister—had mixed up our two distinctly different companies. That was our day in Ottawa.

All of this lobbying would prove sadly academic in the end. As Marc Lalonde had noted, there were people out there who wanted to buy our fine company. Or try to sell it. One of them was Robert Greenhill, the New York investment banker who built the mergers and acquisition business at Morgan Stanley & Company.

Greenhill approached federal Energy Minister Donald Macdonald in the autumn of 1981 to have the new state oil company, Petro-Canada, take over the HBOG shares owned by Conoco. To have Bill Hopper and his gang at the government-owned PetroCan overseeing all that we'd helped build over the years was a personal affront to Gerry and me. As it happened, the deal failed late in the year with the two parties half a billion dollars apart. But before we could take more than a deep breath, up loomed "Smilin'" Jack Gallagher and Bill Richards of Dome Petroleum.

The black Dome Tower, rising beside the HBOG building in downtown Calgary, was a testament to the two men who had created Canada's highest-profile energy company. With assets of $6.5 billion in western Canada, the Arctic Islands, and the Beaufort Sea—sixty million acres in the Beaufort alone—it was exploring on land holdings surpassed in size only by HBOG's. In the previous five years, Dome had become an investor's darling on stock markets around the world as its shares skyrocketed from $1.58 to $25.38 per share.

Chairman Jack Gallagher was a dapper, handsome guy with a trim mustache and a penchant for taking risks, much like the daredevil pilot Smilin' Jack of the wartime comic strips who inspired his nickname. In Gerry's words, Jack was "a great visionary and one of the world's best salesmen." He had a blinding smile and a well-honed pitch of sales patter: "Jack would say the same thing exactly the same way he'd said it a few days before. He had all these things memorized, word for word—pronunciation, enunciation, pauses—everything exactly the same. And I thought to myself, *this guy would make the greatest stage actor in the world*. Unfortunately, Jack and his guys were totally impractical in what they were saying to the public—and the analysts and the media of the day just gobbled it up.

"They were saying that they were going to have oil production flowing [from the Arctic] to Canada within two years. Well, Dome hadn't even made a discovery worth economic development at that time. And coming from the international scene and the North Sea—where it's much easier than the Arctic—I knew that from discovery to production took a minimum of seven years, and sometimes twelve or longer." When Gerry stated this publicly at the time, the media happily picked it up and people from Dome attacked him for being so negative.

Jack was a Winnipeg-born petroleum geologist who'd worked for Shell and Standard Oil in the U.S., the Middle East, and South America before returning to Canada and founding Dome Exploration (Western) in 1950. Three decades later, he'd acquired $4.5 billion worth of Canadian resource properties—among them, $360 million in assets developed by my friends Bill Siebens, an American petroleum engineer, and Harold Siebens, Bill's entrepreneurial father. Dome had also gained a controlling position on the board of TransCanada Pipelines by buying the block of shares held by Canadian Pacific. This was a complex deal—with Dome's earned dividends more than balancing the expenses of financing—that essentially left Gallagher and Company getting them for free.

Bill Richards was another Winnipegger, a smart, workaholic lawyer who'd joined Dome's legal department in 1956. By now, he was really running the company as president. I once asked an executive there, "Harry, what's the organizational structure like at Dome?

"Dick," Harry said, "it kind of runs like the Catholic Church. There's Bill Richards, who's the Pope, and there's a whole bunch of cardinals, who report directly to him."

"And Jack?"

"He's God."

Before the government passed the NEP legislation, Bill had been negotiating with Ottawa to somehow sidestep the new rules. Because of its heavily American ownership, Dome Petroleum was ineligible for the grants and liable for the penalizing petroleum and gas revenue tax. In a classic Richards move, he conceived Dome Canada, a subsidiary to be controlled by the parent company but with a majority of Canadian shareholders—in fact, sixty thousand of them who would buy stock after an initially wary Ottawa finally agreed to this corporate juggling act.

Riding high, Bill went on the hunt for yet another acquisition.

Soon he had his gun sights set on good old wealthy and wisely run HBOG—or "Swampy," as he code-named our company. Jack himself found out about the idea only after walking into a meeting where Bill was discussing the potential takeover with his executives. Dome Petroleum certainly didn't have the ready cash to take on such a major acquisition. But what if they bought shares of Conoco, our controlling stockholder, on the U.S. markets and then traded them for the 50.2 percent of HBOG shares that Conoco held? That kind of trade would be wonderfully tax-free. In fact, such a deal would supposedly allow Conoco to avoid paying $400 million of capital gains tax.

In his encyclopedic history *The Great Canadian Oil Patch*, Earle Gray impartially paints the scene that led to the Gallagher-Richards gamble to bid $4 billion for our company in what would be the largest acquisition in Canadian history:

> HBOG offered a number of attractions. There were large cash flows and earnings that Dome could certainly use. The National Energy Program, with its adverse impact on foreign investment in the oil business, had reduced the price at which HBOG might be bought. HBOG, with its years of profits, was paying a high tax rate, while Dome's aggressive exploration expenditures had created a pool of tax credits that could be used to reduce the taxes on HBOG's revenue. Geologists might search for oil pools but lawyers looked for tax pools. Politically, buying out a controlling U.S. parent based in Connecticut and merging HBOG with a Canadian company based in Calgary would be a winner, based on perception. In reality—unless Dome sold more shares to Canadian investors—buying HBOG would actually reduce Canadian ownership of the oil industry, because of Dome's 60 percent American ownership.

Gerry and I felt frustrated by our lack of power to influence any of these proceedings. And then we were infuriated to discover that the bank that was leading Dome's loan to buy the Conoco stock was none other than the Canadian Imperial Bank of Commerce. *Our* bank—for the past half a century. We were one of their best clients. But Jack Gallagher was on the CIBC board, which in itself shouted, "Conflict of interest!" Frank Duncanson headed up the commercial side of the bank locally. I hauled him into my office and gave him holy hell. Frank was a nice enough fellow, but because every bank in Canada would have loved to back the high-flying Dome, he was blind to the mess CIBC was making. So was Russell Harrison, the bank's chairman in Toronto. When Gerry got him on the phone, he exploded in self-defence, arguing that the bank would never betray one client's secrets to another. (Years later, when I got involved with CIBC, I would make damn sure that directors' relationships were spelled out when the bank backed any party during a takeover.)

The chairman of Conoco was Ralph Bailey, in his late fifties, the stocky son of an Indiana coal miner. He and I had enjoyed a good relationship, which was weakened a bit by the fact he'd been willing to discuss the possibility of having PetroCan take over Conoco's shares of HBOG. Now he seemed to be at least entertaining the idea of Dome's doing the same thing. We bristled at the very idea of getting into an uncomfortable bed with this big-spending, ball-breaking company.

Ken McNeill, our human resources specialist, sums up some of the differences between them and us: "Our executives said, 'Listen, let's not do what's not good for our people.' But Dome would hire an industrial psychologist to interview all the candidates for a job and make them into the same ilk—and then they'd look down their noses at everybody else with equal disdain. And the employees were left to live on the edge—for instance, in the way that their pensions were handled. Dome had a pension plan, but it made the plan very unattractive to get into." (In recent years, Enron Corp., the failed American energy resources trader, used similar incentives to encourage stock ownership for employees instead of pensions.)

Gerry and I flew to New York to meet with the Conoco management. Well, we *attempted* to meet with them: Ralph said his lawyers wouldn't let him talk to us, and so we paced the floor, never learning what the company's intentions were.

Behind the scenes, as it turned out, Bailey and his board were trying to fend off Dome's tender offer, which offered 30 percent over the current market price. When it was made public in May 1981, shares of Conoco, HBOG, and Dome all shot up—ours by 40 percent to $31.75, and Dome's to more than triple our figure. Conoco launched a lawsuit against Dome, and the two companies engaged in a nasty war of news releases (one of Dome's misnamed us as *Hudson* Bay Oil and Gas). Ultimately, Conoco learned that its pursuer might in fact be going after a wholesale takeover of the American company. During Conoco's federal court case in Oklahoma to forestall this development, Jack Gallagher testified, convincingly enough, to help get the legal action dismissed.

In late May, after all the gun smoke had cleared, Dome had paid a little over $2 billion Canadian for 20 percent of Conoco's own stock, with the intention of swapping the shares for the American company's interest in HBOG. Conoco's advisors at Morgan Stanley & Company went looking for anyone but Dome to buy it. They first approached Olympia & York Development (O&Y) of Toronto, owned by the Reichmann family, which bid nearly $1 billion. But that offer was sidelined by one from Edgar Bronfman's Seagram Company. The world's major liquor distiller had huge profits from the recent sale of petroleum properties in Texas and wanted to take over not HBOG but Conoco itself by acquiring 35 percent of its shares. To forestall that bid, the oil company went on the defensive (there was talk at the time that the Jewish ownership of Seagram would harm Conoco's image in the Middle East, where it had substantial operations—but that, frankly, was a crock of bull). Ralph Bailey approached Cities Service of Tulsa, a much smaller petroleum player, to amalgamate instead. But when Seagram offered to buy 40 percent of Conoco for more than $10 over the going price of $62 per share, Cities Service pulled out and two more serious contenders stepped in. E.I. du Pont de Nemours and Company, the major American chemicals producer, made the first friendly ante, followed by the multinational Texaco (as well as unsolicited offers from Mobil Oil, Marathon Oil, and Unocal). Ralph, worrying that the Ronald Reagan government would look dimly on a marriage of two petroleum titans, stayed with du Pont and its $7.6-billion (U.S.) bid.

The subsequent merger proved to be, at that time, the largest ever in American corporate history, creating what was then the nation's biggest industrial enterprise. While Jack Gallagher and Bill Richards couldn't match that record, they did complete the largest such deal to that point in Canadian history when Conoco agreed to trade shares with Dome, after all. That very day, Gerry and I were in Calgary. After Ralph phoned to fill us in, Jack called Gerry and, at his friendliest, said he really liked us and wanted to work with us. I got a call from Bill (he and the equally strong-willed Gerry never got along) as he was flying home. He and Jack wanted to meet us immediately on his return.

We had lunch at the Country Club with the slender, health-conscious Gallagher and the burly, cigar-chomping Richards. They took pains to assure us that we ran a very good company. Hell, we knew that—and we were infinitely bigger and more dominant in producing properties than Dome ever was. Jack was at his charming best as they pointed out, "You guys don't have a lot of money."

Which was true—we didn't enjoy all the stock options that top Dome executives had. Their idea, as it transpired, was to put all the HBOG-ers on the Dome payroll.

"Look," I said, "that's not in the cards. They're separate companies and we've got another 50 percent of the shareholders out there who we represent, as well."

The four of us agreed to meet weekly to discuss the transition, though Jack often failed to show up, or he wandered in late. (Ken McNeill remembers being called over to meet with Bill Richards and his people to discuss the merging of the companies' human resource functions and Bill confiding, "Now, this is between us. No need to talk to Jack about any of this stuff right now.") One point that soon became apparent was that Bill and Jack had the naive notion that, with a merger, they could save the roughly $300 million a year that we paid in taxes. Dome Canada's tax bill was negligible because of the break it got through the NEP. Our position was that we spent money wisely and paid taxes because we were so successful. But they assumed that with some slick accounting, Dome would suddenly get rid of those hundreds of millions in tax charges. In fact, you had to *spend* about $1 billion a year to save that amount in taxes. A third-year accounting student could have figured that out.

Harking back to that time now, Gerry says, "As long as I was going to be there as chairman and CEO, they were not going to get their hands on our cash flow or tell us how the hell to run our business."

Knowing this, Bill and Jack had to go after the other half of HBOG's stock, held by a mixed bag of individuals, pension funds, and the largest minority shareholder, the Hudson's Bay Company, with 10.1 percent. As they were pursuing these shares, Dome's long-term debt had more than doubled to $5.3 billion while the price of its shares was falling. Meanwhile, the Toronto-Dominion Bank had unwisely given the company loans amounting to about three-quarters of the bank's own capital and was now pressuring Dome to sell off its HBOG shares. Instead, the Gallagher-Richards duo met with the Bay at the King Edward Hotel in Toronto. Also present were a lot of lawyers, investment bankers, HBOG's committee of independent directors—and Gerry Maier.

Gerry believed that the price Dome was offering for the Bay stock—the price that the bankers and the independents had agreed was fair—was much too low. In fact, he knew that the Dome negotiators would go higher. In a story I heard only recently, Gerry explains exactly how he knew they were low-balling:

"I flew in from Calgary to Toronto and got checked into the hotel and went down to the bar. There was a bunch of guys standing around there, and some were Dome guys—and none of them recognized me. They were drinking and talking while I was standing right beside them. I listened to everything they said. I'd known before then that they had to take out the shareholders to get their hands on the cash. And I knew from their conversations that there was upward mobility in what they thought the company was worth because of their projection of oil and gas prices in the future. Oil prices were fairly high for that day and age. But they were projecting prices to increase by about 3 to 5 percent per year, ad infinitum. Well, that makes the value of the shares incredibly different. So I knew that if push came to shove, because they needed to have the total company, they'd meet a higher price.

"So I went back and told our guys what I'd heard. I knew then that the number that they had offered—and the number that the Hudson's Bay Company had already accepted—was way too low. It wasn't a bad price, it wasn't that ridiculous, but I knew that Dome was willing to go much higher. I told our people, 'This is our number,' and unless they agreed to it, I'd go and get financial backing to take out Dome and buy HBOG at this number. Of course, I was bluffing. In the end, I didn't get exactly the number I suggested, but very, very close to it. And if I remember right, it meant about $75 million just to Hudson's Bay Company alone. The Bay guys were so damned embarrassed, and they never had the courtesy to thank me."

It was sweet revenge. The final tab to buy out HBOG's minority shareholders reached $2.3 billion. Typically, Dome didn't intend to front real money for the stock: It issued special shares that could be cashed in three years, making the company's cost of acquiring them free of any capital gains tax. A week later, Ottawa decided to change the rules allowing such an exemption, a move that would kill the deal. Marc Lalonde, the energy minister who'd been hostile to Gerry and me, had applauded most of Dome's initiatives so publicly that many in the Oil Patch saw the company as a private-sector instrument of government policy—a blunt instrument, as it happened. Now he convinced his colleague, Finance Minister Allan MacEeachen, to make a last-minute exception and let Dome escape the capital gains levy.

Bill Richards' next problem was to figure out how to finance the deal while the company was so deeply in hock to Canadian banks. This time, he went south to a Citibank-led consortium of twenty-seven American financial institutions. And as collateral for the world's biggest oil-production loan up to that time, he put up all of HBOG's oil and gas wells and promised to pay Citibank $400 million (U.S.) when Dome sold some of our assets. The Canadian lenders were outraged to hear this plan, which would wipe out the collateral value of the HBOG shares they were now holding.

For months, I'd seen the ugly handwriting on the wall, and it hollered, "Get out now, while the getting's good!" In the fall, I finally decided to exercise that option. Fortunately, on their own hook, our directors had long since decided to protect the top seven management people as well as the company itself. They'd worried that, given all the machinations of a possible Dome deal, all of us high-profile guys would bail out of HBOG early. Their solution was to create one of the first Canadian "golden parachutes"—those contracts given to senior executives in the event they lose their jobs when their company faces a hostile takeover. Generally, the contracts offer sizeable severance pay, stock options, and a bonus. Our general counsel had a hard time even finding a precedent for such a provision in Canada. Many parachutes have a double trigger: Not only does your company have to be gobbled up but your job has to be diminished in some way to activate the 'chute. Mine had only the single trigger of a takeover.

And when Dome did snare HBOG, my parachute turned out to be gilded enough—worth $660,000 in total—that, by making shrewd investments at the current interest rate of 18 percent, I could probably have retired then and there. But at my ripe, young age of forty-six? Not a chance. At that time, I was able to put the money into an RRSP tax-free (only two weeks later, Ottawa made such funds taxable), and that's where I parked it while I considered the next rung up on my ladder.

Gerry and I could officially step down in October 1981. While relinquishing his CEO role to Bill Richards, he decided to stay on as a heartbroken chairman till March 1982, when the Citibank loan was to be signed and sealed. I'd already had a number of approaches from, among others, Shell Canada and James Richardson & Sons, the old, established western investment and grain dealers. But the job offer that proved most attractive came from Home Oil, just across the street from the HBOG tower. What convinced me was the encouragement from my friend Ken Burgis, who was retiring as our senior VP. A great advisor, he underlined the fact that Home was part of the supposedly stable and well-heeled Hiram Walker conglomerate of companies, which included one of the world's major liquor distillers. Home's parent was Hiram Walker Resources, and its president was Bill Wilder, whom I knew well when he was chair and I was controller of the benighted Arctic Gas project. Another important influence on my decision was Stan Olson, HBOG's former chief executive, who'd been appointed to the Hiram Walker board.

I agreed to become Home's president and CEO, replacing the outspoken Al McIntosh, who had not been long in the position. My leave-taking would occur just before year's end (by which point, four of the five most senior executives had announced their departures). Meanwhile, I could observe the continuing financial brinkmanship of Richards and Gallagher that—though I didn't realize it then—would lead to the eventual demise of Hudson's Bay Oil and Gas.

As ever, all of Dome's dealings were perfectly legal, but also foolishly risky and politically charged. In March 1982, the company was $7 billion in debt and needed $100 million by month's end to avoid bankruptcy. Only its friend Marc Lalonde's intervention with Toronto bankers saved Dome this time. But the condition attached to the rescue was that Jack and Bill had to resign—which they would, at long last, do at the end of 1983.

After the merger, some insightful employees at Dome (and it had many stars) had begun to realize the fine distinctions between the two cultures. One of those people was Hal Kvisle, who was organizing the production-engineering department of the combined operation. A young man from Innisfail, Alberta, of Norwegian extraction (his name is pronounced "*Quiz*-lee"), he'd started as a production engineer, went on to get his MBA, and was fated to someday lead TransCanada Pipelines: "My introduction to Hudson's Bay was an enlightening experience, to learn a little bit about how a well-run company worked. The purchasing, accounting, and computer-systems departments all worked really well. And they let the technical professionals just get on and do their job. Dome had grown from 330 people when I joined to 6,500 after the Hudson's Bay merger—and nothing worked. Dome had this great entrepreneurial approach but was really quite weak on the administrative and accounting and financial systems. Which was ultimately their downfall."

It had quickly become clear to Dave Powell that, with all Dome's problems, his pride and joy, the international division, would have to be sold off. He'd begun by reporting to a committee of Gallagher, Richards, and senior VP John Beddome, and when that didn't work, to Jack and Bill. "But they were putting fires out all over the place," he remembers, "and we had one meeting which ended up with them quarrelling and me quietly sidling out the door." By the end of 1982, when the international operations had grown seven-fold from the early HBOG days to a value of about $350 million, they were hived off to British Petroleum and Lasmo Oil of London.

Over the next few years, a new chairman tried to staunch the bloody flow of cash, but to no avail. By mid-1987, the badly limping company had the largest debt in Canadian corporate history—$6.3 billion. When Hal Kvisle's $200-million capital budget plunged to zero, he took the lead in convincing the creditor banks to restore 80 percent of the capital funding. Hal went on to work with Morgan Stanley to get a fair evaluation of the Dome/HBOG assets and to find a buyer for the company. They targeted three serious contenders: TransCanada Pipelines, Exxon, and Amoco Canada Petroleum, the Canadian subsidiary of the Amoco Corporation in the U.S. "While I would have loved to see TransCanada do the deal, the Canadian government did not," Hal says now. "It was Mulroney's government, with Michael Wilson the finance minister. They just wanted this nightmare over but didn't want Dome to go bankrupt." That November 1987, after months of negotiation, Amoco Canada agreed to buy Dome Petroleum for $5.5 billion.

It was only a temporary pause in an inevitable decline and fall. Within five years, Amoco sold nearly two-thirds of its oil fields and chopped more than half its staff. By the end of the 1990s, it vanished entirely when its parent company merged with British Petroleum. Most of its remaining properties in western Canada went to Canadian Natural Resources and Penn West Petroleum, controlled by the shrewd Calgary financier Murray Edwards, for $1.6 billion.

The question remained: What the hell really happened here? A newspaper quoted me not long after Dome's takeover of HBOG about the general topic of mergers: "Only one in five corporate mergers are successful. The others are disastrous. Look at Dome: a huge disaster." While acknowledging that the minority of companies—the one-fifth or so—that do succeed in merging well can ultimately win big, I wouldn't change a word of that statement today.

Certainly nobody won in the Dome takeover. Throughout the resulting drastic decline in its share price, stockholders lost big time. The banks lost on the bad loans. Three thousand or more employees eventually lost their jobs and, having bought corporate stock under an incentive scheme instead of contributing to a pension plan, lost their savings for retirement. Canadian taxpayers lost literally billions of dollars in Ottawa's series of subsidies and special tax exemptions to a company in dire straits. There were no winners.

And Canada lost a potential Northern Tiger. I don't see any Canadian companies around today that could have exceeded HBOG, with our combination of an enormous land base, the auspicious discoveries we were making in Australia and Indonesia, and the disciplined people who went on to operate other petroleum giants.

We should have been the ones taking over Dome. But because of the supercharged, overvalued performance of its shares, the stock markets wouldn't allow us to do that. Dome was trading at high multiples based merely on the utter hype Jack and Bill had built up around their unproven Beaufort Sea holdings. Simply far better at promoting themselves than we were with HBOG, and supported by a fawning federal government, they stickhandled us out of existence. There's no question that we should have been more aggressive. Today's oil companies *are*—and the EnCanas and Canadian Natural Resources are far smarter in balancing promise with execution, having learned from the fancy but ultimately ineffectual moves of the high-sticking Domes of the world.

Chapter Four

TAKING IT ON THE CHIN
Home Oil and Hiram Walker Resources

AFTER IT HAD BEEN ANNOUNCED that I was leaving Hudson's Bay for Home Oil, Dave Powell—HBOG's well-informed exploration guy—followed me back to my office to say, "Haskayne, Home is drilling these goddamn wells in Guyana, and the best thing you can do is phone them right now and tell them to stop drilling there."

"I can't do that, Dave. Christ, I'm not going to be there for a month."

"Well, I'm telling you, Haskayne, you want to get out of Guyana as fast as you can because you certainly will never make any money, and not only that, Home is holding the bag there right now."

And that was how I found myself in 1982 on the sultry northeast coast of South America in the office of Forbes Burnham, the hardline socialist prime minister who'd become the autocratic executive president of Guyana. The former British Guiana, which had received its independence two decades earlier, was a bit of an impoverished hellhole and, despite supposedly free elections, no model of democracy. During his twenty-one years in power over what he called a co-operative republic, Burnham had formed alliances with communist nations and his agents were alleged to have been involved in the deaths of a Jesuit priest–journalist and an opposition leader. The country, as usual, was in a state of political upheaval.

Despite this, Home Oil had a majority interest in oil-drilling operations in Guyana, based on the prospect of a big discovery that never did pan out. Getting our drill rigs there had involved a complex mobilization of resources from all over Home's world. The company shipped equipment from Edmonton, and our Houston office flew in pipe and cement on big Hercules turboprop transports. Part of the rigs themselves were seconded from Saudi Arabia, and then our logistics people had to figure out how to float them up the Amazon and into the jungle site. The Brazilian government charged us about $400,000 in duty alone, just for passing through their country. As time went by, our two partners in the deal—Norcen Energy and Ranger Oil of Calgary—pulled out, so Home had to assume 100 percent of what looked like two ridiculously expensive dry holes on the edge of nowhere.

"It wasn't the end of the world," Ken McNeill used to say, with his wonderfully over-the-top turn of phrase, "but you could certainly see it from there. Some of the administration people Home sent down there were guys they didn't want around in Calgary. So there they are with a unlimited spending budget down in the poorest country in the world, living like drunken sailors with a big expense account."

Meanwhile, there had been all sorts of false rumours that we'd found a lot of oil, which would bail the nation out of its misery, but had decided not to produce the wells because of low world prices. In 1982, I had to "discount and deny" a Guyanese government report that said the field, 320 kilometres south of the capital, Georgetown, contained two billion barrels. In fact, we found only a touch of light, sweet crude in one of the wells.

What Dave Powell had realized early on was that well drilled just across the river in Brazil had hit a salt formation that killed the chance of finding much oil on our side. As he explains it now, "The thing wasn't explored properly, and even though I personally wouldn't have gone in there in the first place, if they'd used a rig from Brazil [instead of importing the equipment], they could have drilled those two wells at a fraction of the cost. But the money they were spending then just frightened the hell out of everybody."

And now I was in Burnham's office in Georgetown to explain why we were cutting our losses. Not surprisingly, the windows had bulletproof glass. The quick-witted president of African descent, who led a nation made up of African, Amerindian, East Indian, Chinese, and Portuguese, was a lawyer and a graduate of the University of London. He was using all of his legalistic and political powers of persuasion to convince me to reverse my decision.

"Oh, you Canadians are very good people," he said in his deceptively folksy manner, "I will phone my friend Pierre and get you some assistance." Pierre Elliott Trudeau, the Canadian prime minister whose government enacted the National Energy Program that kneecapped our Oil Patch. Trudeau had stepped down as PM the year before.

"I am not looking for assistance," I assured Burnham. Our conversation was running into its own dry hole. The only hope Home had of saving the project, I knew, was to attempt a joint venture with the national oil company in neighbouring Brazil. I'd get back to Burnham if we had any success.

Home had a large office in Georgetown and a leased Twin Otter aircraft to ferry our people to the rig near the Brazilian border, where we had to build our own airstrip. But I flew there in our little cigar tin of a Lear 35 jet, crossing the vast rainforest—which, from the air, looked like clusters of broccoli—and landing at the big, bustling port of Manaus, the capital of Amazônia State, right on the Amazon River. But the officials of Brazil's Petrobras oil giant were just not that interested in assuming any of our obligations in Guyana. There was no other option but to shut down the whole damn thing. Our unsuccessful South American adventure would cost us upwards of $30 million.

Being a successful CEO means knowing exactly when to fold as well as when to raise the ante. Here, it wasn't in the cards to keep playing.

About three years later, in June 1985, Forbes Burnham went into hospital in Georgetown for what was supposed to be a routine procedure to treat a throat infection. Only Cuban doctors were allowed in the operating room. And there he died on the table—some say murdered, in revenge for the assassination of a Cuba-backed Guyanese political figure that Burnham's government had supposedly arranged.

HOME OIL HAD BEEN FOUNDED IN 1925 by a provincial politician who didn't know a thing about the petroleum business yet developed the company into the biggest independent in Canada. A quarter-century later, the wildcatting son of an oil entrepreneur took Home over and, like Jack Gallagher, risked everything in the Arctic but managed to evade near-bankruptcy and keep it alive— long enough to sell it to a successful Canadian utility. I arrived well after his death and, along with confronting a socialist strongman in South America, I would face a Hollywood tycoon, two reclusive Toronto brothers whose family was one of the world's ten wealthiest, and an Ontario-bred scion of a liquor baron family who made their fortune during Prohibition in the U.S.

Home was the brainchild of James Lowery, an Ontario farm lad of twenty-one who migrated to Alberta in 1905, the year it became a province. He became a Jim of all trades, selling newspapers, hardware, and real estate before running twice as one of the rare provincial Conservatives in that Liberal era and winning the second time. Lowery served with the Canadian Army during the First World War and, after being wounded at the infamous Battle of Vimy Ridge, came home a major. His career was looking up in 1924, when a company co-owned by Imperial Oil drilled in Alberta's Turner Valley and brought in Royalite No. 4, the well that ushered in the province's first petroleum boom. Less than nine months later, he was an oilman, a partner in the Home Oil Company Limited. Its first well struck crude oil and then, within two years, an enormous flow of high-grade naphtha (natural gasoline). It was the largest find in the valley. Building on it, Jim Lowery proved to be a great promoter and, over the next twenty-five years, positioned Home to capitalize on the next boom that was touched off by Leduc in 1947.

He already knew Robert A. Brown, a Quebecer who'd studied electrical engineering at McGill University and worked for Westinghouse Electric Corporation in the U.S. before coming to Calgary in 1906. A few years later, Brown was supervising the city's electric light and streetcar departments and looking for further stimulation. He found it by creating electrical utility companies in rural communities, among them my parents' town of Gleichen. And that's also where, in 1934, the year I was born, Brown and his partners met with a local baker, coincidentally named Robert Brown, and subleased sixty acres of land he owned in the Turner Valley. It took only two years before both Browns were rolling in oil money as Turner Valley Royalties' first well blew in wildly in 1936.

The discovery marked the end of the college career of yet another Robert Brown. The businessman's twenty-two-year-old son, Bob Brown, Jr., was studying accounting at the University of Alberta when that No. 1 came in, and he soon spent more time on the fascinating company business than on his studies. He and his dad launched several new ventures, and Junior (nicknamed the Oil Baby) turned out to be a confident, visionary promoter and an inspired corporate financier. After working in oil supply for the government in Ottawa during the Second World War, he had a brief fling with importing American home appliances. Then Leduc happened, and in 1948 when his father died of heart failure, young Brown became president of the main family business, Federated Petroleums. He wasn't a hands-on operator. As he once told a reporter, "I have an effective arrangement with the senior employees who manage the operations of Home Oil. I find the money, and they find the oil."

The Canadian Bank of Commerce's far-sighted Neil McKinnon, then second-in-command and later president, backed Federated in its takeovers of other oil companies. By 1950, Brown was buying up shares of Home Oil, where Jim Lowery was ready to retire, and within a year, Federated had control of Canada's fourth-largest oil producer.

Under Bobby Brown's leadership, Home made significant discoveries whose names are part of Alberta's oil heritage: Swan

Hills, Virginia Hills, Westward Ho. He was an advocate for the oil industry, promoting the idea of a pipeline to Montreal, becoming the biggest shareholder in the TransCanada pipeline to Ontario, and helping found the Independent Petroleum Association of Canada. But there was another side to the man: Like his father, he was hard drinking, hard driving, and prone to developing heart disease. And he had a penchant for financial risk-taking and over-extending himself, which landed him in deep, dark waters.

In 1959, despite owing the Commerce nearly $20 million on a demand loan, he'd been the first in Canada to buy a Grumman Gulfstream I, the world's original large executive turboprop. Philip Smith, in *The Treasure-Seekers: The Men Who Built Home Oil,* describes Brown's dilemma at the time:

> ...his bank loan was now so large that he could not pay it back without selling a substantial portion of his assets—and possibly losing control of Home. He lived at the time like a millionaire....Perhaps because of his anxiety over this seemingly insoluble problem—or, more probably, given Brown's nature, out of sheer frustration that his upward climb was at least temporarily stalled—he stepped up his already heavy drinking. He was now in his late forties and the recuperative powers which had always been the envy of his friends were beginning to wane: more and more he would show up at the office late and sometimes he would be unable to attend even important business meetings if they were held early in the day.

Brian MacNeill, a Winnipeg chartered accountant who wound up as controller at Home, says, "Not many people had anything bad to say about Bobby Brown—even though most of them got fired by him at one time or another when he was in his cups." In the early 1960s, when I came into the Oil Patch, Brown was mired in debt and soon had the first of a series of heart attacks. Things didn't get much rosier over the years: He bet almost everything on exploring and leasing fields on Alaska's North Slope and trying to

buy control of the much-larger U.S. oil company Atlantic
Richfield. That all ended disastrously (the takeover attempt alone
cost $69 million), and near the end of his life, he was personally
indebted for $26 million.

Finally, he had to yield control of Home to Consumers' Gas of
Toronto. Consumers' was a century-old company that had
switched from producing coal gas locally to supplying much of
Ontario with the Alberta natural gas that the TransCanada line
was now shipping east. Its president was Oakah Jones, an
accountant from Boston who'd operated a similar gas company in
Tulsa. Jones and Brown did a friendly deal in 1971 that saved
Home from bankruptcy and left its CEO in place. But Brown died
early in the new year.

The conservative Jones succeeded him as CEO. But again,
briefly: He died in 1973. He'd sold the Gulfstream but kept the
rest of the fleet of smaller aircraft, the King Airs and the de
Havilland Beavers, that Brown had assembled. His successor, Ross
Phillips, had to do more belt-tightening as inflation and fresh federal taxes reduced exploration throughout the early 1970s. Later
in the decade, after Ottawa and the Alberta government settled
some of their differences, oil finding rebounded. In 1977, Home
had holdings in the province's productive new West Pembina field,
but its sorties overseas in the North Sea and the Mediterranean
were showing little return.

Suffering overall, the company was a takeover candidate when
Hiram Walker–Gooderham & Worts showed up. Canada's second-
largest liquor distiller, wanting to diversify, sought an alliance that
might also help keep it out of the clutches of its bigger competitor,
Seagram. Hiram Walker was named after the Detroit grain merchant who, during the American temperance era of the 1850s,
moved across the Detroit River to build a mill and a distillery in
what became Walkerville, Ontario. His innovative Walker's Club
brand of whisky became Canadian Club, which swept the North
American market. In 1926, the Walker descendants sold out to a
syndicate headed by Harry Hatch, who three years earlier had
bought a smaller Ontario distillery, Gooderham & Worts.

Clifford Hatch, Sr., Harry's son, was chairman in 1980 when he led a merger between a healthy Consumers' Gas and its weaker, wholly owned subsidiary, Home Oil. The new company—at first called Hiram Walker–Consumers Home Ltd.—enjoyed revenues of $2.6 billion and the fifth-biggest profits of any Canadian company. A year later, it was rechristened Hiram Walker Resources (HWR). Hatch was chairman, and two of my mentors sat on the board: Bill Wilder, the president and CEO, and Stan Olson, a director (Cliff and Bill were old war buddies). The idea was to widen the scope of the oil company with revenues from the spirits and gas companies. Presiding over Home, meanwhile, was Al McIntosh, who'd been executive VP of Calgary's Pacific Petroleums when Petro-Canada took it over in 1978. Unhappy about working for a creature of the federal government, he went to a more comfortable Home.

Now, just three years later, I was replacing Al. As I stepped out of the frying pan of a Dome-dominated HBOG, I began to realize what a hellfire I was stepping into at HWR. Bill had told Al to buy something substantial in the U.S. to offset the effects of the new National Energy Program in Canada. What Al found was Davis Oil of Denver. Marvin Davis and his father had founded the Davis oil and gas exploration business, which became one of the premier wildcat drilling operations in the U.S. They bought cheap oil and gas leases in the Rocky Mountain region and then developed them through the booming 1970s. Only three multinationals—Shell, Amoco, and Exxon—drilled more exploratory wells. (Marvin always quoted his friend and fellow oilman H.L. Hunt: "He who drills the most wells wins.") In January 1981, HWR bought Davis lands in Wyoming, Oklahoma, Louisiana, and Texas with an estimated eleven million barrels of proved and probable reserves of crude oil and 173 billion cubic feet of natural gas. The cost: $737 million, which was an astonishing figure to Gerry Maier and me. Within Hiram Walker, though, even Bill Wilder thought the world price of oil would continue to rise and justify the acquisition.

But the deal was done in a hurry to compete with half a dozen other companies and with Davis claiming he had an incurable cancer that was prompting him to sell. Home's due diligence had been obviously deficient—as I now discovered. During the month I'd planned to relax before becoming president and attending my first board meeting in mid-January, I reviewed all the numbers. Hiram Walker itself was having a wonderful year. Consumers' was doing fine, too, but in studying the details of the Davis transaction and the U.S. operation it had spawned for us, I could have calculated the figures on the back of an envelope and known that it was horribly overvalued. We were losing our shirts—and our shorts. I grew more and more disturbed, so much so that I flew to see Stan Olson at his home in Washington State.

"Stan, what the hell is going on with this Davis stuff? You really have to look at the economics of this bloody thing."

"Christ, Dick, I didn't know anything about it," he said.

The directors and their chairman, Cliff Hatch, had relied on an external assessment of the properties. As Cliff's successor, Bud Downing, would explain in a post-mortem two years later: "We had what we considered the best investment banker in North America, Morgan Stanley, doing the work for us. The information they gathered was the information we used [to evaluate the properties]. Admittedly, it was not as complete as it probably could have been."

If the board didn't have a good grasp of the current situation, it had even more surprises in store. Flying me back from a trip to Toronto, our chief pilot happened to ask if I'd be spending the weekend working on "Mountain 2."

"What's that?" I asked.

While he didn't really know, I quickly learned that it was the code name for a scheme to buy a second big batch of Davis properties for $450 million (U.S.). A vp named Ron Watkins told me he and his team were heading to Denver to begin sealing the deal, which was to close in a couple of weeks. "This is really the best part of it, and Marvin Davis will give us an exclusive on it," he assured me.

"You guys are not going," I told him. "You're going to stay home, and I want you to start working on the properties you bought two years ago." My plan was nothing less than to set in motion a severe writedown that would reflect the true value of the Davis properties.

"Well, what will Mr. Wilder think?" Ron asked.

"I'll handle Mr. Wilder." And when I told Bill we were cancelling the second deal, he agreed with barely a murmur.

I also had to tell Marvin Davis. Flying to his headquarters in Denver, I hooked up with a senior Davis Oil guy who was now working for our company. Together, we met with Davis, a big bear of a man (who'd lose 150 pounds near the end of his life). Looking remarkably well for a man with cancer, he sat behind an oversized desk in his ballroom of an office, with its autographed photographs of Davis with three American presidents. The oilman was buying the fabled Twentieth Century-Fox film studio, and a lot of the investors in the oil and gas wells we'd bought were movie stars. In his flamboyance, he was an American version of Jack Gallagher. As *Forbes* magazine would later report:

> Using other people's money has been a hallmark of Davis' empire, going back to his days as a wildcatter succeeding to his father's oil business. He shielded Davis Oil from losses by having investors assume risk for his wells. Davis financed his acquisition of Twentieth Century-Fox in 1981 with bank loans and an investment from [the American tax] fugitive Marc Rich.

This was the billionaire whom I was now informing that our deal for the second chunk of his properties was toast and, as the new CEO of Home Oil, I was sorry for the inconvenience.

Obviously needing our money to help finance his entry into Hollywood, Davis went berserk: "I've saved this thing for the Home people. They got first priority, I've held it off the market, and I've got sixteen people lined up at the door to do the deal— and now you come in and tell me this!"

"Well, Mr. Davis, I apologize for that. If you have some other people, maybe you should sell it to them because I'm not going forward with it—period." I stood to go, figuring my allotted twenty minutes with him was up.

"Dick, sit down for a minute," he said, cooling off. "While I don't like this, you seem like a pretty reasonable guy. Tell me more about yourself."

After we chatted for much of an hour, I told him I'd speak to our directors, see what they'd decide to do, and get back to him.

Soothed a little, he offered to hold the properties until Hiram Walker's upcoming annual general meeting.

Then I went back to our accountants and, working with Price Waterhouse, we struggled to decide exactly how much the write-down of Marvin Davis's first group of grossly overpriced properties should be. After much internal debate, even taking into account some of the good holdings Home had in the U.S. before the Davis deal, we decided the figure was an appalling after-tax $177 million (before tax, it was more like $350 million). My philosophy then, as it has always been, was to confront problems head-on and deal with them directly and efficiently. In other words, to take it on the chin and then get on with life.

Other than telling Stan Olson, I hadn't described the situation in any detail at my first board meeting. But now the directors would have to know how bad things really were. We called them together in a special conference in Toronto—just before the annual general meeting of Hiram Walker, when the parent company was all set to tell shareholders how terrific the past twelve months had been.

Stan and I, along with some other Home executives from Calgary, met that morning with Bill Wilder. After hearing our rationale, he agreed on the number and said we had to tell the board. None of the other directors who met with us in a board-room in the Royal York Hotel was an oilman. They were shocked. In a press release already prepared to announce the writedown, we'd mentioned the company's new management, but Bill had deleted that reference and said he had to take full responsibility as Hiram Walker's CEO.

At the annual meeting, full to the brim with shareholders, as usual, he reported the bad news. There was dead silence and then a barrage of irate comments and questions from the floor as the corporate analysts rushed to the phones. Our high-flying stock dropped to a five-year low. Devaluing the properties would cause Hiram Walker Resources to lose $78 million in the coming year, compared to a 1981 profit of $222 million. At a media scrum after his speech, Bill said, "We'll know in about a month whether we have a case for misrepresentation of information."

Of course, Marvin Davis was incensed. I didn't need to call him: There was a message waiting for me back in Calgary saying that he was suing Bill Wilder and Hiram Walker, probably for tens of millions of dollars. He never did follow through on that threat. And within a few years of buying the film studio, he sold it to Rupert Murdoch. Davis, who had a reputation as a relentless corporate raider, died in 2004—nearly a quarter-century after he'd talked of having terminal cancer. We had only that one meeting.

(There's a strange sequel to this story. Years later, when I was on the board of the Alberta Energy Company, I argued strongly against investing $1 billion in deep oil wells in the same Wyoming area where Home had inherited Davis Oil's questionable holdings. People with more technical expertise assured me that the technology to get the oil had vastly improved since that time, and the directors voted to go ahead with the purchase. "If you find out that any of that land was owned by Home at one time," I said, "don't tell me, because I'll cry." A couple of weeks later, AEC's chief financial officer, John Watson, told me, "You were right: Not only were they Home Oil lands, the discovery wells were the ones you guys drilled in 1984.")

After we'd sorted out the damn Davis acquisition, Cliff Hatch, Sr., took over the Hiram Walker Resources operation on a temporary basis as Bill Wilder stepped down as president and became his deputy chairman. A couple of years later, when Cliff wanted to retire, Bud Downing—a low-key chemical engineer who'd come up through HWR's distilling ranks—stepped up as chair.

RATIONALIZING OUR DAVIS DEAL was nowhere near the end of my challenges with our American operations, though. I still had to deal with the bloating of staff and the spending I was hearing about at our offices down south. By now, Ken McNeill was working with us at Home, where people thought of him as my alter ego. He'd applied with a photo to remind me of what he looked like, a dime to make "telephone contact with the candidate," and a letter that noted: "My background is varied, but I consider that background an exemplary demonstration of my ability to be equally incompetent at any level of responsibility." I was soon calling on his competence—and even his background as a cop—to help resolve deep-rooted problems with some of the 660 people on Home's payroll in the U.S., some of them inherited from Davis Oil.

Ken became our general manager and later VP of administration, a catch-all title that included everything from purchasing to human resources. It was his HR skills that I needed immediately to straighten out personnel problems at our Houston, Denver, and Oklahoma City offices. Ken recalls that time: "The U.S. operation was truly a mess. We were hearing rumours and seeing evidence of some strange things going on. We had one very bright young internal auditor and, knowing my background, he asked me: 'What do you make of all this?' The books did not make any sense. The people down there were going on trips to Mexico, and there were no expense accounts for those or anything else. Obviously, the trips were being paid for by other companies, their suppliers. I ended up getting a private investigator to work down there."

Home's interim chief operating officer, Bill Waddell, had been awaiting my arrival to decide what to do with a Price Waterhouse organizational study of our American operation. To put it mildly, things there were horribly lax. Ken's detective may not have found any actual smoking guns, but we did discover that some people were much too cozy with their service suppliers, to the point of accepting free trips—and even engraved shotguns. As well as ethical issues, there was an ingrained culture of overspending and overstaffing. The two offices were competing with one another and, in this jockeying for position, had duplicated many of their functions, including human resources and accounting personnel. If we maintained the status quo, our U.S. operation simply wouldn't be sustainable. But even on a personal level, it wouldn't be fair to employees to keep them on staff when they didn't have meaningful roles to play, given the duplication in their work.

On a fact-finding trip, I met in Houston with the key operating executive, a former Davis man, in his big office with a bar and a private bathroom. The staff idolized him because he was so lavish in his largesse. It didn't take me long to realize that we should consolidate in Denver and severely downsize our Houston office, which was staffed with employees hired by Home. And he would be one of the many to be let go—in a respectful and financially fair process.

THERE'S A CALLOUS-SOUNDING quotation that reads, "It isn't the people you fire who make your life miserable, it's the people you don't." While that may be partly true, it's a one-sided view that simply ignores the human element involved in severing individuals' links with their workplace and endangering their livelihoods. And here I was soon after with Ernie Hambrook, the administrative VP from Home, to meet with a packed room of maybe a couple of hundred people in Houston as we delivered the sober tidings: Ernie, we told them, was taking the place of the Davis alumnus, and Denver would now be our major office in the U.S., with Houston relegated to more of a field operation.

The situation soon became tense as the employees erupted with anger. *How could we be so stupid to gut the Houston office?* They were crowded around us, menacingly close as they shouted and swore. This was the nearest I've ever come to being physically threatened—in my work and in my life. I felt that if somebody had a gun, he'd have shot me. Fortunately, the ex-Davis guy bailed me out: "Look, this isn't fair. Dick is trying to do the right thing. He's treated me fairly and he's undertaken that we'll all be treated fairly." We escaped with our skins and, though we cut back to a staff of four hundred, Home would still be the biggest Canadian operator in the U.S. for the next few years.

There was excess in the Calgary home office, too. It had come from the top in Bobby Brown's day, with the fanciest formal dining room outside of the Petroleum Club, all antique furniture and thick broadloom, and an art collection that could rival a good small gallery's. Ken McNeill brought in an art consultant who found valuable paintings on employees' walls and in storage rooms—even one by the Group of Seven's A.J. Casson, which we gave to the Glenbow Museum. Coming from the tightly run HBOG, Ken was disturbed by the sense of entitlement at Home: "When I first got there, one thing I blinked at was that people had memberships at the Petroleum Club and would routinely take their friends, and even neighbours, there and write off all these personal expenses to the company. I'd say, 'What are you doing? That's only for business expenses.' And they'd say, 'Oh hell, no, that ain't the way that's ever worked around here, sonny. You're not going to survive long if that's your attitude.' They honestly thought that this was a kind of deserved perk." We soon put a stop to that practice. And I put Ken, with his love of airplanes, in charge of the aviation division, where he had to sell our Lear 35 and the manufacturing positions on one of two Citations and a Dash-8 turboprop that the previous administration had on order.

Besides Ken, other refugees from HBOG joined us at Home. Fred Callaway, for instance, who'd been in several senior management positions there, came on as a corporate vice-president and then, as our international VP, launched oil and gas operations in South America. Fred was Pat Daniel's first boss after Pat fled an undisciplined Dome to run the information technology department and solve the disconnect we were seeing between IT and the customers it was supposed to be serving. And then there was the inimitable Dave Powell.

When Dome sold its international arm to British Petroleum and Lasmo Oil, Dave was courted both by Dome, to run its frontier operations on the east coast and in the Beaufort Sea, and by Lasmo, to work from its London office. Dome's John Beddome called me and asked what I really thought of Dave, whom he wanted to lure away from Lasmo: "We feel if we offer someone a challenging enough job, they'll probably accept it."

And I replied, on the spur of the moment, "I'll tell you what I think: I think we may be rivals for the same guy."

I called Dave immediately to say we were interested in hiring him. Because I didn't want him to meet where people could see us negotiating, I suggested neutral ground: the Coffee Mug café at the Hudson's Bay store downtown. That's where we made a deal on the back of a napkin, which he kept in a filing cabinet for years. He replaced Bill Waddell as senior VP of exploration and production (Bill and I remained friends even after he left the company). Dave began to clean up some of our messes. One of them was closing down the Oklahoma City and Houston offices entirely and overseeing a further reduction in U.S. staff to about two hundred.

Another was our involvement offshore and onshore in the Blina reef play of western Australia's Canning Basin—which he'd also warned me about when I was leaving HBOG. Gerry Maier had been interested in Canning until Dave told him, "I'll drink all the fucking oil that comes out of the Canning Basin." When he joined Home, we were still a partner there with others, including Occidental Petroleum, one of the ten largest American oil companies, controlled by the storied billionaire entrepreneur and art collector Armand Hammer. While Hammer was publicly pushing the merits of Canning, Dave knew from his early days with Burmah Oil that the reefs held very little oil despite some tantalizing shows. He managed to sell a friend in the business the three positions Home had on a floating rig. Australia was far from being a complete washout. We had 55 percent ownership of Home Energy there, with shares trading on the local stock exchange. When all of the subsidiary's assets were eventually sold (long after I'd left), the company even made money on the deal.

Meanwhile, on our home turf, we paid closer attention to the 88.5 percent interest we had in Scurry-Rainbow Oil. A thirty-year-old company that was about a seventh of our size, it had petroleum properties in B.C., Alberta, and Saskatchewan and exploration acreage in the U.S. Early on, we sold off its interest in a large coal project in the Crowsnest Pass area of the Rockies as well as its gold and silver mines in Nevada.

Coming off the financial horror of the Davis debacle, we began positioning Home to take advantage of the National Energy Program's crazy policies to encourage Canadian oil companies. Crazy, because the nation's taxpayers were paying through the nose for them while the corporations were reaping the profits. In 1983, I had the pleasure of watching Dave Powell negotiate a $1.47-billion deal with debt-laden Dome Petroleum while Jack Gallagher and Bill Richards were still in place as lame-duck operators, scheduled to step down officially by year's end. Home and Scurry-Rainbow would earn a substantial interest in Dome's lands in the West and the Beaufort Sea in return for picking up anywhere from 15 to 40 percent of the costs. (As Dave would point out, "A lot of Dome people lower down the ladder felt that the farm had been sold, but in fact, there wouldn't have been a ship sailing in the Beaufort Sea that season if Home hadn't put up the money.") Much of the properties in Alberta were holdings that Dome had picked off with its ill-fated takeover of my alma mater, HBOG.

The sweetener was that under the provisions of the NEP's Petroleum Incentive Program—the so-called PIP grants—Ottawa would reimburse most of our frontier exploration expenses because Home had high-enough Canadian content to qualify. At that point, we were drilling expensive wells off Nova Scotia and had a farm-in arrangement with Esso Resources Canada to explore in the Beaufort (that's an agreement in which the owner of a working interest in a petroleum lease assigns it wholly or partly to another party). But we were spending only seven-cent dollars— the government would give us the rest back (ninety-three cents) in these grants to encourage drilling that we normally couldn't afford to do. As a Canadian, I was embarrassed by what I considered to be a dumb law, but as a businessman, I wanted to keep Home competitive. And as it turned out, we did drill eighteen-thousand-foot wells in the Atlantic.

By 1984, we were in fighting trim again. "I'm on a bit of a high these days," I told the *Financial Times*. "We're really pleased with where we are." Home had more than $2 billion in assets and was generating close to half a billion in revenues. We were the sixth-most-active explorer in Canada and the fourth-ranked in PIP incentives as we received more than $100 million in grants that year.

Somewhere during that time, I got a nice note from Gerry Maier, who'd long since left the remnant of HBOG as it dissolved into Dome. He became president and CEO of Bow Valley Industries, controlled by one of Calgary's great corporate families, the Seaman brothers—Daryl (Doc), Byron, and Donald. Their company had mushroomed in recent years, with oil and gas fields in the North Sea and Abu Dhabi, its uranium venture in their home province of Saskatchewan, and its acquisition of the Flying Diamond Oil Corporation in the U.S. (with a $130-million loan from the Royal Bank, the biggest single loan in Canadian history up to that time). So Bow Valley and Gerry were busy beavers themselves when he dropped me the note, which was high praise coming from him:

> Congratulations, old buddy. You are really doing a first-class job of putting Home back on its feet, and it's good to see your efforts are recognized. The future certainly looks very promising. Keep up the good work—but, please, do leave a few farm-ins for us!

Chapter Five

RUNNING WITH THE REICHMANNS

Interhome Energy and Interprovincial Pipe Line

THE HOPEFUL FUTURE THAT GERRY MAIER pointed out, as well as my own natural optimism, would prevail for the next couple of years. Then came the Reichmann brothers, doggedly on the hunt again. No matter how experienced, forward-thinking, and in-command an executive you think you are, events conspire to control *you*. Unexpected external forces come barrelling down and toss you off your carefully chosen track.

In this case, the unforeseen forces were the reclusive scions of a family that was among the ten richest in the world. Paul, Albert, and Ralph Reichmann were casting a large shadow from their headquarters in Toronto. I'd probably heard by then that the roots of this ultra-orthodox Jewish family harked back to at least eighteenth-century rural Hungary (where an ancestor adopted the Germanic surname meaning "wealthy man"). Their story would unfold in magazine articles and books throughout the 1980s, and it described how the family's descendants moved to Austria and lived there until the anti-Semitism of the '30s propelled them to Paris. Then, with the Nazi occupation of France, they settled in Tangiers, where the patriarch, Samuel Reichmann, became a wealthy currency trader. In the early '50s, his sons began to migrate to Canada, first to Montreal and then to Toronto. And there, in 1964, Paul and Albert formed a small industrial development company, Olympia & York. Two decades later, with Ralph and their parents as equal partners, they'd shaped a multi-billion-dollar enterprise that was building the four towers of New York's enormous World Financial Center at Battery Park City and, in 1986, was a year away from opening London's massive Canary Wharf development, featuring Britain's three tallest buildings on reclaimed east-end Docklands.

Over the years, they'd acquired the English Property Corporation of London, which had ten million square feet of office space in Britain and Europe. Through that company, they held a fifth of the shares in Canada's third-largest developer, Trizec of Calgary, and had another 58 percent jointly with Edper Investments, owned by another important Jewish-Canadian family, Edgar and Peter Bronfman. The Reichmanns also controlled most of Block Brothers Realty of Vancouver, the West's largest real estate firm. But there was so much more beyond property in their portfolio. They'd bought Canada's Abitibi-Price, the world's major newsprint producer, and Cassiar Resources, which was rolled into Brinco Ltd., the huge natural resources company. And they'd held the largest piece of Royal Trustco and minority positions in the forest giant MacMillan Bloedel of Vancouver, and for a while, even Bow Valley Industries, where Gerry had presided until 1985.

And of course, they'd made that play for Hudson's Bay Oil and Gas a decade earlier. When that failed, the brothers began buying up shares in the conglomerate I was about to join, Hiram Walker Resources. In time, they discreetly assembled a 10 percent bloc that cost $200 million. They had a couple of objectives: One was simply to hold sway over a flourishing enterprise, and the other, to convince Bill Wilder to help them acquire another oil company. Bill had been executive VP of Gulf Canada, our second-biggest petroleum producer, before leaving to become chief executive officer of HWR. In an attempt to do what they hadn't done with Conoco, the Reichmanns planned to hold enough stock to induce Gulf Canada's controlling American parent, Gulf Oil, to sell its Canadian subsidiary. But when they announced their intention, neither Bill nor Hiram Walker's Hatch family would entertain the idea of collaborating with them.

That was then. In 1986, the Reichmanns finally got Gulf Canada, which was generating revenues of $5 billion a year. In the U.S., Chevron had bought Gulf Oil that year, but the Brian Mulroney government insisted the Canadian subsidiary must be offered to domestically controlled buyers. Up stepped Olympia & York. In a typically complicated transaction, the brothers actually acquired Gulf Canada by persuading it to buy their pulp-and-paper company, Abitibi-Price, at the same time—in effect, Gulf was helping to finance its acquisition with its own money (and paying double what the Reichmanns had). Arguing that they were saving a Canadian company, the brothers also managed to finesse a half-billion-dollar tax break from Ottawa by capitalizing on an intricate and heavily criticized legal loophole called "the Little Egypt Bump" (after an old-fashioned stripteaser). Peter Foster described the loophole in his book *The Master Builders*:

> Gulf Canada's oil and gas assets were on the books at much less than their market value. Oil and gas assets, moreover, could be written off against income. So, if the assets' book value for tax purposes could be "bumped up" to their real value—or even more—then there would be correspondingly larger amounts of depreciation available to be set against future income. Assets depreciated once could be depreciated all over again.... This was clearly not the intention of the legislation, but it was the law.

My friend Stephen Jarislowsky, the outspoken Montreal investment manager, said, "It was hypocritical of the Reichmanns to raise the issue of patriotism to justify their huge tax break on the Gulf deal. These patriots have made most of their fortune in New York." The loophole was soon legislated out of existence. It helped the deal to have the advice of the president of Paul Reichmann's private holding company, lawyer and tax expert

Marshall (Mickey) Cohen, a former federal deputy minister of energy, industry, and finance, who among his other government duties helped craft the National Energy Program.

With one oil company in hand, a determined Paul and Albert came after the second one that had spurned them in 1981. In a finely calculated raid that could make your head spin with its complexities, they made a bid for Hiram Walker Resources, Home's parent. Bill Wilder had left as chief executive while staying on the board, Cliff Hatch, Sr., had retired as chairman, and Bud Downing was now chair and CEO. Among HWR's holdings was Toronto-based Interprovincial Pipe Line Ltd. IPL, founded in 1950 to transport crude oil from Edmonton to eastern Canada and the U.S., became the longest such pipeline in the world, with assets of $1.7 billion and a healthy balance sheet. In 1983, in an early defensive move, HWR had acquired more than a third of the line, making it the major shareholder in a stock exchange that also made IPL the largest single shareholder of HWR, with about 16 percent.

The Reichmanns' initially friendly takeover attempt of the pipeline, our oil company, and the liquor business would derail my career track. Because Bud was close to sixty-five, Cliff and the board had asked me to consider replacing him in Toronto. My wife, Lee, wasn't that crazy about making any move but said that if we kept our Calgary house and I had a local office as well as one in the east, she'd support me. As I wrote to Noah Torno, chair of the board's management-resources committee, "I would be the sole determinant of the allocation of my time." We were just working out the timetable of the transition when the Reichmanns sideswiped us and cancelled my decision to climb a notch up the ladder.

Their offer for Hiram Walker Resources was $8 per share lower than the $40 value that analysts had determined was fair. Downing and his directors fought back, placing bold ads that suggested Olympia & York was stealing the company and urging shareholders not to sell their stock. Meanwhile, HWR's investment bankers canvassed the world for a white knight to buy the conglomerate's liquor asset, Hiram Walker–Gooderham & Worts, where Cliff Hatch, Jr., had become president. In fact, they found a real knight, Sir Derrick Holden-Brown, head of Allied-Lyons PLC, the London-based food and drink multinational (Baskin-Robbins ice cream, Teacher's scotch). With the funds from such a sale, HWR could battle the Reichmanns for control of the remaining company, including Consumers' and Home. Olympia & York sued to prevent Allied from buying the distillery, but lost in court.

By this time, another suitor had appeared: TransCanada PipeLines, where Gerry Maier had become president and CEO in 1985. He'd known the Reichmanns while he was running Bow Valley Resources, in which they had a heavy investment. But he'd met them earlier, in his time at HBOG, when he approached Paul Reichmann to make a competing bid during the Dome takeover. Paul had been interested, but the Gallagher-Richards team deked him out. Now Gerry wanted Home Oil, so he decided to negotiate with Paul rather than compete directly against him. But he wasn't aware that Interprovincial Pipe Line also wanted Home and that Paul was simultaneously talking to Bob Heule, an engineer who became IPL's chairman, and Ted Courtnage, an Exxon and Imperial alumnus who was president.

TransCanada, backed by its biggest shareholder, the mighty Bell Canada Enterprises, bid $36.50 cash per share for HWR—while agreeing to accept the $2.6-billion sale of the distilling subsidiary to Allied and planning to sell off control of Consumers' and possibly enlarging its stake in Interprovincial. It looked like a done deal.

But challenged by the competition and determined to get their prize—which for them was the liquor company—the Reichmanns finally offered $38 a share, or $3.3 billion. It was reportedly the largest sum that had ever been tendered for a company in Canada at that time. This time, HWR's outflanked directors reluctantly gave in, all the while hoping that TransCanada would up its offer. Gerry and his directors, however, decided the price to capture the petroleum assets was way too high and withdrew from the bidding contest.

In accepting the Reichmanns' offer, HWR had insisted that the sale of Gooderham & Worts to Allied proceed. Yet once in control, the brothers talked of pulling out of that deal. Allied counterpunched by launching a staggering $9-billion legal action, a Canadian record to that point and the second-largest lawsuit in the world. The Reichmanns—despite politicking in Ottawa and lobbying in the distillery's home of Windsor, Ontario—were forced to visit London and make an arrangement with Sir Derrick's company to sell it a 51 percent interest in Gooderham & Worts. The agreement contained a clause that would eventually allow Allied to buy them out entirely. As things would transpire in 1988, though, the canny Reichmanns traded their stake in the whisky business for $370 million in cash and enough stock to make them Allied's biggest shareholders.

One unfortunate aftermath of the deal was that with the British company as the active partner, the nerve centre of the company moved from Windsor to England. As financial officer Jim Ferguson, one of the few senior executives left in the original Hiram Walker distilling offices, told *Saturday Night* magazine, "With the money we spent on Davis Oil in the early 1980s, we could have taken over Allied-Lyons.... Had we been more aggressive, more proactive, Canada would have still had a proud public company." Another potential Northern Tiger down the tubes.

And in the end, what had the Reichmanns got for their trouble? A weakened conglomerate, which had spent $35 million trying to ward them off (after the acquisition, Bud Downing lost his job but left with a golden parachute of $3 million or so). They got a distilling operation that was in decline as North American liquor sales continued to drop. And even Home wasn't quite as attractive as it had been at the start of the takeover bid: In early 1986, oil prices had plummeted to what was only a third of their value the year before—another example of surprising, controlling forces surfacing from the outside. In the wake of the painfully public Gulf and Hiram Walker Resources deals, Paul Reichmann told the *Globe and Mail*'s David Olive, "If I'd known all this would happen, I would rather not have gone ahead with it."

The actual disposition of shares in the sale of Hiram Walker proved to be as convoluted as the hostile takeover had been. Seventy percent of its stock was tendered to the Reichmann-controlled Gulf Canada, 11 percent went to their GW Utilities Ltd., and 16 percent to Interprovincial Pipe Line, which was the largest single shareholder of HWR—and now Gulf, in total, would own 40 percent of the pipeline, nearly double the holdings of the only other large investor, Imperial Oil. It takes the minds of an accountant, a lawyer, and an investment banker to track all of this.

Where did all this fancy dealing leave Home Oil and me? In limbo, until late July 1987. That's when Hiram Walker Resources announced it would be selling Home to Interprovincial for $1.1 billion (which excluded our assets in the U.S.). For the second time in a row, a company I was running had been sold out from under me.

At that point, I could have quit Home with my own golden parachute. When the Reichmanns had come after HWR, its board gave eight senior executives what had become standard employment contracts to deal with takeover situations. The idea was to create incentives to keep the current management in place during a transition from one owner to another. Mickey Cohen, whom I'd known from my days at Hudson's Bay Oil and Gas, was negotiating for the Reichmanns, and my hard-nosed friend Bob Peterson, Imperial Oil's CEO, represented his company. If the takeover happened and I simply walked out the door, my agreement would have given me options and a pension—all in all, amounting to about $4 million. Instead, they were offering an increase in my salary and a stay-on-board bonus of $330,000. Bob said flatly, "You can't quit. You're key to putting these two companies together."

"Then you guys have an obligation to make sure that I get the same benefit if I stay on," I replied. In return for my forgoing the lucrative terms of the parachute, I suggested, "Give me another five years on my pension. It's cheap as hell for you, and it keeps me here on an ethical basis." (Bud Downing had encouraged me: "The one thing you've got to remember is that the Reichmanns need you more than you need them.")

They agreed to my demand. I also received the $330,000 sweetener to become president and CEO of both companies, a bonus that led to press reports saying I got this "spoonful of sugar...not as solace for being kicked out into the cold, but for moving between affiliated companies." In fact, I would have been about twice as better off financially if I had just parachuted out. And I felt comfortable about my deal, knowing that the employees who worked for me were also being treated fairly during the transition. (I'm happy to say that never once in my career did a company I headed face a legal challenge about the financial settlement in an employee's severance package.)

As president of Interprovincial, I replaced Ted Courtnage, who'd been criticized for making reports to the board that were so technically oriented that they often went over the directors' heads. Of course, he had also backed the Reichmanns in the takeover battle. That twist also prompted mentions in the media. As the *Financial Post* reported,

> The affair became a symphony of corporate misunderstanding. Hiram Walker management suspected their counterparts at IPL had been plotting with the Reichmanns. IPL management claimed they had not, and that they only climbed into bed with the billionaire brothers because Hiram Walker management would not talk to them.

The *Post* also noted that I was well regarded by the Reichmanns. They and the articulate and engaging Mickey Cohen had been keeping in touch with me. A few years later, I'd get to take Paul's measure in more depth. But Albert, who was on Interprovincial's board, had called with assurances that they wanted me to run the combined IPL-Home operation. Mickey and I had come to know one another when he was a deputy minister and I was still at HBOG, involved in a consortium planning an oil-sands project. During an Ottawa meeting, the participants were seeking more tax incentives until Mickey asked, "Do you remember what Porky Pig used to say at the end of the kids' cartoons? 'Th-th-that's all, folks'." Then he walked out of the room.

At an early board meeting of the combined operation, Mickey asked, "Now, Haskayne, what are you going to do at this company? What's it going to be when it grows up?"

"Mickey, I guess the answer is simple," I replied. "When oil prices are over $30 a barrel, we're going to say this is one of the best exploration production companies in Canada—which it probably will be. When oil is down, I'll say this is the longest crude-oil pipeline system in the world with a stable rate of return."

We had a good board, with strong people such as Bob Peterson, the Maclean-Hunter publisher Don Campbell, and the Royal Bank deputy chairman Doug Gardiner. My first momentous decision, in early 1987, had been the logical move of the pipeline's corporate office from Toronto, where the major investors and refiners like Imperial had their headquarters, to Alberta—where the producers of the oil were based. Even so, I had to make as many as forty trips a year to Toronto for meetings.

THAT FALL, I TOOK TIME to do a self-analysis, a habit I've continued over the years, writing down and rating how I felt about my various involvements. In the areas of career, travel opportunities, personal contacts, and club memberships, I rated my situation (humbly, of course) as "O" for Outstanding. I felt in excellent shape in terms of my academic credentials and financial investments, which included my membership in syndicates with the specialist insurer Lloyd's of London and my property holdings. I'd bought farmland around Gleichen and a farmhouse outside town that had once been the Salvation Army's Eventide Home for Old Men. As well as those ongoing links to my boyhood, I partnered with friends to develop land near Calgary around the rural community of Bearspaw. This was all involved with looking after me and Lee, of course, but I also rated us well for our contributions to charitable causes—following the counsel of Albert Schweitzer, who once said, "Even if it's a little thing, do something for others—something for which you get no pay but the privilege of doing it." But I gave myself only an "A" for Average on my participation in cultural and recreational activities and the number of corporate directorships I held—the only major ones were Manulife Financial and the Canadian Imperial Bank of Commerce. Assuming I wasn't going to be a CEO again, I could probably sit comfortably on as many as six boards. All in all, I was feeling good about my life.

My career was proceeding well, too. The company had assets of $2.9 billion versus liabilities of $1.9 billion and a plan to spend $7 billion on ventures over the next decade. We were expanding the Interprovincial pipeline to the tune of $1.1 billion alone and would be investing up to $400 million a year on Home's projects. Early in the new year, we'd decided to rename the amalgamated company to reflect both of its divisions. Rejecting the suggestions outside consultants offered, we had a contest for employees to come up with a name, with the proviso that it couldn't incorporate either "Interprovincial" or "Home." Of course, the winning entry broke that rule: Interhome Energy. A new logo in the shape of an oil drop blended the colour gold with Home's red and Interprovincial's blue. Dave Powell points out, "It didn't escape your notice that the logo looked very much like the old Hudson's Bay Oil and Gas logo. It was the same consultant who designed both of them." Despite the new overall identity, we continued to call the separate divisions by their original names.

A quartet of key players in Interhome's success was well in place. Allen Hagerman, who'd wanted to leave Hudson's Bay Oil and Gas when Dome took control, was one of my first hires at Home. He came on as corporate secretary and my administrative assistant, and he became treasurer as we put Interprovincial and Home together. Pat Daniel had moved from overseeing information technology to heading a special task force on productivity to being our planning director. A newcomer, Brian MacNeill, had never worked with me before, though we'd crossed paths when I was at HBOG. Brian, from Winnipeg, had started at Home as an accounts-payable clerk in the Bobby Brown era of the 1960s before going to college and articling in the U.S. Returning to Home, he became the vice-president of finance. After the Reichmann takeover, he moved to Toronto as VP of treasury for what was then called Hiram Walker Consumers' Home, and he worked on a dozen financings to complete the Davis Oil deal.

Needing a new chief financial officer in Calgary, I invited Brian to take the job and asked the current CFO to stay on as treasurer. As Allen says, "Brian was unassuming. He's not very tall—he was the only one able to stand up in a Lear jet. Laid back, but very intelligent. And nothing seemed to get Brian excited." It was just that quiet nature and his reluctance to speak out forcefully at management meetings that convinced some people Brian didn't have enough fire in his belly. I had to lecture him about getting off the fence and asserting himself. Which he did, when we named him chief operating officer to run the Interprovincial office in Edmonton. His astute performance in that job would give him wings to fly to the top of the heap in the Oil Patch.

Dave Powell, meanwhile, ran the Home Oil division in Calgary and had Allen reporting to him on the financial side. ("My main job with Allen often was trying to keep him calmed down," Dave says. "He was a workaholic, and you literally had to push him out the door to get him home. But he was a great team person.")

With both our distinctive divisions under the same Interhome umbrella, there was a real potential for conflicts of interest. Because Interprovincial dealt with other producing companies, we had to create a Chinese wall of written policies that protected their confidential information from leaking to Home—and vice versa. That sort of detail was the only thing the Interprovincial and Home people couldn't discuss with each other when they met. One group of seven VPs—which Ken McNeill nicknamed "The Silver 7"—was like an executive committee that came together regularly as required. An operating committee gathered weekly at Monday-morning meetings. Both groups were designed to build consensus by bringing every department together—their managers, not just the vice-presidents—and allowing all of them, whatever their background, to understand and participate in the company's decision-making process. Pat Daniel says now that he earned his MBA while sitting around the table at those meetings, and he later went on to schedule the same sort of sessions in running Enbridge Inc. Another device for building community was the piggybank I placed on the table—anyone from either division who used the words "them" or "us" instead of "we" had to pop a buck in the bank.

Dave Powell, deputy chairman of the operating committee, was so impressed with this style of interdepartmental meetings that he brought it along with him when he later became Home's chief executive officer. For both of us, consensus was the Holy Grail, but at times, you, as CEO, have to make the final decision. As Dave says, "There were some occasions when everybody wanted to go one way, but I felt that that was not the way, then I would invoke my majority of one. At that point, you have to trust your own instincts and judgment That was very infrequent, but it happened. And that's the prerogative of any chief executive officer, you know— that old Harry Truman thing: 'The buck stops here.' The decision was accepted, and everybody threw their weight behind it."

That sort of solo decision-making became known in the office as "white-tanking." When we'd gone to Australia to officially open the Blina-reef operation, I spoke at a gathering of dignitaries at a storage-tank farm being erected in Darby, where Home shipped oil from the Canning Basin. Apparently I told them, "When you look up and see this big white tank, you'll know Home Oil was here." To which Graeme Stephens, our man in Australia, responded, "Thank you, Dick, we'd planned to have the tank in a buff colour, but I guess now it's going to be white."

IN 1991, *FORTUNE* MAGAZINE ranked the Reichmanns as the world's fourth-richest family, with a combined wealth of $12.8 billion (U.S.). And by then, Interhome—of which they controlled about 60 percent—was percolating along nicely while the brothers had been staying in the background, not interfering—or so I thought. What I didn't know until recently was that Paul

Reichmann was ready to sell us to a Calgary company called PanCanadian Petroleum, created in 1971 as a merger of Canadian Pacific Oil and Gas Company and Central-Del Rio Oils. Twenty years later, it was still under the control of the CP Ltd. conglomerate, and its new president was David O'Brien, a Montreal trial and commercial lawyer who later became general counsel and CFO at Petro-Canada. While there, he helped negotiate PetroCan's acquisition of Gulf Canada's downstream refining and marketing assets from Paul. "I never saw anything in my dealings with the Reichmanns that indicated that they were not ethical," David recalls, echoing most people's view of the business family. That was my experience too: They were opportunistic and often operating out of their depth, but never once in our dealings were they ever dishonest with me, nor did they ever treat me in anything but a fair manner. Biographer Anthony Bianco writes in his exhaustive and even-handed book *The Reichmanns: Family, Faith, Fortune and the Empire of Olympia & York*, "The leading lights of the North American establishment extolled Paul and his brothers as the epitome of old-fashioned integrity in a corrupt, mercenary era."

O'Brien remembers, "They were very private, so everything was shrouded in mystery. And they had a way of negotiating that if you ever compromised on something, and they compromised, the next day they'd [have] forgotten what they compromised on and started all over again from your compromise. That's just a negotiating strategy.

"In 1991, I'd been at PanCanadian for about a year and someone gave me the idea that Interhome was for sale. So I got into a very heavy negotiation with Paul Reichmann, and when we were getting reasonably close, I then had to go to the CP board in Montreal because it was such a big transaction—about $2.5 billion. And I sold them on the mix of the pipeline and the oil and gas really bringing us to a whole new level. After I had their authority, you could see Reichmann trying to ratchet me up on the price, thinking this young guy must be anxious now. At one meeting in a Toronto hotel, when we were probably $3 apart and there was just the two of us and we weren't getting together, he excused himself very courteously and walked down the corridor. I watched as he got to the elevator, pushed the button, and then turned around and walked back. And what he was doing was seeing if I was going to say, 'Oh, Paul, come on back'—he was testing me.

"But we still didn't agree, and ultimately what the problem was—and I had just a hint of it at that time—he'd got into trouble in his New York project, Battery Park [the World Financial Center], and was under enormous financial pressure and really needed this deal. But what I was offering him was a little cash and a whole lot of PanCanadian shares. And he said, 'It's not enough money for me.' But I wasn't going to put PanCanadian at risk—and so we fell apart.

"The end of the story is that about two months later, the word had come out the Reichmanns were in financial difficulty. One day I'm in my office at PanCanadian and there's a call from Paul Reichmann: 'David, is there any chance we can get together again to discuss this?' And I said, 'Paul, I used up all of my political goodwill with the CP board, and it didn't work. There is *no* chance.'"

I had been getting hints of the Reichmanns' challenges for some time. Although I got on well with them, we'd had one major disagreement. The brothers wanted to place the U.S. assets of our pipeline division into a master limited partnership, an MLP that blends the tax benefits of a limited partnership with the liquidity of publicly traded securities—like the income trusts that became so popular in Canada until Stephen Harper's Conservatives plugged the tax loophole in 2006. The only reason for doing the MLP was to extract a fortune in funds from investors. Our company didn't need the infusion of cash, but I knew the Reichmanns did. And I didn't want thirty thousand unit-holders in the American portion of the pipeline badgering us about rates of return and other stockholders' concerns. During my tenure, I managed to keep the idea at bay, though Interprovincial later did an MLP on the line down south.

I also had the words of Howard Blauvelt ringing in my ears. Howard, who'd hired me at HBOG before becoming head of Conoco, was on the board of Abitibi-Price with the Reichmanns. One day at breakfast in Toronto, this shrewd, circumspect man told me that he'd cautioned them that if they raided the assets of a company like Hiram Walker, they'd be perceived not as builders but as takeover artists destroying companies: "They didn't listen to me, Dick. And the Reichmanns have now abused the privilege of debt."

Meanwhile, I was seeing Paul Reichmann on the board of the Canadian Imperial Bank of Commerce, where I was now a director. From my contacts with him and Mickey Cohen, I'd known that the family was now involved in a bewildering array of rocky investments, from building their own gargantuan Canary Wharf development to being the second-largest shareholder in Ottawa-based Campeau Corporation, one of the top developers in North America but facing financial disaster. Paul Reichmann was the public face of the company, the master juggler dealing with the family's four main Canadian banks and a dozen or more international ones. Canada was deep into a recession, with the gross domestic product decreasing and unemployment rising above 10 percent. Real estate values were collapsing across North America and overseas. The bankers were naturally nervous. Anthony Bianco describes this period of time in *The Reichmanns*:

> [Paul] Reichmann's increasingly desperate efforts to retain the confidence of Olympia & York's lenders led him to what amounted to a double life. In private, he was the Harry Houdini of real estate, scrambling continuously to extricate himself from the spike-lined coffins and padlocked strait-jackets of Olympia & York's excessive indebtedness. In public, he carried on in the mode of magisterial invincibility he had adopted in taking over Canary Wharf. Although Reichmann did admit that his diversification drive had not panned out, he conceded nothing to critics of his Docklands project and seemed to welcome the recession as a fresh opportunity to display his contrarian will.

Then early in 1991, the brothers hit me with a bombshell: They wanted to split Interhome apart again into its pipeline and oil-company divisions—all the better to sell off the pieces. Strongly disagreeing, I met with Paul a couple of times, to no avail. His secretary called to request another meeting on the day of a farewell party in Calgary for Keith McWalter, who was retiring as president and CEO of Gulf Canada. I was speaking at the event, but even though the Reichmanns had been such big players in Gulf, neither they nor their representatives were attending. I held Paul off till the next day, flying overnight to Toronto.

His secretary called me at my hotel that morning to say Paul was running late and had pushed our meeting back an hour. Their headquarters was in the family's proud flagship, First Canadian Place, which they shared with the Bank of Montreal and Hiram Walker Resources. It was at the heart of the Bay Street financial district. At 72 storeys, it was Canada's tallest office building (and the world's tallest bank building). When I arrived at the thirty-third floor, Paul came out of the boardroom and politely apologized for a further delay. He introduced me to a half-dozen dapper-looking American railway executives who he was seeing. The Reichmanns were the largest single stakeholder in the Santa Fe Southern Pacific railway and real estate conglomerate.

Cooling my heels, I looked at the model of the Canary Wharf project Paul always showed me on my visits and realized again how its burdensome debt was crippling Olympia & York. He finally bid the railway guys goodbye and called me in for what I knew would be a critical meeting about the future of Interhome— and me. We were alone—not even Lionel Dodd, the overworked accountant who was Mickey Cohen's successor, was with us. Nor was Gil Newman, who'd started as an outside auditor and became his chief administrator. As always, Paul at age sixty was serious, soft-spoken, and well mannered—yet what Anthony Bianco describes as "a most aggressive introvert." Full-bearded, wearing a yarmulke and his trademark beautifully tailored charcoal suit, he appeared to be (in the words of a Canadian banker) "more of a wise man than a developer." We met for an hour, and his essential message was that Interprovincial and Home were worth far more split up than they were together.

"If you want my opinion," I said, "that is not what we've been planning to do, and that's not the way to support earnings."

"Dick, I have no trouble making U-turns in my life."

Paul asked if I agreed with the idea of Brian MacNeill running Interprovincial and Dave Powell Home Oil. Obviously, I did. But the brothers also wanted me stay on to be chairman of the two companies—which is not the job I wanted to do.

In the end, knowing of the Reichmanns' desperate need of cash, I said, "The point is if you want to go ahead with the split, we'll work on it. But it's not going to be easy because of the intertwined financing and the fact we're in a regulated industry."

Our session done, Paul would be meeting later with Chuck Schultz of Gulf Canada and then dealing with the bankrupt Campeau Corporation. Afterward, I wondered how this one man could dip into industry after industry—railways, real estate, pipelines, petroleum—in a single morning, with no advisors in the meetings with him to debate or buttress his opinions while he decided the fate of major corporations. I understood then that Paul was personally stretched as thin as the family finances. The media had been saying that Olympia & York was run more like a corner grocery store than a multinational colossus. And, as much as I wanted to keep running our company, I knew my best course of action now was to beat a rapid retreat from the Reichmann empire. I would leave with a financial package that prompted some smart-ass friends to commission a cartoon that still hangs on my office wall. It shows me clutching a big money bag as I descend on a parachute to a waiting CIBC armoured car while three planes fly above me, labelled HBOG, Interprovincial/Home/Interhome, and Hiram Walker. Below this, there's a medal—based on a remark by Bart Rombough of PanCanadian Energy: "Haskayne's been taken over so many times, he's earned a Distinguished Flying Cross in golden parachutes."

A year later, laden with the heavily indebted Canary Wharf project and other troubled real estate holdings, Olympia & York

Development went bankrupt. The brothers managed to salvage enough assets out of bankruptcy protection to create a new company, Olympia & York Properties, but most of their prize holdings were gone—including Interprovincial Pipe Line. In 1992, the original O&Y became a broadly held company when they turned over control to its creditors and essentially walked away from their once-proud enterprise.

Home Oil suffered the most in the fallout, bearing a $540-million debt load and having to sell $110 million worth of property. Though the Reichmanns had owned three-quarters of the stock in Gulf Canada, which controlled Home, the shares were pledged to a consortium of domestic and international banks as security for loans to Olympia & York. In 1993, Gulf and the creditors of O&Y sold their combined 60 percent interest in Home into the market. Two years later, Amoco Canada Petroleum (Amoco)—an arm of Standard Oil of Indiana—made a hostile bid for the company.

Through all of this, Dave Powell was CEO: "The Reichmanns had been more hands-on than Hiram Walker were, but they weren't too bad. The problem was that with the split-off of the two companies, Home Oil was left with an enormous amount of debt and we had to reduce it. Our debt-to–cash flow ratio was about seven times, and by the time the hostile bid from Amoco came along, we'd reduced that to about four. But it meant selling off a lot of properties and reducing staff by about 40 to 50 percent. So there were some tough times. I couldn't explore much.

"But I'm proud of what we did: put Home on a safe footing [and] reduced the debt, and we were coming out of it. And that was the time when the Canadian dollar was only about seventy cents to the U.S. dollar and gas was running about sixty to seventy cents U.S. MCF [per thousand barrels] compared to the $7 or $8 now, and oil was between $15 and $20 dollars a barrel [compared to $75-plus a dozen years later]. I look at the prices now, and think, *Jesus Christ, if only we could've hung on, you know?*"

Home held off Amoco long enough to let a white knight, the colourful James Carl Anderson, take it over instead. J.C., a blunt

Nebraskan who came to Alberta as chief engineer for Amoco, launched his own oil company in 1968. His one-man operation evolved into Canada's seventh-largest gas producer. In 1995, Anderson Exploration bought Home for $1.2 billion and he promptly fired four VPs. Dave Powell left to be a consultant and sat on the boards of two resource companies, including Talisman Energy, where he was chairman (and more recently retired to Panama). Despite Anderson's lean style of operating, his company was a sitting duck when Devon Canada, the subsidiary of a Houston energy corporation, bought it for $4.6 billion and became the third-largest independent gas producer in Canada—but not in any sense a Northern Tiger.

On the other hand, Interprovincial—which came to be called IPL Energy—did eventually take on Tiger status. In 1994, it repatriated Consumers' Gas, which British Gas Overseas Holdings now controlled. At the time, Brian MacNeill was the pipeline's CEO and Pat Daniel was overseeing corporate planning and business development. It was Pat who recommended that IPL buy Consumers' for about $1.5 billion and Brian who led the secret negotiations (just before the sale was announced, an unknowing headhunter offered Brian the CEO's job at Consumers'). "There is no doubt," Pat says, "when we did that deal and effectively doubled the size of the company, that was the turning point."

He then ran the pipeline division in Edmonton: "We finally convinced the industry that we should embark on a series of expansions, so we were plowing a lot of capital in there. And we'd done an incentive deal with our shippers, a cooperative agreement that forged a whole new relationship. We, as managers of the pipeline company, would attempt to reduce costs, and for every dollar saved, we'd give the shippers half of it." In its first five years, the deal yielded $117 million in productivity gains and cost savings.

With the acquisition of Consumers' and other companies, IPL was becoming so diversified that it changed its name in 1998 to Enbridge—for "energy bridge." Three years later, Pat succeeded Brian as CEO of an enterprise that now runs a crude-oil and liquids pipeline system through Canada and the U.S.—the world's longest—and the major Canadian natural-gas distributor, supplying commercial and residential customers in Ontario, Quebec, and New York State. The company's international reach includes energy projects in Colombia and Spain and its own pipeline-simulator technology that it provides on a consulting basis around the world. And with a staff of more than 4,400, Enbridge has been named one of the country's top one hundred employers for its innovative management.

Brian MacNeill, who has since become chairman of Petro-Canada, believes Enbridge has become a Northern Tiger. Pat Daniel thinks it isn't quite big enough—yet: "We are a very conservative, disciplined company, but we are also very aggressive. We really worked hard to grow this damn company, and I think Canadian companies should have a bigger role to play on the world stage." He's working hard to make that happen and is fully capable of reaching his target.

SO, IN THE AFTERMATH OF the Reichmann takeover, two companies emerged from the morass and, after I'd left, both were run by men I thought of as protegés. While Home was swallowed whole by another company, Interprovincial morphed into a world-beater in the years to come.

Ken McNeill and I had quit Interhome at the same time in the spring of 1991 when the companies were split. For him, this was a real retirement to a life in the country with his sweet wife, Lyn, as the airfield brat and former cop pursued his passion for flying his own Cessna Cardinal and riding a Honda ST1300s motorcycle with his buddies.

As for me, I took my pension from Interprovincial and looked around for something challenging to do. But while I was pondering my future, there were other challenges in my life to preoccupy me—most of all, the health of my wife, Lee.

In December 1992, Lee—my cherished partner of three and a half decades—and I sent out our very first Christmas letter to family and friends. Her contribution to the message was brave but heartbreaking:

> It was so nice to hear from you and you will be pleased to know that we are carrying on with our life in the same fashion and seem to be out at some type of function almost every night. While I can't speak, I am able to communicate in writing and currently use a magic board and many scratch pads. Saliva is a bit of a bother because my swallowing is impaired and therefore I notice it more. I have difficulty eating but by watching my diet and blending my food, I am able to eat reasonably well. Also, my left leg is weak but I have a companion (Doreen) to assist me in continuing my many activities. Doreen is a good friend and although she is not a nurse, she is most helpful to me.
>
> So, with Dick's help and the enormous support from family and friends, I am able to carry on with most of my former endeavours. I still go to Dick's office on Mondays and Fridays to work on projects. For example, I have recently organized all our photos over the last ten years and have already filled five new albums....

A year earlier, as I was leaving Interhome, I began noticing some disturbing signs whenever I called Lee long-distance while on the road. I always made a point of phoning home at 6:00 p.m. Calgary time, wherever I was. She had a polished manner on the telephone—she'd been a receptionist at a local TV station for years—but now, she would sometimes stumble or sound hesitant in speaking with me.

"Lover, what's wrong?" I'd ask.

"Oh, I was just about to have supper," she might reply, excusing her little flubs.

Both of her younger twin sisters were nurses, so finally I asked Louise, who lived in town and was close to Lee, what she thought was happening. "I think it could be hypoglycemia—low blood sugar," she speculated.

Over Christmas 1991, we holidayed in Hawaii, and being alone with Lee for long periods, I saw the difficulties she often had speaking and even swallowing. Back home, out for dinner one night with Louise and her husband, John Giffen, I quietly told her sister that Lee's condition probably wasn't hypoglycemia because it was surfacing all the time. John, overhearing us, asked what we were talking about—and when Lee and I got in the car, she asked me the same question.

"There's something wrong," I confessed. "You just don't seem to be yourself." She admitted that she was feeling confused but didn't quite know why. Meanwhile, her bosses at the station—where she was like a beloved Mother Superior to the staff—had sent her a letter noting that some people there were having trouble deciphering her announcements on the PA system. My frat brother Don Campbell remembers her phoning him and Marlene: "There'd be a pause, and then all of a sudden, she'd get the words out. That went on for a few months. We weren't observing any other physical signs then." But Lee, a fashion plate, had taken to wearing sneakers to work because, as I learned later, she was concealing signs of drop foot, a weakness in the muscles that flex the ankles.

Her doctor agreed she needed more specialized help and sent her to a local neurological clinic for test after test—X-rays, needles, blood work. At one point, two of the top station executives came to see me, and as they nervously tried to open the conversation, I told them I knew why they were there, that we were having her tested, but had no answers yet. To my friend Ken McNeill, I let it all come out: "What if they come back tomorrow and say it's Alzheimer's? What am I going to tell her?" But a panel of three specialists in Calgary finally admitted they couldn't find any medical reason for her condition.

I'd had checkups at the Scripps Clinic, the multi-specialty medical group and clinical research institution in San Diego. Now I took Lee there for an intensive series of further examinations by Scripps's crack team of experts. After studying all her medical records, the chief neurologist said he and another doctor had to do one more test, which involved needles in the mouth. After going out for lunch, we came back to hear the news: "This is what she has," the doctors said. "Amyotrophic lateral sclerosis."

ALS.

Lou Gehrig's disease.

LEE HAD A BORN-IN-IRELAND beauty and sense of humour as well as a voice that sounded sweet when she sang and proved an asset in her long-term job as the morning receptionist at CHCT. It was Alberta's first television station, which with changes in ownership became CFAC and CKKX during her time there. Ron McLean, CBC-TV's renowned sportscaster, likes to recall how warm and welcoming she was when he showed up one day as a green announcer from Red Deer. She came home to tell me about this bright talent who should land a job at the station in sports—which he did.

One of the people who knew her then was Shauna Ryan, who was working for a local fashion boutique. "I knew all the wives of the businessmen," Shauna remembers, "and I admired Lee because she always maintained her own status as a working wife. She was very independent. And she was particular—very friendly at the station, but she had a few special people in her life, very much 'I pick *you*.'"

Lee and I had a wonderful relationship, even though we never had children. When we were first married, living in a basement suite, I was busy articling for my CA and still helping out at the butcher shop. At one point early on, Lee thought she was pregnant but really wasn't, and after that, she seemed to feel apprehensive about having a child. Yet we both liked being with kids. Her folks had their much-younger twin daughters still at home, and we often acted as surrogate parents for the girls, taking them on holidays and helping to finance them through high school. And I felt like a very special uncle to my brother's daughters, Leslie and Laurie.

It's a cliché, but my wife was my dearest friend. We shared most things, except I drank and she didn't. We loved to escape the Alberta winters and refresh our marriage in warm oases like

Hawaii and southern California. Along with pursuing her own work, Lee played the role of the executive spouse with grace and charm. One of her nice old-fashioned habits was having a hot bath waiting for me when I called from the airport after a road trip. She sometimes travelled with me on special business occasions—while I was at Home Oil, she came to France to christen the world's largest drill rig at the site of our two deep offshore oil wells. But she didn't want to move house from the Calgary area when Hiram Walker Resources asked me to run the company from Toronto in a relocation that thankfully never happened.

In early 1991, after leaving Interhome Energy, I agreed to join the board of directors of a Calgary pipeline and chemical company, NOVA Corporation (as I describe in the next chapter). By then, I had started to notice Lee's health problems. She'd had other medical challenges. For many years, she suffered from peripheral neuropathy, which caused anything from numbness and tingling to a burning sensation in her feet. Just before learning about the ALS, she had quit her job at the station and came twice a week to the comfortable downtown office I'd subleased, where she answered the phone, organized my calendar, and handled mailings. Lee was still driving then, though I worried about her coordination behind the wheel. And finally in June 1992, she was diagnosed with Lou Gehrig's disease.

We soon discovered that this terrifying condition (named for the New York Yankee slugger who died from it) has no cure. It's a quickly progressing disease that attacks the body's motor neurons, which normally transmit electrical messages from the brain to the voluntary muscles. When these impulses are interrupted, the muscles begin to atrophy and eventually die. The average life expectancy after diagnosis is two to five years. Yet ALS doesn't affect the senses and only seldom the mind—which is a mixed blessing, as we found, because the victim is painfully aware of the devastating deterioration of the body.

Overnight, our whole world shattered. At that time, there was a theory that a form of the Salk vaccine, originally developed for polio, might help with ALS. Although our local doctor couldn't get the vaccine from the Toronto company that produced it, I acquired it through the help of Dr. Bill Cochrane, who'd been founding medical dean and then president at the University of Calgary. But, after all, the medication didn't help and Lee's health kept deteriorating. We were out for dinner with the Campbells one evening when Lee was walking to the door of a restaurant and then keeled over backward. I just happened to catch her. It was one of the first major physical manifestations of her condition.

When she started losing the use of her limbs—badly enough to require a wheelchair—and eventually lost her speech, we hired a driver, young Kelly Bagley, and a woman friend who became her boon companion, Doreen Cordingley. Eventually, we also had compassionate nurses who offered the care that helped Lee maintain her independent spirit. Kelly would drive her and her caregivers somewhere every day, perhaps to go out for tea or to have her hair done. And we had the ongoing support of good friends such as the Campbells, the Culberts, the Maiers, the McNeills, and of course, her most trusted friend, her sister Louise.

By year's end, I was chairman of NOVA as well as of the board of governors of the U of C and a director on a half-dozen other corporate boards. But my time for business began to be severely limited. Over eighteen months, I never left Calgary so that I could always be there with Lee every evening and weekend. Near the end, we had to brush her teeth for her, purée all her food, and create a board with pictures she could point to without speaking. At one stage, Ken McNeill brought me together with Lee's sister Louise, the nurse, and Dr. Bob Hatfield, a local co-author of two books on death and dying. The very good idea was to offer me advice about my situation. And Dr. Bob said, "You had better keep doing what you're doing to keep your mind occupied. You cannot do any more for Lee. If you try, you're going to go under too—and what will that do for her?"

Aside from a week she spent in hospital after a fall, Lee was never confined to her bed—until the day before she died. God, she was courageous through her ordeal. Sometimes she became so frustrated and angry that she'd send a nurse packing. Yet she always insisted on getting dressed with considerable help in the morning and presenting the best possible face to friends and family. My heart was broken every day.

Lee Mary Haskayne died on October 1, 1993. She was fifty-seven. We had been in love for nearly forty years. Her funeral service at Grace Presbyterian—led by Jack Stewart, a minister Lee had taken a shine to—attracted 1,100 friends, and there were several hundred contributions to the ALS Society. Her television station offered a heart-rending tribute to her that evening and a special commentary from her old friend Ed Whalen, the TV voice of the Calgary Flames. (And more recently, Ron McLean paid a terrific tribute to her at a Calgary Business Hall of Fame dinner.)

Afterward, along with all the other memories, I kept recalling two highlights of our life together. I'd written one of them down earlier that spring as I described the depth of our marriage, and I noted, "The best summary of this is made by Lee and me in the past ten years where we have consistently said that if anything happened to either one of us, that nobody should feel sorry for us because we have had a complete and satisfactory life and accomplished more than we ever expected."

The other recollection was more recent. When Lee's condition had declined so she couldn't speak, I used to take her to the Country Club in Calgary, where immigrant Polish members of the staff—especially Josephine Siemak and Maria Mlodzianowski—would take special care of her, seating us in a quiet corner of the dining room and doting on her. Lee communicated to me that Josie longed to go back to Poland for a visit and that we should give her the money to make the trip. I didn't know how to make that gesture diplomatically. It wasn't until after Lee died that I gave cheques in her name to several of the staff, including Josie. And she was the very first person to call me the next morning, to thank us and say, "*Now* I can go to Poland." As usual, Lee had been right all along.

HER ILLNESS AND DEATH WIPED me out mentally and physically. Yet not long after, I sat down in my usual calculating accountant's way to sum up all the advice I'd been getting during the past year and a half as I was grieving her imminent loss.

One of the key advisors was my niece Leslie, the elder of my brother's daughters. Dr. Leslie Haskayne is a gifted psychiatrist who got her MD at twenty-three and long ago moved to England, where she practises at the Yorkshire Centre of Forensic Psychiatry. She and her younger sister, Laurie Lunseth, were there for me in the week after Lee died, never leaving me alone in our home.

Leslie and I talked long and hard after the funeral, and on a series of pink notes she listed the "many needs" a person in my situation has: physical ("including sexual"), social ("relationships/family, friends"), intellectual ("using one's brain to its potential"), creative ("creativity in the widest sense"), and spiritual ("your inner self—make sure you leave time for contemplation rather than just keeping busy"). And as I noted about any future socializing, "Leslie said I may want to develop a 'consort' or 'escort' relationship with people to accompany me where there are no possible motives other than friendship or family—when I need a companion for certain functions."

I'd already been warned about the approaches some aggressive women—"casserole ladies"—can make to recent widowers. As I wrote, "It put me on notice that my usual behaviour of a loving person may NOW be suspect and misinterpreted. So in conclusion BE CAREFUL about motives of women (but not too skeptical) and CAUTIOUS—also watch my own behaviour."

There *were* some casserole-bearing women in the months that followed. But I had my own female support team to shore me up during that dark winter. One of them was Laurie, who took over when Leslie returned home to Yorkshire. Laurie and her contractor husband, Les, live with their two sons in Bossano, where her dad—my brother—had his butcher shop. She's both the school librarian and the manager of the local golf clubhouse. An obvious Haskayne, she thinks she looks like my father, and I think she acts like my mother—warm and caring. As a teenager, she would come to Calgary with her friends and waltz into my office at HBOG to say hello and drop off her shopping bags. She lived with Lee and me while going to business college, and afterwards, we always spent Christmas mornings together. When I phoned from the Los Angeles airport to tell her that Lee had Lou Gehrig's, we were both in tears.

Laurie spent a lot of time with me on the weekends following the funeral. I was with her family in Bossano on Christmas Eve and the next morning, which was a tough one for me. At one point, I sat staring out a bay window at a corral and said, "I can see your dad out there."

Stan had once convinced me to back him in a small cattle business. After we bought some frisky cows at auction, he said we'd have to brand the things right away. Later, as we sat in our sweaty clothes with beers in our hands, he announced, "We could've had them branded for fifty cents apiece at the auction mart, but I thought this would be more fun." (As his daughter shrewdly points out, "He had his little brother with him, and life was good.") When Stan died in 1983, I told Laurie, "I've lost my brother, my second father, and my best friend." Now my best female friend was gone, too. Leaving Laurie's family that Christmas day to have dinner with Lee's sister, Louise, I stopped off in Gleichen to visit my parents' graves.

Chapter Six

OUT OF THE SHAMBLES
NOVA Corporation

BOB BLAIR WAS ALWAYS A MAVERICK: a Liberal in a Conservative town, an oilman who never went to the Petroleum or Ranchmen's clubs, and one of the rare Albertans who supported the National Energy Program. But this shy yet aggressive engineer had built the provincial government's former Alberta Gas Trunk Line into NOVA Corp., a petroleum powerhouse that operated around the globe and, in partnership with Hong Kong multibillionaire Li Ka-Shing, had acquired Husky Oil, controlled by the Neilsen family of Wyoming and Calgary. I'd encountered Bob during my brief tenure with the Arctic Gas consortium in the mid-1970s, where he chafed under the bullying by representatives of some big American corporations. At one point, a couple of days before a meeting Bob had booked with me well in advance, Alberta Gas Trunk surprised the industry by announcing it had created a consortium with two other pipeline companies that intended to compete directly with Arctic Gas. At our session, I was surprised when Bob asked me to be a senior manager in this Maple Leaf Project, which I refused to do. After Bob bought Husky in 1978 and I was back with Hudson's Bay Oil and Gas, his assistant Joan Dennis (who'd worked for me at HBOG) called with a cryptic request to meet Bob and his long-time associate, Bob Pierce, one mid-afternoon in Fuller's Restaurant downtown. This was the last place you'd want to have a serious meeting, but that's where, sitting over tea, they invited me to become president of Husky—and once more, I refused.

Thinking they might be third-time lucky, the two Bobs blind-sided me yet again in 1991 during the partitioning of Interhome Energy into Home and Interprovincial Pipe Line. I was in a slightly more vulnerable position this time because of my opposition to the proposed split. That spring, Joan called and said Bob Blair wanted to get together—in my office, at least, not Fuller's—without revealing the nature of the meeting. Alberta Gas Trunk had since evolved into NOVA, which had both pipeline and chemical divisions. I believed that NOVA was simply one of several suitors hoping to buy the flourishing IPL. In fact, I had our chief financial officer, Allen Hagerman, and our general counsel, Bob Perrin, waiting in the wings to witness the expected offer. When Blair and Pierce arrived, I triggered my office's automatic door lock and told them I wanted to have my colleagues present for the bid.

"Oh, no, we don't want to talk about IPL," Bob Blair said. "We want you to come to NOVA and be president of the pipeline." They were also about to split their divisions—in a project code-named "Primrose"—and spent the next two hours trying to convince me to take the job.

Bob was an inveterate writer of memos, and in one to his directors that May, he accurately summarized my response and present circumstances:

> He wants a month or two to make the choice of whether to go back to big company executive work after a vacation. If he commits to such full-time work it will definitely be for NOVA—he has crossed that bridge. But he needs time to reflect on whether he should or should not go back to industry full time. He expects he should—what can be so satisfying as work? He regards CEO of NOVA as the best job in Alberta, the company to be a good and proud one to connect with and therefore the opportunity as impressive. But he needs some time.
>
> He does not need money, happens to be getting another $2 million plus settlement now. For 1990, his salary was $525,000 and bonus $110,000. He has options

for 40,000 shares at $48 to $50 and their options stay in force for 4 years after departure. I gave him some numbers on higher NOVA bonuses of the past and to understand that our share option plan has higher allocations.

Typically, in deciding whether to get involved with NOVA, I sought the advice of friends. One of them was Bartlett Rombough, a former president of the hugely successful PanCanadian Petroleum, born of an amalgamation between Canadian Pacific Oil and Gas and Central Del-Rio Oils, which had its roots in a wildcat operation just after Leduc came in. Bart said, "Be careful of NOVA," and pointed out that I had other alternatives, including TransCanada PipeLines and Alberta Energy Company (AEC). Meanwhile, I had just accepted a directorship with TransAlta, the prominent international power-generation and energy-marketing company and the country's largest investor-owned electric utility.

Another good friend was even more forthright about the NOVA position. Ron Southern heads one of Alberta's First Families of business, which include the Mannixes and the McCaigs. The hard-driving, tough-minded entrepreneur had fashioned he ATCO Group into one of Canada's most prominent family-run conglomerates, with billions of dollars of assets in a boggling array of ventures ranging from natural gas and prefab housing to travel agencies and the highly esteemed Spruce Meadows Equestrian Centre in Calgary. Ron's brother-in-law, John Wood, was running ATCO's Canadian Utilities and had wanted me on his board for a long while.

Ron is a proud man, so I was determined to tell him, before the newspapers announced it, that I'd gone on the board of TransAlta instead of its competitor that also supplied residential natural gas, Canadian Utilities. Getting that off my chest as we sat in his pleasant atrium-like office, I then mentioned the possibility of the NOVA position. The story around town was that Ron had long ago resigned as a NOVA director in what was described as "a huff," but nobody knew exactly the reason why. *Alberta Report* magazine speculated, "The ATCO chief, as a NOVA director, tried hard to have Mr. Blair deposed for his misadventures in non-pipeline activities."

"Ron, I don't want to ask confidential questions, but I know you left the NOVA board, and now they're offering me a job," I said.

"Well," he replied, "I would be very careful about that. Blair is a difficult man."

"The thing is, I don't want to betray a confidence, but Bob is going to retire—in fact, he's been involved in recruiting me."

"That makes a helluva difference," Ron said, with excitement in his voice. "What are you going to do?" When I explained about my other options, he exclaimed, "Christ almighty, man, it's one of the most important jobs in Calgary and this province and it's in a goddamn mess—and that's why I left. You're the current Wayne Gretzky of the business world, it's the third period of the Stanley Cup finals, and you're saying you won't skate?"

In the end, knowing my time with Interhome was done, I agreed to go on the NOVA board that May of '91 and said if they really did restructure the company, I would head the pipeline side, which had interests in Husky, Pan-Alberta Gas, and a pipeline operation in Italy.

HAVING LEFT INTERHOME and being not yet on full-time with NOVA, I moved into my own office downtown and soon had two special women working with me who remain to this day. Wise and well-organized, pleasant in personality and appearance, they brought some order to my world when it had begun falling apart with the diagnosis of Lee's ALS.

The first was Nancy Matthews, who'd studied fine arts at the University of Calgary and took a year of business college before joining Home Oil as an assistant to the human resources manager a few years before I arrived there. At age twenty-two, while continuing to work in HR, she became secretary to Ross Phillips, who was Home's CEO. She left for a year and a half to be executive assistant to the CEO of Morris Petroleum, a small oil and gas company where she set up the office and even handled its land bids.

Returning to Home, she worked for Fred Callaway, vp of corporate development, and that's when I came to know her. Fred was confident enough of her organizational and accounting abilities to give her a lot of latitude. With the birth of Interhome Energy, she also assisted Dave Powell when he was president of the petroleum division. At thirty-five, married to Randy and with one child, she left the company again, and this time she wrote and published a book that showed off her dry wit and powers of observation. (*Golf Your Way: The No-Stress Game* is full of cartoons and funny lines like "Never, ever tell anyone how long you have been golfing. The look on their face will kill you.")

When I first asked her to work part-time for me in the spring of 1991, she declined but then relented and started up the office I took as a director and, later, chair of NOVA. We stayed in that space for a year before moving to a handsome suite on the twentieth of fifty-two storeys at Bankers Hall, the dramatic stone-and-glass twin towers at the heart of the city. Lee decorated the offices, one of which Ken McNeill took to have some digs downtown. Through it all, Nancy was terrifically sensitive to my wife's ever-worsening condition. A year and a half later, I hired a full-time assistant to complement her—by a nice coincidence, Shauna Ryan, who, in one of her several careers, had sold clothing over the years to Lee.

Shauna had come to Canada as a four-year-old with her family from England (her father, an aeronautical engineer, wound up working for Domtar and designing the beer carton as we know it today). She studied advertising, public relations, and human resources at a community college in Edmonton. After graduating, she wrote advertising copy for Woodward's department stores there and in Calgary and Lethbridge, where she'd moved with her new husband, Murray, an air-traffic controller at that time. When his job took them north, she did PR for the federal public works department in Inuvik, Northwest Territories. After they came home to Calgary with their daughter, Shauna spent a decade managing a prominent local boutique, where she met Lee, who became one of her regular clients.

Looking to spread her wings, she took a couple of university courses and did job placements for a friend's personnel firm, which had supplied staff for Home Oil. Ken called the firm on my behalf and interviewed Shauna for the job of general assistant. When she said she knew my wife very well, I went home and told Lee, who wrote on her notepad, "She's wonderful!" And she is. When the personnel firm wanted her back, I said, "No damn way."

Wherever you go, the Irish proverb says, *have a woman friend.* There are women in a man's life who become very good friends, which is the role Shauna and Nancy have played in mine. But they also eventually became the "partners" in my personal company, Haskayne & Partners—and we typically call each other "Partner" rather than by name. Many years later, in the fall of 2004, when we leased a suite on the thirty-eighth floor of Bankers Hall, I gave them carte blanche to supervise the interior design of the empty space to their taste and to outfit it without skimping. Consulting with experts, they finally invited me to see their handiwork for the first time six months later. I was delighted at how they'd put all the pieces together, chose the perfect colours to complement all the art Lee and I had collected, and created a homey yet sophisticated ambience. My two partners would continue to work seamlessly together as a team, with Nancy focused on the financial and corporate concerns and Shauna on my busy calendar and a string of donations. And both of them would host the countless visitors dropping by for a chat and, with their husbands, join me for many of the social and corporate occasions I attended. As Shauna has said, "It's an intimate, loving relationship where we're all considered equals."

AS I CAME ABOARD IN 1991, NOVA had some interesting directors, people such as Willard (Bud) Estey, the retired Supreme Court of Canada judge; Doc Seaman, head of Bow Valley Industries (where Gerry Maier had gone); and Harley Hotchkiss, something of a legend in town. Harley—a farm boy from southwestern Ontario with an honours degree in geology from Michigan State University (where he played college hockey)—worked in Calgary for CIBC in the first petroleum department of any Canadian bank, and that's where I got to know him. Harley later worked with the Seaman brothers, Doc and B.J., before launching his own company, Sabre Petroleums Ltd., and selling it for $24 million in 1976. But most Calgarians knew him as one of the founding partners, with the Seamans and three others, in the NHL's Calgary Flames. This warm, generous guy would become even better known as the league's diplomatic six-term chairman of the board of governors and one of the community's sterling philanthropists.

Until my first board meeting, I didn't appreciate that NOVA was now a shambles, laden with $4.2 billion in debt. It had diversified into a host of activities totally unrelated to its core businesses, manufacturing things like trucks and cellular phones. One director, Bill Howard, whispered to me, "Dick, I bet you're sitting here wondering why you took this job"—which is exactly what I was thinking. That year, the company would lose $937 million. It was bleeding about $15 million a month in the chemicals business alone, and yet the executives and directors were listening to investment bankers pressing them to send the two divisions out on their own as separate entities. They wanted to free the pipeline, with its guaranteed returns, from the chemicals arm that was hurting the collective credit rating. At Interhome, it had taken us years to split Home and IPL, and here NOVA was about to leap into a similar venture with very little forethought. A third-year commerce student would have known better than to make chemicals a stand-alone, no longer relying on the strength of the pipeline's balance sheet.

The board even offered me a contract based on the supposition that NOVA would be split in two. Despite the fact that it offered generous golden-parachute provisions, I couldn't in all conscience sign it because I simply believed the company should stay whole. I came on board without a contract.

By the fall, Bob Blair (one of the highest-paid executives in Canada) had finally retired as chairman and CEO, as predicted, and Doc Seaman was the interim chair. And for the time being, I acted as special advisor to a distinguished newcomer recruited from Toronto—Ted Newall. He would head the petrochemical company, Novacor Chemicals, and serve as NOVA's chief executive while the company was being reorganized.

J.E. Newall was a hell of a fine catch, a senior statesman in the Canadian business world. Bob had approached him early in the year when Ted was still chairman, president, and CEO of DuPont Canada, a subsidiary of the American-based multinational famous for developing synthetic fibres. He was the current chair of the Business Council on National Issues, had chaired the Conference Board of Canada, and served on advisory groups to Prime Minister Brian Mulroney and Mike Wilson, when he was the international trade minister. Yet for a guy who was a director of the Molson Companies, the Royal Bank, and Alcan Inc., he had a surprising liberal bent, admitting he'd been known to vote NDP and considered Tommy Douglas to be the most admirable Canadian politician.

Ted knew me through Carl Jones, HBOG's former president, who was on DuPont's board. The two of us hit it off from the start. I like journalist Sydney Sharpe's description of him: "A tall, burly man who looks like a friendly Henry Kissinger." Aside from the fact that he stood four inches taller than me and counted six siblings to my one brother, we had a lot of things in common. He was born only a year after me in small-town Alberta, and his Scottish-bred father was, like mine, an artisan—a champion butter-maker with Burns Creamery. Ted worked there summers to pay for university, watching his dad and learning what customer service was all about. He got a commerce degree, too, but at the University of Saskatchewan, where he was also a bit of a party animal (though those hijinks were cut short when he met his wife-to-be and budding social activist, Margaret).

He came to NOVA off a thirty-three-year career with DuPont Canada. The subsidiary of the American chemicals, materials, and energy corporation had begun as a nineteenth-century explosives manufacturer, branched into making cellophane and nylon products, and was now producing everything from consumer paints and automotive finishes to polyethylene resin and film. Just out of college, Ted had started there in the accounting department before moving into sales promotion and direct sales of new nylon and Lycra products in Ontario. Bouncing between Toronto and the Montreal head office, he became a marketing manager and then group director of fibres, the largest division, and eventually vice-president of corporate development in 1974. Under his inspired direction, the company developed a major polyethylene resin polymer plant in Ontario.

Within four years, at age forty-two, he was CEO of a suddenly money-losing DuPont Canada. Fixing it, he streamlined thirteen management levels down to an average of five. The following year, he chaired the company, and later, also oversaw all the non-American operations around the world reporting to the parent company's international department. He then talked the head office into eliminating the department and giving the regional subsidiaries more autonomy. Yet he was a big enough man to acknowledge mistakes, as when he misread the marketplace and DuPont lost about $50 million in developing, killing a polyester plant. All in all, he had a good mix of boldness and humility: Ted Newall seemed just the fixer to turn around NOVA's failing chemicals division.

Bob Blair had caught him just as Ted was planning to retire. Bud Estey, whom he knew from the Business Council, convinced him to take on the task back in his home province. Before deciding, Ted approached the chairs of several banks that propped up the chemicals company, particularly the Bank of Nova Scotia's Ced Ritchie and CIBC's Don Fullerton.

"These guys want me to go out to Calgary and run this company and it wasn't in my plans to do that," Ted recalls telling them. "You know, I'm not the least bit interested in running NOVA if I'm going to be at the beck and call of the banks, worried about these loans all of the time. I need some breathing space to get the place fixed."

And the bankers responded by saying, "Go out there and get things fixed, and we're with you 100 percent. If you need any help from us, just ask."

As special advisor, I greeted him when he arrived in town by offering, "Tell me anything I can do to help you get this bloody place fixed, and I'll do it."

Knowing nothing about the pipeline side, he was grateful to have me battle with the producers who thought NOVA was making too much money from shipping their petroleum to market. Years later, *Globe and Mail* columnist Mathew Ingram criticized NOVA for what he called its "typical arrogance," pointing out that we finally had to agree to modify our pricing for a group of gas producers—primarily PanCanadian Petroleum and Vancouver's Westcoast Energy—who'd planned a competing pipeline project. He said in this situation and similar ones, we should have "tried to understand the concerns of producers...instead of ridiculing them." It was a reasonable argument: While the gas producers always tried to nickel-and-dime us, to be fair, I'm not sure NOVA handled their concerns with enough understanding.

I also inherited the job of co-chair at Husky Oil. If NOVA was a mess, Husky was in even worse condition, both because of the low price of natural gas and lax management. The Royal Bank was hounding it about $400 million in corporate debt, and while the company had roughly the same amount tied up in a capital program, the cash flow was only $100 million or so.

"Doc," I asked, "do you realize what shape Husky's in?"

"Oh, no," he said, "they make presentations once in a while, and they seem to be okay."

"This goddamn place is going bust."

When I asked Art Price, Husky's president and CEO, why it was teetering on the abyss, he said his masters at NOVA had urged him to expand: "It's a private company, and so you can go ahead and lever things up because you know you have two big strong outfits behind you [NOVA and Li Ka-Shing's conglomerate]."

Then I met with Bob Blair, and—while not wanting to be critical—I asked, "How had Husky come to such a sorry state?"

"Well, Dick," he replied, "K.S. [which is what he called Li Ka-Shing] promised us a billion dollars, and that didn't come through; and I promised the price of gas would be $4 [per thousand cubic feet], and that didn't come through."

We had to sell Husky. The logical acquisitor was our partner, Li Ka-Shing. But first, I sought a local buyer. By now, I was good friends with David O'Brien, Bart Rombough's successor as CEO of PanCanadian Petroleum.

"David," I said, "I have got a hell of a deal for you!"

When I told him what it was, he just about threw me out of his office: "Haskayne, that company is a dog, for Christ's sake. You can't sell that to me."

Chastened, Ted and I decided we had to go to Hong Kong to talk with Li and his people at Hutchison Whampoa, his public company. Because Bob Blair still hadn't cut all his connections with NOVA and felt he had an in with the Asian magnate, he came along, too. We stayed at the Hilton, where exotic bottles of cognac awaited us in our rooms, because it was not only located across the street from Li's skyscraper but owned by Li, as well.

We were certainly trying to make a deal with him on his home turf. This is the man who operated most of the local port, the world's largest, supplied electricity to the Chinese mainland, and was one of Hong Kong's leading retailers and property owners. Li is an intriguing character who'd started out as a Chinese refugee sweeping factory floors in Hong Kong. (He still liked wearing cheap watches and setting them eight minutes early because in Cantonese that number sounds like the word "prosperity.") The three of us had lunch with him in the corporate dining room to set up the ground rules for negotiating the sale. Li, sixty-three then, was unfailingly polite and, though his English wasn't perfect, was easy to understand. Ted reflected afterward, "I felt like I was a first-year university student and here was a hugely respected prof who knew everything there was to know." Between us, Ted and I suggested to him, "We're the new management on the block, and if you prefer to have Bob sit in with us, that's fine. But if you think we might have some different views than Bob..."

We began negotiating with his assistants—without Bob. Among them were his quiet son, Victor, who would become the conglomerate's deputy chairman, and Canning Fok, his aide-de-camp, a round, smiling chartered accountant from Australia who would stay in touch with me over the years. Canning took the lead on their side, and I handled NOVA's interests in negotiations that reached several roadblocks. Before I left Hong Kong, Li asked for a private meeting with me. Surprisingly, it turned out to be an hour of chatting not about Husky but about CIBC, where I was now a director. He was a big investor in the bank, and the bank had a 5 percent piece of Husky, and we both considered Don Fullerton, the chairman, to be a friend.

The complex talks resumed in Calgary, this time with Husky's legal expert, Bob Phillips, a partner in Blake, Cassels, and Graydon. Again, we hit stalemates that kept us bargaining long into the night until Canning came up with a solution and an agreed-upon price. We had been mandated by NOVA's board to accept anything over $175 million for Husky. In the end, we got a comfortable $375 million. Frankly, I believe Li's people just didn't appreciate how deep a hole Husky had dug itself. At the time, we thought we were striking a good deal for ourselves, but in later years, I wished we'd sold the bloody chemical company and kept Husky because I saw how successful the new owner was in reviving it. Under the dynamic leadership of John Lau, the financial and operating results have been simply outstanding—he's built the business into a Northern Tiger.

Near the end of 1991, fellow directors were urging me to become chairman of NOVA as well as run the pipeline operation. Ted Newall remembers, "I went to Doc Seaman and said, 'Look, I know you don't want to be the chairman of NOVA, and the board doesn't want to have a situation again where the CEO is the chairman. You know they don't want me to be chairman, so why don't you propose to them that we make Haskayne the chairman?'" As usual, I sought opinions from informed outsiders, in particular Don Fullerton, my friendly banker.

"Don't touch the chairman role," he cautioned me. "You'll have all the responsibility without the authority to handle things. For all practical purposes, you have a chairman in Ted, and he'll continue to act that way—even though you both get along. Your problems will start when things go wrong—and they might, because the chemical business may not be out of the woods for two years or more. And Ted may not last more than two years."

I argued that Ted was a very good executive who'd impressed me with his performance.

"I'll wait and see," Don replied, "and hope I can agree with you later."

Despite his misgivings, I agreed early the next year to become a non-executive chairman, holding no other positions in the company and operating independently from an office outside the NOVA headquarters. As it turned out, Lee's health began failing at about that time, and in my regular exercise of chronicling the seven benchmarks of my life, I'd written about the present state of my career: "Perfect at age fifty-eight—DON'T WANT TO BE CEO AGAIN." I'd happily leave that role to Ted Newall. And my faith in him was repaid in spades.

With our board's blessing and the help of outside consultants, he and eight top managers began an eighteen-month strategic review. As Don predicted, the first couple of years were as tough as they come, rife with the restructuring of the chemical company and fire sales of defective assets, including several chemical plants in Sarnia, Ontario. The chief casualty was Polysar Energy & Chemical Corp., which Bob Blair had acquired in 1988 for a steep $1.9 billion in an overreaching attempt to become a world-class petrochemical enterprise. "And all of a sudden, the chemical business is losing money like there's no tomorrow," Ted remembers. He sold Polysar to Bayer AG of Germany for $1.25 billion. The writeoff on the company's books during his first year on the thirty-sixth floor of the NOVA Building would total $923 million— "which at that time was the largest loss in Canadian corporate history." Doc Seaman simply asked him, "Are you sure you've got it all?" Though NOVA's shares dropped by about half in value, they shot up again a week or two later as analysts decided Ted meant business. Within six months or so, we released two equity issues because investors were demanding stock. And Ted was announcing that the plan to divide NOVA into two companies was "deader than a doornail."

Meanwhile, he confounded most other North American chief executives by refusing to take any salary as president and CEO, preferring instead to be compensated only in NOVA shares. "It sends a very clear message to investors that I'm one of them," he explained. "And they know I'm not captured by suicidal impulses."

By 1992, thanks to his disciplined, team-building approach and with natural-gas sales humming along nicely, NOVA had a profit of $164 million, our shareholders enjoyed a 24 percent return, and the managers among our 6,300 employees benefited from an incentive plan tied to the performance of the company, each business unit, and the individual. Along with everything else, the Native Employment Services of Alberta was soon to name us "Company of the Year" for our Aboriginal hiring practices. Not bad for an old nylon salesman, as Ted liked to call himself.

He and I became as tight as brothers. (And I admired his wife, Margaret, a former music teacher who was so horrified by the Montreal massacre of fourteen female engineering students in 1989 that she created an action network devoted to research and the frontline treatment of victims of violence and abuse.) Early in 1993, I wrote Ted a letter of appreciation on behalf of the board:

> Ever since your appointment in 1991, NOVA has been pro-
> vided with exceptionally strong leadership in overcoming
> a number of challenges such as dealing with the financial
> community to restructure the Company's balance sheet,
> resulting in the successful issuance of common shares,
> establishing a plan to address serious problems in the
> chemicals business, rectifying corporate governance issues,
> completing the sale of Husky, improving relations with the
> producing companies and establishing senior management
> development as a priority.

Later that year, Ted returned the compliment when he was named "Canadian CEO of the Year," chosen by a group of his executive peers from companies such as Bombardier, McCain Foods, and Shell Canada. In his acceptance speech at a gala evening in Vancouver, he recalled having known only a few key people in his new line of business: "I'd met Dick Haskayne. Dick became my chairman, and he's been one of the best coaches I've ever worked with. I credit Dick with helping me make the transition to the energy industry."

What I'd done was pretty basic: introducing him to the right people and warning him off the wrong ones. I knew the economics of pipelines and had spent my whole career in the Oil Patch. Ted took the puck from me and then put it in the net.

Chapter Seven

THE URGE TO MERGE
TransCanada Corporation

IN 1994, I WAS AT MY OWN AWARD ceremony when I shot my mouth off, as usual, about the downside of mergers. In Edmonton to receive the Canadian Business Leader Award from my alma mater, the University of Alberta, I was speaking to seven hundred people, including my executive colleagues and Premier Ralph Klein. Unable to resist pontificating on a pet topic, I pointed out that in my experience, most mergers fail because of issues such as corporate egos, the desire to grow for the sake of "bigness" alone, and the taking on of too much debt. Only three years later, I was wondering whether I'd have to eat my words with a side dish of humble pie, when the merging of NOVA with a major Canadian company suddenly loomed as a practical—and desirable—possibility. Would it be the one in five such alliances that beat the odds?

In the intervening years, NOVA had expanded on the chemicals side as we acquired a quarter stake in the multinational Methanex Corp., the world's largest methane producer; more than a third of Natural Gas Clearinghouse, a gas marketer and vendor based in Texas; and even a polyethylene plant in Sarnia owned by Ted's old employer, DuPont Canada. Yet though the 1996 earnings were the third-highest in corporate history, a year later our shares were treading water as investors couldn't come to grips with a company operating both a pipeline and the more volatile business of petrochemicals. Reluctant as Ted was to split NOVA into two distinct ventures, we were all concluding this was the only answer to making forward progress.

American corporations were expressing interest in taking over NOVA. "A large pipeline company and a large chemical company had studied NOVA nine ways to Sunday," Ted remembers. "They knew everything there was to know about us. So my CFO and I had a meeting with the number-two guy from the pipeline company and the number-one guy from the chemical company. We met at the airport in Tucson, where Margaret and I have a little home. They gave us this big pitch on how wonderfully the chemical and pipeline shareholders would do and that, of course, they would keep me on as the CEO and I'd become very wealthy—and all this bullshit. And finally after we went through this for two or three hours, I said, 'Well, the truth of the matter is I didn't come out here to sell NOVA to the Americans. So long as I am the CEO, that is not an acceptable outcome.'

"One of the things that triggered our announcing the split was the fact that these two guys were sitting like vultures on the doorstep. Because the government of Alberta had a vote that wouldn't let anybody take over NOVA without its approval, the Americans knew they couldn't do a hostile on us. It had to be a friendly takeover, and they couldn't figure out quite how to do it. But we knew that sooner or later this was going to happen if we didn't get the split done."

It was at that point my former colleague and long-time friend Gerry Maier showed up on our radar. Gerry had been CEO and was now non-executive chair of TransCanada Pipelines. A proud Canadian, he was the right man at the right time in the history of a company that was born in political turbulence.

Four and a half decades earlier, a cross-Canada pipeline had been the brainchild of a Texan named Clinton Murchison, who owned the major American gas producer Delhi Oil. Finding good supplies of gas in Alberta, he conceived a transmission system to bring it to North American markets in the east. But the federal Liberal government of Louis St. Laurent—and especially his formidable trade and commerce minister, C.D. Howe—

insisted on having substantial Canadian content in the project. With Ottawa providing sizable loans, Murchison became equal partners with a consortium of domestic investors called Western Pipe Lines. Passing the legislation to approve the enterprise led to the Great Pipeline Debate of 1956. Howe, using closure tactics to stifle debate and compromising the neutrality of the Speaker of the House, fast-tracked a bill to authorize the construction and bulldozed it through Parliament. The fallout from the government's arrogant attitude led to the defeat of both the Liberals and Howe and the victory of John Diefenbaker's Conservatives in the next election.

TransCanada's first president and the engineer who supervised the building of the pipeline were Americans, but most of the buyers of its first mortgage bonds and original shares were Canadians (thirty-five thousand of them became stockholders, compared to six thousand from the U.S.). By 1962, 90 percent of the company was in domestic hands. One of the major investors was Home Oil's Bobby Brown, Jr., who became a disruptive director until his death in '72, when the CPR acquired his shares as the single biggest shareholder. Only six years later, the railway sold its 49 percent to my nemesis-to-be, Jack Gallagher. But Dome Petroleum was soon hemorrhaging so badly that he had to sell out to an unlikely eastern saviour, Jean de Grandpré's Bell Canada Enterprises Inc. The telecommunications colossus was seeking, among other things, access to the pipeline's right-of-way across central Canada to lay fibre optic cable for long-distance telephone lines. By 1993, Bell had sold off all of its stock, and TransCanada was its own master five years later when Gerry and his chief executive, George Watson, came calling on us at NOVA.

While the pipeline division of NOVA—originally a creation of Ernest Manning's Alberta government—held a near-monopoly on gas collection and distribution in the province, it had to link with the TransCanada line to get its natural gas to eastern Canada and the U.S. As veteran oil commentator Frank Dabbs described the two companies,

> TransCanada and NOVA are corporate Siamese twins
> joined at the hip in Alberta's postwar energy boom.…
> While not direct competitors, and in fact both enduring the
> undying hostility of gas producers and consumers, the
> companies have been locked in four decades of often-bitter
> sibling rivalry, trying to outgrow and outdo one another.

Former Premier Peter Lougheed had labelled TransCanada as one of Alberta's two public enemies (along with the CPR) because it seemed to be a lot friendlier to consumers than it was to producers.

TransCanada was no longer merely a Canadian utility but a great North American network with stock prices soaring to the highest peak in a decade. As I'd done with Interprovincial Pipe Line, Gerry had moved the head office from Toronto to Calgary, an action that helped to begin healing the wounds between TransCanada and the Alberta gas producers. For about a year now, he and George Watson had been contemplating the common sense of melding their company with NOVA. As Gerry recalls, "It seemed unnecessary to have an entity in Alberta gathering gas and another company [transmitting it to the east]. And I saw the dealings between TransCanada and NOVA were often lengthy and complex—producers and shippers had to deal with two entities. There seemed to be some potential synergies and cost-savings here that were very important in the short to medium term. But in the longer term, I perceived that a much stronger entity in North America was going to be required because of the potential competition from other companies in the United States. To me, it just made great business sense."

A complicating factor in all this was the threat of a pipeline planning to compete with TransCanada's monopoly situation. Alliance Pipeline Ltd. was proposing to the National Energy Board a $3.7-billion gas line between western Canada and the U.S. Alliance was a consortium of industry goliaths, including Gulf Canada, North Carolina's Duke Energy Corp., Alberta Energy Company, and Crestar Energy. Interestingly enough, I was now on the board of AEC and Crestar as well as NOVA's and had to excuse

myself from any discussion involving those two producing companies and TransCanada.

AEC was another creature of the Alberta government, designed
to participate in oil and gas projects. It later invested in forest
products, petrochemicals, coal, and steel. In 1975, the government
had sold half its interest as a public share offering and, in '93, tendered its remaining shares. Within two years, AEC was focusing
entirely on petroleum investments. Its president was a young man
destined for loftier perches, Gwyn Morgan. I'd met him when I
was running Interprovincial and he was on the board of the
Independent Petroleum Association—the producers who were
beating the hell out of us to get more price breaks. Gwyn was
prominent among those attacking me, and I wondered, *Who is
that smart-alec but smart young bastard?* And all these years later,
Gwyn had made sure that AEC was one of the original investors in,
and champions of, Alliance. I now felt like a mentor to him, and
we had many discussions about the idea of including NOVA in the
proposed pipeline. Playing the diplomat, I even had him and Ted
meet in my office for what turned out to be a frustrating attempt
to make a deal.

Gwyn had also met with George Watson, TransCanada's president and CEO, the former chief financial officer whose career had
blended the investment banking and energy resources industries.
At one point, George seemed inclined to partner with Alliance
until lawyers warned that such an arrangement might contravene
agreements with his company's American distributors.

That left Gerry even keener on completing a possible
TransCanada-NOVA union. He'd already talked with me about the
concept and then later with Ted. (The two of them had become
friends when Gerry was on the DuPont board, and Ted even consulted him before taking the NOVA job.) At the time, though, we
were still trying to figure out what to do with NOVA's two divisions. Because TransCanada had no wish to ever get into the
petrochemicals industry, the idea of a merger just perched on an
unlit back burner for a year. Then in November 1997, Ted
announced that NOVA Corp. would, after all, be sundered into two

public companies operating in separate spheres: petrochemicals and natural-gas pipelines and marketing.

The next day, George Watson got Ted on the phone: "I just think you've solved both our problems."

Ted warmed to the suggestion of a deal: "It made so much sense. Putting two pipeline companies together was going to create a much stronger pipeline company, which would get higher valuations from investors. And it would particularly create a helluva lot of value on the chemical company side."

I was holidaying in Hawaii then, and came back to chair a meeting that would consider the approach from TransCanada. NOVA's stock had sunk to the level of two years earlier—about $11 per share—as we diversified into the midstream business of processing gas as well as trading it on the open market. Of course, TransCanada was into the iffy trading game too, following in the footsteps of an American company called Enron Corp. that was making a splash in this business—and that would one day create even bigger, bumpier waves.

George and Ted, meeting under assumed names at a local hotel, first discussed the general mechanics of the deal. Then both parties put three representatives apiece on a committee to oversee the nitty-gritty negotiations being worked out by the companies' financial and legal people. NOVA's trio was me, the Bank of Nova Scotia's ex-chair Ced Ritchie, and Harley Hotchkiss, who had been on our board since 1979.

On the TransCanada side, the committee members were Gerry, ex–Royal Bank chair Allan Taylor, and Harry Schaefer. Harry, an engineer's son and graduate in commerce from the University of Alberta a year behind me, was a chartered accountant who'd articled in Calgary at the same time as I did. He'd served as a long-running CFO of TransAlta, and at this point, had been a TransCanada director for a decade. While managing people wasn't his strong suit, he was a whiz with balance sheets, regulatory hearings, and corporate governance. Smart as hell, hard-working, and dedicated, he became one of the deans of Canadian audit committees.

Despite my general bias against mergers, this appeared to be the one in five that could work. It would be billed as a marriage of equals even while Gerry and his colleagues believed TransCanada held the higher cards in the game. The plan was to create "a pooling of interests," which, under securities regulations, means a merger of companies of similar size and with no controlling shareholder. The new board of directors would have equal representation from the two previous boards. Rather than any cash being exchanged, shareholders were to receive equity in the combined company—in this case, 520 common TransCanada shares for one thousand of NOVA's. Meanwhile, the deal would also create an independent company, NOVA Chemicals, which would take an appropriate amount of debt with it. A NOVA stockholder would get 520 shares in NOVA Chemicals for every one thousand of NOVA's.

The talks went on through the Christmas season, and on January 24, 1998, the boards of both companies approved the general terms of agreement. What we came to realize was that this merger would create the fourth-largest energy-services company on the continent, operating in six provinces and seventeen states with 6,300 employees and boasting annual revenues of $16 billion and assets of $21 billion. The $14-billion deal itself broke the record as the biggest in the history of the Canadian energy sector to that point. Analysts welcomed it, as did virtually all the shareholders. The only critics were Gwyn Morgan and his colleagues who were promoting the three-thousand-kilometre Alliance pipeline from Alberta to Illinois—which was soon approved by the National Energy Board and began operating at the end of 2000.

Ted became non-executive chairman of the new NOVA Chemicals (leasing an office next door to mine, downtown). Gerry Maier stayed on both boards until his mandated retirement. The head office and the senior executive team—headed by president Jeffrey Lipton, an American—moved to Pittsburgh in 1999, supposedly to be closer to its markets. Ced Ritchie, among others, is still upset by the transplanting of an Alberta-built enterprise down south. But the company went on to become North America's largest producer of polystyrene and to run the world's largest ethylene complex, in Red Deer, Alberta.

I replaced Gerry as the non-exec chair of what came to be called TransCanada Corporation. Our directors ranged in background from Wendy Dobson, a professor at the Rotman School of Management and director of the Institute for International Business at the University of Toronto, to Paule Gauthier, a senior partner in a prestigious Quebec law firm and a long-time chair of the Security Intelligence Review Committee, the agency that oversees the Canadian Security Intelligence Service. Joining them in the next year or so would be two of my compatriots, David O'Brien, former head of Canadian Pacific Ltd., and Barry Jackson, a past president and CEO of Calgary's Crestar Energy.

I asked the board to give me a year without pressure to sort out what we should do with the company. As it happened, I needed that time. In April 1999, I really hadn't been taking particularly good care of myself. I weighed about two hundred pounds, about fifteen too many. For weeks I'd been constantly out of breath, and an aching feeling gnawed at my chest. One day while in California just before Easter, I was having a bad bout of pain and called Shauna to make an appointment with my internist in Calgary, Dr. Derrick Thomson. Cardiologists Dr. Eldon Smith and Dr. Henrik ter Keurs soon had me on the table for an angiogram to check for blockages in my arteries. I had six of them, and one was in the main artery—the widow-maker. Two days later, I was in hospital having a quintuple bypass as a very fine medical team headed by the surgeon Dr. Andrew Maitland used parts of my healthy blood vessels to detour around the plugged sections of the coronary arteries.

Interestingly enough, I wasn't scared at the time. A Canadian professor named Roby Kidd, an international expert in adult education, once wrote, "It isn't so much that dying is tragic, for death comes to us all, but dying without meaning." Like this lifelong-learning guy, I guess I'm a fatalist about death: It comes when it comes, and if you've done as much as you've wanted in life and enjoyed the doing—which I have—you can accept the end graciously. Not that I wanted to take leave then, nor do I now. But if I had to choose any way to go, it would be exactly how my mother went: a heart attack that took her instantly. In my case, I didn't even have an attack—just a warning that led to the life-saving bypass surgery.

While I was away, some board members were already questioning George Watson's capabilities, even though he was an accomplished dealmaker. Our share price had dropped to $20 per share from $31 at the time of the merger, and when George was asked at a board meeting when the price would recover, he replied, "I don't know—five or ten years."

A new director we'd recruited, Doug Baldwin, witnessed this exchange and wondered if he'd made the right move in joining the board. Doug had been the highly ethical president of Esso Resources and a senior VP of Imperial Oil. A high school principal's son and chemical engineer from Saskatchewan, he'd worked for the largest oil company in Canada and its parent, Exxon, for forty-one years. Within a year of the merger, George Watson was gone, and the next day, Doug was our interim CEO, aged sixty-three.

Earlier, Doug had suggested we could act something like a tag team in the post: "Look, if you become the interim CEO, I'll be there for you. I'll back you."

I checked with my old buddy Ken McNeill, who said, "Haskayne, you can't do the job jointly with somebody else. Somebody has got to be boss." And then I called Bob Peterson, who'd been his colleague at Imperial, and asked him for a confidential, frank opinion of Doug as a potential leader of TransCanada.

"There is absolutely no technical or other reason he could not do the job," Bob said. "The only problem is I'm not sure he is tough enough—he's too accommodating to people."

Well, I preferred Doug's softer side to the typical Exxon approach, so I convinced him to take the temporary position. Before accepting, he told the directors, "I'll take the job on the basis that I'm not working for the board. I'm not your guy. I *will* talk to Dick and ask for advice because I don't have the background he does." In fact, we did get together every week, and I attended some management meetings for a while until Doug said this wasn't helpful to him anymore because my presence suggested I was running the joint.

At the board level, I *was* among those overseeing the reorganization of the company while it slashed costs and divested unprofitable assets. When the board cut the dividend to shareholders, there were dire warnings from stock analysts, but we had a massive mess to clean up. Like NOVA, TransCanada had leapt into the energy-trading area as well as the midstream business—the processing, storage, and transportation sector of the industry—and was losing potfuls of cash. Harry Schaefer, chairing the audit committee, and I started tearing the balance sheet apart and discovered the midstream assets were being financed with 87 percent debt, which would have infuriated the gas producers if we'd had to reveal that at a National Energy Board hearing (which we eventually did—after making things right again).

We also realized that the company's involvement in energy trading and marketing was a disaster waiting to happen. Traders were peddling futures of natural gas, taking short positions that made them vulnerable, and there were rumours of the false reporting of trading data in an attempt to manipulate the gas market. TransCanada, as the largest mover of gas on the continent, felt it was important to be in that market, buying the resource from suppliers and reselling it—in transactions that were totalling $10 billion a year. But in the day that Harry and I spent among the few hundred folks on our trading floor, we couldn't figure the business out—all we old number-crunching CAs found was gobbledygook about the tight controls our traders were supposed to heed.

Fortunately, Doug, Russ Girling (the new CFO), and a young up-and-comer in the company, Hal Kvisle, shared our unease. I'd never met Hal while he ran the production-engineering department at Dome Petroleum as it took over Hudson's Bay Oil and Gas and I made my exit. He was well-known to George Watson, who wanted to hire him at TransCanada, but I insisted on interviewing this Harold K. Kvisle one whole afternoon at a headhunter's office.

He was forty-seven, wise beyond his years, and a pretty ingratiating guy. As Amoco was buying the remnants of Dome, he'd been the point man to negotiate the price. Turning down a good job with Amoco in Chicago, he went out on his own, finding partners to put together million-dollar deals to build gas plants for a couple of years. My friend Ron Southern was on the board of the Fletcher Challenge resource group in New Zealand, which was looking for oil and gas investments. Ron told his fellow directors they should consider western Canada. Hal, meanwhile, had fashioned a $120-million deal to acquire Amoco's assets in eastern Alberta—and as the twain met, he was persuaded to come on as president of the new Fletcher Challenge Energy Canada. He left a decade later when the company was sold for more than $1 billion. One thing that impressed me was that he'd convinced the Fletcher parent company *not* to get involved in several dubious deals.

Doug describes Hal well: "Quiet, witty, can be very intense, extremely intelligent, good strategic thinker, a tough dealmaker. He knows when to cut bait and knows when it's time to leave the water, too." That kind of informed naysaying was what we now needed at TransCanada. Interestingly enough, it was only after George Watson's sudden leave-taking that Hal had actually joined us. Admiring Doug, he'd decided to follow through and accept a senior position, which soon evolved into executive VP of trading and business development, focusing on North American power and pipeline ventures.

His eventual goal was to rebuild a reorganized company that had been downsizing rather than developing—in Doug's words, it had "too many moving parts." As Hal says, "The big decision was that all of our international business and all of our midstream business had to be sold, and there was quite a bit of pressure on to sell all of our power assets. The midstream assets were the large Alberta liquid-extraction plants and as many as twenty gathering and processing plants scattered all over western Canada that were performing poorly." The blue-chip extraction plants went for a great price to the Williams Companies Inc., the Oklahoma-based pipeline and exploration conglomerate. TransCanada also sold its gas pipelines and marketing businesses in Mexico to Gaz de France. In the first year alone, it sold non-core assets for more than $3.4 billion and then repaid $1.75 billion in term debt to strengthen the balance sheet. Many employees shifted to the new owners' payrolls, and over the next four years with the help of efficiency programs, our staff count dropped to an astonishing 2,600 from 6,300.

Hal didn't want to sell the power-generation assets, which were then worth only about $500 million but had real potential for growth. "Our power guys were saying they'd sure like to participate in the power purchase-agreement auction where the government was about to sell off these long-life, twenty-year interests in the output of different coal plants in Alberta. But they knew we didn't have the money, so I did everything I could to convince Russ Girling and Doug Baldwin that this would be a good idea. We got board approval to do one of those coal deals—and that really was the foundation of our whole power business here in Alberta, which has turned out well. In parallel with this, we did a number of co-generation projects [using natural gas to produce electricity] as that provincial market was unfolding." Power generation has climbed from about 5 percent to a quarter of TransCanada's business.

Observing all the sell-offs and not realizing the potential in the power field, wary investors had pushed our stock down to below $10 per share by early 2000. "I was worried whether the company was going to make it," Hal recalls, "because we had all kinds of hostile parties making noise about taking us over—there were rumours all the time."

That January, the toughest job awaited him: Trying to take control of the trading department. "I became very uncomfortable with the way they'd portrayed their business at the end of 1999," Hal says. "It's compensation and bonus time, and the guys that are running the marketing and trading group would have me believe that they'd just had an absolutely stellar year. I wouldn't say they were cooking the books, but they were only presenting half the story. So I terminated them and turned the business over to the only guy in the senior group there that I really trusted, who wasn't part of that culture. I said, 'Do you trust the people reporting to you?' and he said, 'Yeah, know them real well.' And I said, 'You know, we've really got to make sure that we understand what's going on here and that there aren't manipulative things being done by the marketers and traders to make their results appear better or to make the risk appear less than it was.'"

About a year later, we hired the executive search firm Spencer Stuart to begin an international hunt for a successor for the retiring Doug Baldwin as president and CEO. What's fascinating today is that while Hal was pinpointed as one candidate, two of his rivals for the job were executives from Enron, the electricity, natural-gas, and communications company that would soon become a global symbol for corporate greed. The search committee finally decided that Hal was clearly the best choice. As chairman, I had the happy task of telling him the swell news. When I said we had to discuss the terms of his employment, he replied, "Dick, I want to do the job. I'm not looking at it as an opportunity to negotiate or to hardball on a lot of little details. I'm sure whatever you figure out will be fair." And it was. He's since said he appreciates that during my tenure, the TransCanada board never suffered from the "sort of backroom diplomatic manouevering that characterizes a lot of boards."

But as the new CEO, he was about to walk on hot coals as the trading department's troubles flared up again. I'll let Hal tell the story: "In November of 2000, our corporate controller, a great guy, Lee Hobbs, came to me and Russ Girling, the CFO, and said something was quite wrong in marketing and trading. The risk-management systems were saying we've got no exposures and we're not losing any money, but according to some brilliant accounting work, Lee had detected that there was something gone awry. The guy running marketing and trading said, 'No, nothing like that's going on, there's no problem.' I told him to dig into it because I smelled something really wrong. He came back two days later, ashen-faced, and said, 'You know, we've suffered a loss in the $70-million range.' And this is in the last month of the year. This is just like net income time, and you really don't want to get this kind of surprise. It was a situation bordering on fraud—we could have made the case that we had a certain group of traders that had put a fraudulent arrangement together.

"And our lawyers and I concluded there was a group of counterparties to these deals—big industrial gas users—and it was their risk: If there was a loss, they would absorb it; if there was a gain, we'd share the gain. But it was clear to me that we had been doing things we shouldn't and these people weren't going to take that loss; they were going to sue us.

"First of all, we just stopped all trading in about half of our business. The other half you couldn't stop because we had big open positions and if you walked away on them, you could be sued for billions of dollars—the magnitude of the disaster we were facing was unbelievable. So I took it to my first board meeting as CEO in April of 2001 and said, 'We've got to get out of marketing and trading. If we can't find a buyer, we've got to take eight months to do an orderly shutdown, and during that time, I'm going to have to pay an ungodly amount of money to certain key people—some of them quite bad actors who had made this mess— to keep them around here because if they walk out the door, we don't know how to manage this thing.' I asked Russ to take on the job of selling gas marketing and trading. We put together a deal to sell the business to Mirant—a U.S.-based marketing and trading company that wanted to become the big trader in Canada. They would pay us a fair bit of money to buy the business and would take on all the liabilities and all the people, and it would be their business going forward."

The deal, however, was being negotiated against a backdrop of emerging scandal in the U.S. as Enron Corp., the vaunted energy-resources trader—once the model for other North American companies in this business—began ripping at the seams. In October 2001, Enron reported a $638-million third-quarter loss and a $1.2-billion reduction in shareholder equity, partly because of falling stock that was designed to hedge inflated asset values and keep hundreds of millions of dollars in debt off the books. The Securities and Exchange Commission launched an inquiry into the company's finances, which eventually revealed massive corporate fraud at the highest levels.

"It was the end of October," Hal continues, "and to sell a marketing and trading business, you've got to cut off the books at the end of the month because that's the only clean break. And if we can't get it done by the end of October, we'll have to run it for another month. That's what happened." Meanwhile, Enron told the SEC it was revising financial statements for the previous five years to account for more than half a billion dollars in losses. On Friday, November 28, Enron's stock tanked to below $1 per share.

"So it was the last trading day of November, a Friday. We all agreed we'd just work hammer and tongs, twenty-fours a day, over the weekend," Hal remembers. "And Russ let me know at six o'clock on Sunday night the deal was done, our money was in the bank. I went home and had a nice glass of wine and a big dinner and went to bed. And I got up at six o'clock on Monday morning because I wanted to read the press releases about our deal on the news wire. I turned on my computer at home, and there was nothing about TransCanada—because the news was full of the fact that Enron had gone bankrupt on Sunday. We sold that business twelve hours before Enron went bankrupt"—and before its collapse caused a meltdown in many other companies mired in the energy-trading market. Without any inside knowledge, TransCanada's people had been lucky enough to get out in time and emerge unscathed.

(Just how vulnerable the company could have been was underlined again recently when a former Calgary natural-gas trader, now working for Amaranth Advisors LLC, a hedge fund in Greenwich, Connecticut, was deemed largely responsible for $5 billion in losses incurred in that firm's gas trading—which led Amaranth to shut down in the fall of 2006. The trader himself, meanwhile, earned an estimated $75–$100 million [U.S.] the year before.)

Hal Kvisle is one of the best chief executives I've ever known, running one of the best and biggest gas-transmission companies in North America, as he was to prove over the next four years. It's now one of the largest private-sector power businesses in Canada, with a net income about equal to TransAlta's. A decade from now, TransCanada plans to have half its business in power generation— and anywhere from a third to half of that could be nuclear power. The company is one of four all-Canadian partners in the private-sector Bruce nuclear power facility northwest of Toronto, the largest such plant on the continent. The future is also in conventional power and pipeline projects: the proposed 3,000-kilometre Keystone heavy-oil line, from Alberta to Illinois, and the enormous potential of the Mackenzie Delta and Alaska North Slope pipelines from the far north.

When after seven years I handed off my chairmanship to Barry Jackson in 2005, TransCanada's share price was hovering around the $30 range—more than $20 higher than it had been five years earlier. Just as important in my eyes was the reputation we had for good corporate governance and ethical behaviour. The company's operating principles are often summed up by the acronym "SPIRIT": Social responsibility, Passion, Integrity, Results, Innovation, and Teamwork. "Integrity" is the cornerstone of these values. Each year, all employees are required to read the "Code of Business Ethics" and complete an online certification to confirm their knowledge and compliance with its contents. If staff—or contractors, consultants, vendors, customers, or other stakeholders—observe or suspect irregularities in the company's operations, they can also make anonymous calls to a toll-free Ethics Helpline.

The morality of doing business involves not only how a corporation treats people but also how it respects the environment. TransCanada has a strategy modelled on ISO 14001, an international standard for environmental management systems. Its systems cover everything from risk assessment and management through training and awareness of employees and contractors to rigorous performance audits and reviews. Acknowledging the reality of climate change, the company also has a strategy to reduce the emission of greenhouse gases and nitrogen oxides (NOx) produced by its pipeline and power facilities. And in 2005, Hydro-Québec awarded twenty-year contracts to two companies—including Cartier Wind Energy, co-owned by TransCanada and Quebec-based Innergex II—to build wind farms in the Gaspé region during the next decade. They'll supply enough power for two hundred thousand homes. On its own, Cartier will be the largest wind-energy producer in the province.

In a recent KPMG/Ipsos Reid poll, leading CEOs had recognized TransCanada as being one of the twenty-five most respected Canadian corporations; *Canadian Business* magazine said it had one of the top-ten boards in the nation; and the Certified Management Accountants of Alberta gave us their province-wide Business Award of Distinction for business ethics. In mid-2006, *Corporate Knights* ("the Canadian magazine for responsible business") ranked the company highly among the fifty best corporate citizens, based on its actions and responses to an array of ethical issues.

After some bad bumps along the way, TransCanada Corporation had become a stalwart and esteemed Northern Tiger through a combination of clever strategy and superb execution by the management team.

Chapter Eight

HIGH FINANCES
Manulife and CIBC

WATCHING NOVA GROW AND MERGE with TransCanada, which continued to prosper mightily, had helped to make up for my sadness about the loss of HBOG and Home Oil through external forces. During the rockiest years, I also took comfort in my involvement with another company that did nothing but flourish. If any one Canadian corporation can be counted among our great Northern Tigers, it's the financial services powerhouse Manulife, where I was a director. If any executive officer can be credited with training a Tiger to jump through the hoops on a world stage with strength and style, it's Manulife Financial's CEO, Dominic D'Alessandro. In contrast, for many of the same years I was also on the board of another enterprise, the Canadian Imperial Bank of Commerce. Once our second-largest bank in market capitalization, it has since fallen to fifth place, after the Royal Bank, Toronto-Dominion (TD), Scotiabank, and Bank of Montreal. Manulife hasn't made a major misstep in its expeditions into the financial jungle of the United States. CIBC, meanwhile, has stumbled in its American forays, most seriously in having to pay out hundreds of millions of dollars because of its exposure to Enron. It's not surprising that a few years ago the media were reporting on a possible merger of the insurance company and the bank.

The grand old banking institution had roots dating back to the birth of Canada in 1867. That's when it opened on Toronto's Yonge Street under its founding president, the businessman and philanthropist William McMaster. Manulife was slightly younger: The Manufacturers Life Insurance Company opened in the Ontario capital in 1887 under founding president Sir John A. Macdonald, Canada's first prime minister. And its record in the U.S., where it began operating sixteen years later, has continued to be exemplary after all this time. In Manufacturers' first, successful year, the press was already calling it "the Young Canadian Giant," and within five years, it had begun growing overseas, starting in Bermuda and then moving into the rest of the Caribbean, South America, China, and India. It weathered the Depression, prospered during the Second World War, and by 1961, had assets of $1 billion.

Nearly a century after Manufacturers' birth, a couple of its directors who knew me, one of them from Hiram Walker, put up my name for the board while I was Home's president. I came on in 1983, flattered to be asked to join my first big national board—a small, influential group of advisors for one of the country's oldest companies, which was then owned by its policyholders and hadn't yet gone public. The headquarters were still in the same neo-Georgian limestone building on Bloor Street that it occupied since 1925, on grounds groomed like a putting green. Sir John A.'s portrait still hung in the handsome boardroom, along with one of his successor, George Gooderham, once Ontario's wealthiest man. (Yep, he was a member of the original Gooderham & Worts distilling family, which sold out to Harry Hatch, whose company later became part of Hiram Walker Resources.) By the time I arrived, Sydney Jackson, a veteran with Manufacturers', had been running things for the past decade. Under his risk-taking, bottom-up style of leadership—letting employees play a major part in decision-making so that they buy into any changes—it had become the nation's second-largest insurance company; over a dozen years, its assets grew eight-fold to $16.4 billion. In 1985, Syd became chairman, and his president and CEO was Tom Di Giacomo, the first of two Italian-Canadians to lead the corporation.

Tom and I were soon friends—I really liked the man—though that didn't stop me from seeing his limitations. His strengths were many. Bespectacled and balding, looking like the caricature of an insurance executive, he'd been one of the more astute investment managers in the industry, doing a good job of getting the company into real estate and equities. He didn't much care about actuarial and administrative details, yet as president, he had to deal with any challenges to corporate morale and organizational structure.

Because he was weak on human resources, our board welcomed the arrival of Rose Patten in 1987 as head of HR. For a few years, she did a hell of a good job in beginning to streamline the organizational structure and dealing with the people problems. One of those she won over was Tom himself, who married her— after which she went to the Bank of Montreal as senior executive VP of human resources (and was named one of Canada's one hundred most powerful women by the Women's Executive Network). Meanwhile, he was moving the company deeper into Asia, from South Korea to Indonesia, buying a British bank, and taking over several Canadian trust companies to create Manulife Bank.

In 1990, the year Manufacturers' became known as Manulife Financial, he was named chairman as well as CEO after pressing the board for the title. That was the biggest mistake we ever made because, other than us directors, he didn't have any mentor to keep watch over him. He was a dealmaker, not a natural-born leader for a corporation Manulife's size who could inspire by his own example. In 1993, knowing he was in trouble, Tom flew from Toronto to see me as I stayed put in Calgary during Lee's last months.

"Look, I'm over twenty-one and I understand the situation. There's a train coming down the track—initiated by a small group of directors—and it isn't likely to stop," he said. "But we're good buddies, and that will continue."

I was one of those upset directors, on the audit committee that was chaired by Gail Cook-Bennett, the clever economist who'd taught at the University of Toronto as well as helping run the C.D. Howe Institute. She had sterling credentials: chair of the Crown's Canada Pension Plan Investment Board; a director of the Bank of Canada, Manulife, and Petro-Canada; and a member of the Canadian Group of the Trilateral Commission. She and I had bluntly told Tom he had a problem with organization—and he had no answer when I asked how many people reported to him.

I was concerned about the timeliness and accuracy of Tom's financial reporting to the board. For example, in 1987, during one of the biggest market crashes, we didn't know the company's position for several weeks. On the CIBC board, I was used to getting thorough and regular reporting from senior management. In one meeting, I'd become so angry about Tom's operating style that another director, my friend Don McGiverin of Hudson's Bay, lectured me later: "Dick, that was inappropriate."

After my session with Tom in Calgary, I wrote notes to myself, as I often did regarding important conversations, and summarized what had to be done: "Loss of confidence is THE ISSUE.... MUST ACT NOW." We had a very strong board, which included former GE Canada chair Bill Blundell, Canadian National CEO Paul Tellier, and C.D. Howe Institute head Tom Kierans. They did act, launching a search for his successor. Coincidentally, the headhunters pinpointed Dominic D'Alessandro. I had the chance to interview him, and I found a compact and candid forty-seven-year-old with a great financial mind and a worldly view. And an occasionally surprising, left-field opinion that probably springs from his working-class boyhood—as when *Maclean's* magazine quoted him telling his grown-up sons why he doesn't mind paying taxes: "If it's not people like myself who are going to pay the tax, then who is?"

His was the classic Canadian immigrant's success story. Dominic had come to Montreal as a three-year-old with his family during the big postwar wave of emigration from Italy. His childhood was a tough one after his father, a construction worker, died in an accident on the job and his mother had to run an inner-city rooming house to support her four children. Skipping two grades, he finished high school at fourteen, winning scholarships to study mathematics and physics at Loyola College. Early on, he displayed his love of travel, which would stand him in good stead when it came to running a global company: He gave himself a year off in Europe before returning to study chartered accountancy at McGill University. Taking evening courses and working days at Coopers &

Lybrand, he won the Canadian Institute of Chartered Accountants'
bronze medal for his final-exam marks. After spending a year in
Paris for Coopers, he resettled in Montreal, joining Genstar Ltd.,
Imperial Tobacco's far-ranging subsidiary that operates in such
diversified fields as development and building materials.

Dominic went abroad again as general manager of a Genstar
subsidiary, a transportation and materials-handling company in a
technology-poor Saudi Arabia. Two years later, he was in San
Francisco as VP of Genstar's materials and construction group. In
1981, missing home, he took a job as a deputy controller in the
Royal Bank's head office in Montreal and was soon controller, the
youngest-ever vice-president, and eventually, executive VP of
finance. Before the decade ended, his management skills and imag-
inative and entrepreneurial approach made him an ideal president
and CEO of the Laurentian Bank of Canada, a small Royal subsidiary. During his five-year reign when Laurentian bought
Standard Trust, its assets nearly doubled to just shy of $10 billion,
its growth topped the industry, and it ranked among the country's
most profitable financial institutions. While Dominic was the best-
paid banker in the country—at $3.5 million a year—as a strong
federalist, he began looking around when Laurentian was taken
over by Quebec's sovereignist Desjardins credit-union group.

When our Manulife board considered the candidates for a new
CEO, he was the ripest plum for the picking. This time, the directors wanted to avoid the problem we'd had with Tom Di Giacomo
and decided to name a non-executive chairman. I believe that Tom
might have survived if he'd had a strong, independent chair above
him—someone like Bill Blundell, whom we voted in as Dominic
D'Alessandro came aboard. Bill described Dominic at the time:
"We were looking for someone who could lead by vision and
strategic skills, someone with business instinct who also had a
good track record in the financial institutions sector." What
Dominic said then was sweet music to all our ears: "My goal is to
make Manulife one of the world's leading insurance companies."

He hit the ground galloping in 1994, selling off more than
$150 million of the company's real estate investments and its

minor American group life and health insurance portfolio while developing the profitable individual insurance and estate-planning business in the U.S. Significantly, he deked out both Great-West Life Assurance and CIBC to pick up the group-insurance assets of Canada's failed Confederation Life Insurance. Confed was the fifth-largest company in a field of about 150 competitors in a mature domestic market. A year later, Manulife acquired a shaky North American Life Assurance (its first president had been our second prime minister, Alexander Mackenzie) and nosed out Sun Life Financial to become Canada's largest insurance provider, with $47 billion in assets.

By that time, I had decided to cut my ties with Manulife. In 1988, five years after becoming a director, I'd also joined the board of CIBC. In those days, there was no potential conflict of interest in being on both an insurance board and a bank board. But only four years later, Ottawa finally agreed to let Canada's banks sell insurance through their subsidiaries, though they couldn't use their own branches as sales offices for most types of policies, including life insurance, nor could they mine their banking-client databases for insurance marketing purposes. The rules prevented tellers from even mentioning insurance to bank customers. Yet it was only a matter of time, we all thought, before the government would remove those restraints and the banks would be more head-on rivals with Manulife. (In fact, while still banned from peddling policies through their branches today, some banks are selling through the Internet as well as by mail—and in 2006, the federal *Bank Act* was scheduled for review under a new Conservative government.) Facing the same problem as me, Gail Cook-Bennett, who was a director of the TD Bank as well as Manulife, later decided to resign from the bank's board.

Beyond the possible conflict in my two board positions, there was also my relative lack of interest in the insurance business. I enjoyed the financial side of things but not necessarily the products themselves. And my contributions to CIBC, especially with my experience in the oil business, seemed somehow greater than to Manulife. Syd Jackson, no longer a director, urged me to stay on:

"Dick, the insurance company has a much better balance sheet than the bank's, and it's a smaller board." Despite such encouragement and the pleasure I had in working with Dominic, I stepped off the board in 1995.

We've remained fast friends ever since, both of us with analytical accounting backgrounds and a penchant for plain speaking and getting down to the no-BS brass tacks of a situation. And I was often left to wonder if I'd chosen the wrong board as I watched Dominic help extend Manulife's reach so widely around the planet. I had such tremendous respect for him that we invited him on to the board of TransCanada, where he was a tower of strength during that company's most difficult period.

Although the company had a stronghold in Canada, he was looking well beyond this limited market for more growth. Manulife got its first licence to sell life insurance in mainland China in 1996, and a decade later, it was operating with a state partner in a dozen cities (and by 2010, it's expected to be in forty). In a joint venture with a minority Taiwanese partner, Manulife became the first foreign-owned insurer in Vietnam and, within three years, had 150,000 policyholders. And it has made major inroads in Japan (where it sells a billion dollars' worth of variable-annuity products).

In 1999, the company went public—demutualized—in Canada's largest initial public offering, with the $2.48 billion raised from shareholders devoted exclusively to paying out its former owners, Manulife's policyholders. As Dominic noted, "The fact that we're not raising any equity capital with our IPO means we don't need any capital." A year later, the company was the first Canadian insurer to post a profit of more than $1 billion. And at this writing, it was sitting on a cash pile of more than $3 billion.

Bill Blundell has acknowledged that Dominic's drive and interventionist style can put off his executives, and the man himself concedes that he's an exacting, detail-oriented boss—without apologizing for it. Yet in dealing with the outside world, he's won laurels as the Canadian CEO most respected by his peers in 2005 (and second only to EnCana's Gwyn Morgan in '06) and, in an industry-wide survey, the one offering the best relations with the investment community.

Most important for the board when I was a director, he quickly put firm controls in place. It was never the "Mystery Hour" when we read his financial statements. We felt comfortable that he was running the company well, despite being a highly opinionated and sometimes contrarian thinker. "Why the hell don't we let Citibank come up here to buy the Commerce?" he once asked a reporter. And then answered his own question, "Of course, if that happened, we wouldn't have a country."

Like me, he's a strong believer in Northern Tigers (and even suggested I write this book). As he told one annual meeting of Manulife shareholders, "There are no fundamental reasons why Canada shouldn't be home to more world-class companies.... Those of us who are supposed to lead some of Canada's most significant enterprises haven't been doing our jobs. As a group, we have been far too timid and cautious."

He really shouldn't have included himself in that group. In 2003, Manulife failed to take over Canada Life in a hostile bid (but saw its 9 percent stake in that company rocket to $300 million when Great-West Life won the war). So Dominic went south and did a $14-billion stock deal to acquire John Hancock Financial of Boston and its Canadian subsidiary, the Maritime Life Assurance Company. It was the biggest Canadian buy of any American corporation ever made. The merger created North America's second-biggest life insurer, and the world's fifth-biggest, by market capitalization, not to mention being Canada's biggest public company. John Hancock, also public and named for the first man to sign the U.S. Declaration of Independence, was (according to the *New York Times*) one of the twentieth century's most powerful brands. The timing of the purchase was swell: Manulife's shares were near record levels while Hancock's were suffering, even though its net income that year would be $806 million, an increase of 61 percent from 2002. It was just a pleasant coincidence that the president of the American company was also a D'Alessandro, though David, an ex-journalist, was no relation to Dominic, an ex-accountant. The flamboyant American jumped from the company with a golden parachute worth more than $20 million (U.S.), leaving the hard-nosed, disciplined Canadian in charge of the combined operation. By 2005, Manulife was registering its best annual results ever—good news for Dominic's fellow Canadians, who make up 60 percent of the shareholders.

That was also the year the company faced its most public embarrassment. Manulife Securities International, a subsidiary, and its independent advisors had referred thousands of clients to Portus Alternative Asset Management, a Toronto hedge fund that was forced into receivership. Manulife Securities' clients had invested $235 million in Portus. What impressed me in the wake of the collapse was how Dominic reacted so strongly and swiftly. His immediate response was to reassure all the investors that the parent company would absolutely guarantee their funds; it would "stand in your shoes," as he put it. And then he went after the executives in the subsidiary who had not done their due diligence—they were either incompetent or unethical—and fired them, including the CEO, chief compliance officer, and chief legal counsel. Dominic and his directors, particularly my pal Mike Wilson, the former federal finance minister, triggered an extensive internal review. Given the public-relations disaster it could have been, Manulife Financial emerged from the scandal remarkably undamaged, thanks to his precipitate actions—he even got a round of applause from shareholders at the next annual meeting.

Dominic and I share the same sense of ethics. We both have zero tolerance for the merest hint of corruption in the marketplace. I remember what he'd said at an earlier annual meeting when discussing the Enron scandal. Calling for "vigorous enforcement of existing laws"—heavy prison sentences and the forfeiting of embezzled funds—he told his shareholders, "I'm convinced that will do more for chilling the occurrence of future Enrons than writing a thousand laws."

SEVERAL YEARS AFTER I'D LEFT the board, it was reported that Dominic entertained the possibility of a merger between Manulife and the Canadian Imperial Bank of Commerce. Blending their strengths and different market niches, I thought, was a better idea than having Canada's major banks merge. He'd gone so far as to hold a series of talks with John Hunkin, the bank's CEO. They pursued the prospect over a few months until the federal Liberal government indicated its utter disapproval of any such marriage in late 2002.

By then, I was also off the CIBC board. But I knew, because of my knowledge of both companies, the union of the two financial institutions would have made good sense.

Joining the bank's board in the late 1980s, I'd brought some useful information with me from my dealings with CIBC over the years. At HBOG, treasurer Ken Burgis had come from the bank, which had always been the company's major financial institution. Back then of course, when Dome was taking us over, Jack Gallagher had been a director of CIBC, though the bank underestimated the conflict of interest and lent him a pile of money in order to attempt a hostile takeover—which Gerry Maier and I reacted to by raging against all levels of the bank's management.

In 1987, stock markets around the world had collapsed in the second-largest one-day percentage decline in history for a variety of reasons still debated by financial experts. When I became a CIBC director a year later, all the Canadian banks still considered that Black Monday to be a sobering lesson. The Commerce, our second-largest bank, was operating in twenty-three countries with assets of about $88 billion and nearly thirty-four thousand employees. It had recently acquired Wood Gundy, the Toronto wealth-management company and our major international securities dealer, after the federal government agreed to allow banks to own investment dealers. That acquisition would have profound repercussions later on.

Don Fullerton was CIBC's hard-driving yet personally warm chairman and CEO, and he became a great friend to me (on his visits to Calgary, we'd been known to get slightly into the sauce and close the Petroleum Club). Nearing sixty, he was a Vancouverite who'd joined the bank after getting his BA from the University of Toronto. Our ties went back to the HBOG days, when he was the bank's president and chief operating officer. And even with our anger at the bank for supporting the Dome takeover, he was instrumental in sorting out the mess. Before my arrival, Don had restructured the company into distinct strategic operations—"the four pillars"—each with its own president to decentralize decision-making.

Now, amid the toughest recession since the Depression, he went on the attack again to get rid of what he called "the middle-management mush" who were mired in mediocrity and acted like a "sponge or insulator." And he added, "The challenge for senior management is to ensure, in an industry where the numbers can seem to be all that matters, that ethical standards are nurtured, as well." Meanwhile, Don was also improving the bank's credit policies and computer systems and expanding CIBC's overseas presence. One of his closest foreign alliances was with Hong Kong's Li Ka-Shing, who'd had a fifty-fifty real estate partnership with the bank that grew into a $100-million joint venture in merchant banking involving parties from several nations, Japan among them.

One of Don's most troublesome decisions was hanging in with the Reichmanns as their empire collapsed. Of course, Paul Reichmann was on the board then, along with other high-profile directors such as former politicians Ron Basford and Bill Davis, the food magnate Galen Weston, Noranda's Alf Powis, MacMillan Bloedel's Ray Smith, and Hollinger Inc.'s Conrad Black)—and then there was me. As the head of Interhome, a company the Reichmann brothers controlled, I was in a delicate situation. Paul Reichmann was on the CIBC board, so I spoke to Don in private. Without revealing any confidential information, I explained my concerns about the number of businesses they were involved in— information freely available to any close observer—and, based on my personal observations, how stretched they were from a management point of view. At the time, CIBC had made massive loans to Olympia & York. But when the bank had to put aside $1 billion to cover the resulting losses, I had to give him full credit for publicly taking the bullet for the debacle.

In 1992, Al Flood was named his president. More of a backroom guy, Al had come to the bank fresh out of high school and had worked everywhere, from domestic branches to the U.S. and Latin American operations. His international ventures spelled trouble in '90 when the bank had to write off $1.2 billion in bad loans to debt-ridden Brazil, Argentina, and particularly Mexico. Yet he was Don's heir apparent and took over as chair and CEO four years later. Al put his stamp on the company, and one of his first sweeping actions was to create a new management structure.

Al was also keen to effect a merger of CIBC with the TD Bank. In 1998, the Competition Bureau of Canada recommended against the proposal, arguing that it was "likely to lead to a substantial lessening or prevention of competition that would cause higher prices and lower levels of service and choice for several key banking services in Canada"—primarily branch banking for individuals and businesses, credit cards, and securities. The fact is, as a director I voted in favour of the merger, rationalizing that if the government was going to approve such consolidation, the Toronto-Dominion was the most complementary bank for the Commerce.

Some of my well-informed friends agree with the merging of Canada's major banks with one another in a bid to compete internationally. But Dominic D'Alessandro had once argued against the idea: "If [the banks] start off by saying 'The only way we can compete is if you give me total dominance over the Canadian consumer,' the implications of that are awesome." Now he recommends bank/bank, bank/insurer, or insurer/insurer mergers if domestic competition is somehow preserved—*and* if banks aren't allowed to sell insurance through their branches. Brian MacNeill, the Petro-Canada chairman, says, "The banks need to merge to become *real* Northern Tigers." Yet I was, and remain, hesitant about the ultimate worth of melding financial powerhouses operating in the same business. Canada has had a strong banking system, as opposed to the U.S.'s, with its thousands of bank and savings-and-loan institutions that underperform for shareholders and are much more prone to bankruptcy. And clearly, the more banks we have, the more competitive they'll have to be in attracting customers. Yet I express my hesitation rather than saying I'm dead-set against all such mergers, because the arguments for and against them are extraordinarily complex and I honestly can't come down strongly on one side or the other.

CIBC proved to be my most challenging board. Part of the problem was its approach to the vital strategy of effective succession planning, which has been called the "ultimate act of leadership." Most boards I've served on worked hard at succession, even though their corporations might have fewer opportunities to develop people for top positions. Oil and gas companies, for instance, should have seniormost people with overall knowledge of such distinct divisions as exploration and production—which is hard to accomplish in that industry. Even as a member of CIBC's management-resources committee, I was unable to influence improvements in that area of the business. Many of the problems that later surfaced could have been avoided by better succession planning.

The man who followed Al was John Hunkin, a thirty-year veteran with the bank, mostly on the commercial side. More recently, he'd got into investment banking as Don's handpicked choice to run the Wood Gundy brokerage house when it became CIBC World Markets. In a high-profile competition, John's rival for the post was the more conservative Holger Kluge, who was president of the retail banking operation. I have to admit preferring John. (And unfortunately, as he became both chairman and CEO, I lost my old argument to split the roles and name a non-executive chair.)

John's father had spent more than four decades with the bank, ending up a regional manager, and his son took his first job there after getting his MBA. A risk-taking senior VP in the U.S. when Wood Gundy was acquired, he went on to oversee two American companies that the bank acquired: the Argosy Group, an investment house involved in high-yield securities such as junk bonds, and Oppenheimer & Co., a private-client and asset-management venture that added equity products to CIBC's U.S. mix of offerings.

NOT LONG AFTER HE BECAME head honcho, I began thinking about retiring as a bank director. I'd had the heart bypass that Easter and, recovering nicely, wasn't treating the event as a not-too-distant early-warning signal to slow down a little. At least not till my friend Don Taylor, a former executive vice-president with Shell Canada, suffered a stroke. I'd got him on the board of Interprovincial Pipe Line, and he'd been hopping between Toronto and a new house in Florida. The pressures on him had been just too heavy. A few weeks after his attack, I stopped off to see him on the way to the airport in Toronto. Don was in a wheelchair, his whole left side was paralyzed, and he was having trouble speaking. I thought, *What a dumb bastard you are, Haskayne. Here you are doing the same things that Don did, running like crazy.* (Eventually he did recover courageously and well enough to stay on as a director and, later, chair of what became Enbridge.)

As well as Don's situation, I observed that three outstanding but elderly directors were anxious to stay on the CIBC board past the official retirement age of seventy. I believe that none of us, good as we may be, is that crucial to the ongoing operation of a twenty-nine-member board. And if you don't know by then what you'll do at that age, what in the hell is another year or so going to do for you? As I told my second wife, Lois, I don't ever want to be in the position where I'm pushing to be kept on as a director.

The day before my sixty-fifth birthday on December 18, I was at the point of looking everywhere for signs to support my decision to leave CIBC, even in my horoscope in the *Globe*, which I sometimes read for fun. This one seemed strangely appropriate: "Don't waste time trying to convince partners and colleagues that what you are doing is right. As long as you believe in it, nothing else matters." A few days later, I told Don Fullerton my reasons for taking leave, and he assured me that my rationale was "sound and defensible" and urged me to call John Hunkin.

John said he understood my health was still "an issue" and that I had my "plate full" even without CIBC. During our conversation, he sought my advice on inviting Bill Etherington, who'd been a senior VP and group executive with IBM Corp.'s global operations, to become the bank's lead director. Knowing Bill as an exceptional leader and realizing the relevance of his background as technology continued to drive the banking universe, I gave John an enthusiastic yes.

Bill would be the first lead director. During my stint at the bank, I was a member of the executive committee and the management resources and compensation committees. Just recently, I'd been working with Sir Neil Shaw, the retired chair of the British sugar company Tate & Lyle, on a much-needed review of CIBC's corporate governance. Among our recommendations that were adopted was eliminating the executive committee (to avoid having two classes of directors), replacing the pension trustees with a corporate trustee, reducing the board to twenty-one or fewer directors, and appointing a lead director who would also chair the corporate-governance committee. This director would essentially co-manage the board along with the chief executive officer. We polled all the directors to see who'd be interested in that position for themselves and who they thought would be the best choice. Two of my fondest wishes for the board eventually came true: In future, a CEO could no longer remain as a director after completing his or her term, and lead director Bill Etherington became CIBC's first *non*-executive chairman.

Even before my own chairmanship of NOVA, I had a bee buzzing in my bonnet about non-exec chairs. Recently, I wrote the foreword to a highly readable book by my old friend and fellow director, Bill Dimma of Toronto, who's served on fifty-five corporate boards and on another forty not-for-profit boards. In *Tougher Boards for Tougher Times: Corporate Governance in the Post-Enron Era*, Bill gives a damn good justification for keeping a firewall between chairperson and chief executive while describing the demands of each position. It's the same stance that I've taken in my stints as a permanent board chair separate from the CEO:

[A non-executive chairman] needs to be as versed on the important issues and decisions as the chief executive officer. He needs to know enough that he cannot be "snowed" by a strong-willed CEO who may have his priorities wrong.

Unfortunately, there's an endemic problem. Every practising director knows that it exists and that it's serious. This problem is that it is almost impossible for directors to obtain and maintain sufficient and full knowledge on a real-time basis. Knowledge at this level is held almost exclusively by management. But this dilemma is usually glossed over on the grounds that, since not much can be done about it, "let's do the best we can and live with it." ...

Which brings me back to the independent board chairman who can play a pivotal role in helping to bridge this knowledge gap. If boards are to be more effective, both in general and in helping to avert the occasional disaster, one answer, at least for larger, widely held companies, is not merely a fully independent chairman but one who devotes much more time to his critical role than has been or is customary.

As I was formally resigning at the annual meeting in early 2000, John was quarterbacking another of CIBC's leaps into the American marketplace—in this case, supermarkets. Though skeptical, I had voted for the decision to introduce a network of electronic financial-service kiosks at Winn-Dixies in Florida and Safeway supermarkets on the West Coast, similar to the bank's successful private-label President's Choice outlets at Loblaws in Canada. I was reluctant because we were marching into somebody else's market, thinking we knew more than our American competitors, and because many Canadian companies—especially in the retail field and in the petroleum business, in particular—had suffered a high failure rate in such forays. Yet it was an intriguing idea, backed by consultants' favourable reports. The rationale was that we had already developed the technology domestically, which would allow us to compete against the big American banks in a manageable way. They had nothing like this, ostensibly because they didn't want to cannibalize their existing branches with a low-fee service.

But I should have gone with my gut and voted against the scheme. While I wasn't familiar with the reasons, apparently what we hadn't realized is that Americans had a different style of banking and not enough of them used the services that the bank had hoped would offset the expenses to operate the 364 kiosks. Shutting them down in 2002, after only three years, cost CIBC a hefty $366 million.

That was the same year the bank unloaded its Oppenheimer division, selling it to a New York brokerage house for $334 million less than the 1997 purchase price. All this retrenchment indicated the bank was retreating to Canada and getting back to its basics. I remember one of CIBC's investment bankers on our human resources committee sidling up to me at a cocktail party one evening and saying, "Haskayne, old buddy, we need to take some action. Our costs are higher than most other banks', and what John Cleghorn's doing at the Royal are the right actions. For example, getting rid of the corporate jet."

"Well, my view, for what it's worth," I replied, "is that our costs are higher, but the jet is just such a small part of it."

"It's embarrassing to have a corporate jet," he said.

"If anybody needs a jet," I replied, "it's a bank—you're spread all over the damn place. And the only thing that's embarrassing to me, sitting on the bank's board, is how much you investment bankers get paid versus the CEO. Your numbers outweigh the corporate jet by a factor of ten to one."

That was the last I heard about the jet. But it wasn't the last time I bristled at the compensation the senior people in our investment banking divisions were taking home. CIBC was just one of the major Canadian banks to acquire such operations, which had been basically partnerships—in which the partners took significant risks and received generous compensation if the businesses succeeded. When the banks took over the partnerships, those same compensation mechanisms remained. But in my view, the firms were now part of large financial institutions that could shelter them from the worst of the downside risks. Meanwhile, the upside potential was just as huge and unreasonable—many investment bankers continue to make more than the CEOs of those banks, and there's little incentive for them to aspire to being chief executives. It's possible that John Hunkin would have earned more if he'd stayed as an investment banker.

And then came the collapse of Enron Corp. CIBC and the energy trader had links dating back to 1991, when the bank's London-based brokerage arm partly financed a huge British power project built by a company controlled by Enron. I can recall only one commercial loan we made to Enron during my time as a bank director. I was skeptical about the company's apparent profitability, based on my experience with the energy-trading operations of TransCanada Corp, but I had no reason to question the standard loan.

Enron was founded in Houston in 1985 to trade natural-gas commodities, but eventually focused on a wide range of commodities trading in deregulated markets. It wasn't until the fall of 2001 that the U.S. Securities and Exchange Commission enquired into Enron's finances. By year's end, the corporation went bankrupt, triggering one of the most complex criminal investigations ever conducted into financial failure. The major charges were disguising corporate debt, inflating profits, and selling stock before any fraud was uncovered. Various traders and senior executives have since pleaded guilty. Chairman Kenneth Lay was convicted in 2006 of defrauding a bank, investors, and his own employees, while former CEO Jeffrey Skilling was convicted of fraud and insider trading. Lay died of a heart attack before he had to serve any prison term, but recently Skilling was given twenty-four years for his part in the scandal and ordered to pay $45 million in restitution.

(Richard Kinder left Enron in 1996 after he didn't get the top job, bought the company's liquids pipeline, and co-founded Kinder Morgan Inc., which became an $11.3-billion success. His career is a fine example of the importance of following sound strategy with clever execution. Among other things, he immediately slashed $5 million in pipeline costs, financed operations without a heavy load of debt, and capitalized on a tax advantage in his partnership structure that avoided corporate income tax if it distributed virtually all of its earnings as dividends.)

Early on, the American court-appointed examiner charged that CIBC was one of many banks—the Royal and Toronto-Dominion among them—that helped Enron commit accounting fraud to conceal billions of dollars in debt and overstate profits as it swindled investors. CIBC supported the company with securities offerings and commercial lending, including loans that Enron misrepresented as cash flow rather than debt. While the bank recognized it had a potential liability, it underestimated the amount. In 2005, while not admitting guilt, the bank settled a $2.4-billion class action lawsuit with Enron investors, the largest to date of any financial institution implicated in the scandal (including J.P. Morgan and Citibank). That settlement, and others, forced CIBC to take the charge in its next quarter, the biggest in Canadian banking history—which amounted to one-quarter of its book value.

While John Hunkin as CEO accepted CIBC's role in the Enron disaster, I was not familiar with who actually structured the loans, but some observers identified the man in charge of investment banking as primarily responsible. That was David Kassie, who was running CIBC World Markets at the time. Between 1999 and 2003, Kassie got a reported $17 million in salary and bonuses, not including the more than $50 million in deferred compensation he walked away with. As the *Globe and Mail*'s Derek DeCloet pointed out to him in a column I clipped and saved because it buttressed my point of view about many investment bankers,

> It was your job to make sure your underlings took only smart risks. That's why you got paid the big bucks—and did you ever.... When anyone complained about your pay, the bank always had a ready response: David Kassie gets paid for performance, and CIBC World Markets is making a lot of money. And so it seemed. But Enron sure changes the record, doesn't it? By our math, World Markets earned

about $3.4 billion from fiscal 1999 to 2004. Subtract $2.5 billion from $3.4 billion, and World Markets would go from being one of the most profitable big investment dealers to one of the least.

In fairness, others have explained that because CIBC gave Enron commercial loans (with unusual conditions), they weren't even in the investment banking area of responsibility. And with the appointment of Gerald T. McCaughey as president and CEO, replacing John Hunkin, and the settlement of the outstanding Enron claims, the bank's stock has since recovered dramatically, which demonstrates that the balance sheet of a Canadian bank can withstand such a substantial financial hit. After all this, CIBC announced it would spend $50 million on various ethical and corporate-governance initiatives. Among them was advanced training for the 1,200 staff who handle complex financial transactions; an online course for all thirty-seven thousand employees, designed to teach them how to deal with risks to the bank's reputation and legal vulnerability; and a hotline to let employees report anonymously any irregularities in day-to-day business. (As to whether such hotlines work, the Association of Certified Fraud Examiners in the U.S. says, "The most common method for detecting occupational fraud is by a tip from an employee, customer, vendor or anonymous source.... [O]rganizations with hotlines can cut their fraud losses by approximately 50 percent per scheme.")

Should the board members in place during these years have been more thorough in their oversight of the bank? Maybe—but as corporate-governance guru Bill Dimma says, it's virtually impossible for a company—especially one as large and complex as a bank—to have the same handle on its operations as its managers have:

Especially when the chairman and CEO roles are combined (with or without a lead director) but even when the roles are separated, there is almost always a profound gap between the depth and breadth of business knowledge held by management and that held by independent directors, including non-executive chairmen. These latter are almost invariably busy people with many other commitments and too little time to overcome the knowledge gap.

But Bill and I agree that a non-executive chairperson should have much more awareness of operations. When CIBC appointed its first non-exec chair, Bill Etherington, in 2003, most of the Enron investments had already been made.

It's easy to second-guess, yet I still wonder what I would have done as a director during the height of the Enron involvement. My suspicions of the energy company were high because, as I've explained, TransCanada Pipelines had been patterning itself after Enron in commodities trading. Then as a TransCanada chairman in 1999, I was involved in the decision to end our $400-million exposure to Enron. But of course, a year later, I was no longer a CIBC director.

Departing, though, I had given the bank a gift. I'd been asked to recommend a successor, someone who could serve the board with deep-seated integrity as well as financial smarts. My nominee, who was accepted, was Steve Snyder. He was the remarkable young president and CEO of Calgary-based TransAlta Corporation—where I'd been a director as it emerged from a troubled past and started to become the immensely successful enterprise it is today.

Chapter Nine

SHAKING UP THE CORPORATION
TransAlta and Crestar Energy

FERNANDO FLORES IS THE FORMER economics and finance minister of Salvador Allende's ill-fated government in Chile. He was imprisoned for three years by Allende's successor, the military dictator General Augusto Pinochet. After his release, Flores took a PhD in philosophy at Stanford University and started four companies in California, one of them called Business Design Associates. BDA supposedly builds on his revelation in prison, where he endured mock trials and solitary confinement, that "communication, truth, and trust are at the heart of power." Translating that idea into the corporate world, often charging $1 million or more for his services, Flores used verbal shock tactics to change the behaviour in an organization. One of the companies BDA tried to transform was TransAlta Corporation, where I went on the board in 1991, at the end of my time with Interhome, and then became chairman five years later. In 1992, the first of Flores's people arrived at TransAlta to work on about thirty different training programs. His style then was to confront employees and managers over their weaknesses—sometimes calling them "assholes" or worse—and to push them into voicing strong and often highly critical assessments of their colleagues. In TransAlta's case, his methods backfired badly.

TransAlta's roots go back to 1911 and Calgary Power, Alberta's first large-scale electric-energy company, which harnessed hydro power generated on the Bow River. Its base was in Montreal, and its founding president was the Canadian business tycoon Max Aitken (who was later owner of a major newspaper chain and a cabinet minister in England, where he was knighted as Lord Beaverbrook). In 1947, the year of the Leduc gusher, Calgary Power finally relocated its head office to the city it was named for. By then, it was supplying 99 percent of the province's power and soon turned to thermal generating plants fuelled by coal and natural gas. A decade before I became a director, it became TransAlta and was well on its way to being Canada's largest private power producer in a capital-intensive industry.

There was a long-standing invitation for me to join TransAlta's board. I was a friend of both Marshall Williams, who had been the well-respected chairman of Calgary Power, and TransAlta's current chief financial officer, Harry Schaefer, who had done Arthur Andersen audits with me during our articling days. So in 1991, as I was deciding to play more of a director's than a CEO's role in future, the company seemed an attractive place to be.

As a regulated business that had been in a near-monopoly position for decades, it had a good rate of return on investment, a high dividend payout, a nice cash flow, a strong balance sheet, and one of the very best credit ratings. But for all its apparent achievements, the company began to have problems. It had tried, and failed, to get into the oil business, for instance, and its expensive strategic alliance with a local software company that was developing a communications link among various word-processing programs seemed to be like tossing money down a dry hole.

By 1993, earnings of $169 million were down slightly, and the following year, as the executive team feared the rise of independent power producers, it cut 350 employees in the first-ever wave of layoffs. The remaining staff was placed on notice. As Ken McCready, the current president, put it, they were "polite and friendly people who would listen to customers, agree with them, and then go away and do their own thing." The sledgehammer solution to reverse this attitude was to call in Flores's Business Design Associates and use techniques that were originally developed and paid for by Werner Erhard, the founder of the controversial, cult-like EST (Erhard Seminar Training) movement.

Ken himself was part of the problem. There's no question that he was a forward-thinking leader who pioneered co-generation projects that use power stations to generate both heat and electricity at the same time. An electrical engineer, he'd been with the company since 1963, becoming president in 1985 and then CEO only two years before I came on the board. The senior role, which paid him about $1.5 million a year, seemed to go to his head as he became a director of other companies and spent too much time outside TransAlta on causes like sustainable development (which has been defined as any kind of development that meets the needs of the present without compromising the ability of future generations to meet their own needs). Meanwhile, the economics of the co-gen plants didn't appear sound enough, initially. In one case, our directors took exception because Ken didn't even have the figures on hand to justify a project because he was too busy doing other things. He was losing the confidence of the board.

Harry Schaefer, the chief financial officer, explains Ken's style: "He would have lots of projects and people studying them and was not quite sure which were the right ones to do. Then time would run out, and he would just pick one—as opposed to a true leader, who picks out the direction you should be taking and shapes it. In the end, he turned to an outsider to get the sense of direction for the company."

One of Ken's most questionable decisions was to bring in Fernando Flores and BDA. Their deal was to get a share of any savings from cost reductions that they produced. But an old established company like TransAlta should have tried to make the bulk of those cuts first and *then* called in experts to trim the final 10 percent or so. Worst of all, BDA's tactics appeared as bullying to many of our 2,100 employees, causing them to burst into tears, to attack one another, or even to resign in shame and disgust. One employee who quit later told the *Financial Post*, "They want people to be blunt and not spare another person's feelings. I felt emotionally abused when this was brought into the day-to-day work environment." Another sent an anonymous letter to TransAlta's regulator, the Alberta Public Utilities Board, complaining that the staff had been "subjected to humiliation and psychoanalytic sessions"—like a form of brainwashing.

TransAlta had another problem that needed fixing: Harry and Ken McCready had risen through the company together, and when Marshall Williams retired as chairman, the directors tried to be fair to the two competitors who were bidding for the top positions. So they appointed Harry chair and Ken chief executive officer. Now Harry was both the CFO reporting to the CEO as well as the chair supposedly overseeing the CEO. What an unworkable situation.

Just before the problems with the BDA consultants reached the media, Harry and Ken asked for a luncheon meeting with me and another director, Ross Phillips, the former Home Oil president. We were told that an American television program was about to report on Fernando Flores and his controversial projects, including the one at TransAlta. And then I saw a local TV show that contained footage of our employees being berated and crying in front of their peers. I was so damn mad because nobody within the company had previously informed me or the other board members that this totally unacceptable behaviour had been happening under our noses. It was embarrassing that in the relatively small business community of Calgary, we hadn't heard about this mess.

I was furious, and my anger was multiplied by the fact that some well-placed rivals in the industry *had* known. After the situation became public, I was flying back from a Hawaiian holiday with Ron Southern and his wife, Margaret, who confided in me, "Dick, I feel badly now that *we* didn't tell you what was going on. I can't believe that you wouldn't have known. We didn't want to tell you because we were competitors [with ATCO's Canadian Utilities] and it would sound like we were bad-mouthing TransAlta."

Ken had commissioned a study by Stephen Murgatroyd, who ran the Centre for Innovative Management at Athabasca University, the distance-learning institution in Edmonton. Reporting in December 1994, Murgatroyd said, in the jargon of his trade, there was a "disconnect between [the] top, middle and bottom of the organization" and "between personal transformation and organizational transformation in the minds of many employees." As a result, the company "needs to be concerned that some able, talented and dedicated staff who are producing value are beginning to look to their future outside of TransAlta and are looking at TransAlta as a place where the promise may not be matched by performance." In other words, a fine mess.

In January 1995, Ken McCready announced that staff no longer had to take Fernando Flores's training—though in a face-saving move, he said it was still available for those who wanted it. The following November, the corporate board set up a special committee to delve into the continuing morale problems. Heading it was Gerry Maier, a director for more than a decade, and its two members were me and Charles (Chuck) Hantho, our strong chair of corporate governance, who used to run C.I.L. Inc. Our mandate included analyzing McCready's capability to lead the company into the coming deregulation of the Alberta utilities industry and also considering his potential successors. We brought in my semi-retired colleague Ken McNeill, with his sterling human resources background, as an advisor reporting only to us. His contract ended with the caution: "Time is of the essence."

In no time at all—January 1996—Gerry and I told McCready, "Ken, it's all over." The board found an interim president and CEO for TransAlta Corp. in Walter Saponja, a salt-of-the-earth engineer who was the highly efficient president and chief operating officer of its subsidiary, TransAlta Utilities. I'd become non-executive chairman of the parent company, replacing Harry Schaefer—but only after Ted Newall checked with the NOVA board whether any of its directors saw a conflict in my accepting the TransAlta position. One of them, former Scotiabank chair Ced Ritchie, immediately called me to say, "This is an important company in your part of the world, and it's your civic duty to accept it."

My first major task, along with a search committee of directors, was to find a permanent CEO, someone who could shepherd us through deregulation, when any new facilities would have to compete in a free and open provincial marketplace. We found two terrific candidates—neither of them with any experience in the utility industry. One was running a Canadian agricultural-products giant. The other was Steve Snyder, who had a superb track record as an entrepreneurial leader focused on business development and marketing—two key areas that would shape TransAlta's future. His most recent position was president and CEO of Noma Industries, which Canadians knew as the Christmas-lights company. But we were most interested in Steve's role as chairman and CEO of GE Canada, the domestic subsidiary of the global General Electric Corp. colossus.

Steve was a youthful-looking forty-seven-year-old with rapid-fire speech and hands and arms that were endlessly in motion—an aggressive yet personable guy. The son of a clothing store manager, he called himself "the classic Canadian—born in Montreal, went to public school in Alberta (Edmonton and Jasper), high school in Montreal, university in Ontario." Steve took a chemical-engineering degree at Queen's and then, after a year with marketing-oriented Colgate-Palmolive, felt in need of an MBA, which he got from the University of Western Ontario. He went to work for GSW Inc., the sole Canadian-owned, full-line appliance company, streamlining the shipping of products to cut costs. The privately run GSW merged with GE Canada to create a joint venture called Camco, which bought the Canadian major-appliance division of Westinghouse. That launched Steve's fourteen-year career with GE. He was vice-president and general manager of GE Lighting and marketing VP and, eventually, president and CEO of Camco, which was then a public company doing about $600 million in business. The two partners in Camco had an antagonistic relationship, which Steve found challenging but fun to mediate.

In 1989, a few weeks after he'd become chief executive, his wife died, leaving him with an adolescent son and daughter. Two years later, GE offered him the managing director's post at Eurolec PLC, its appliance company based in Brussels. After quickly realizing that all the European travel was alienating him from his children, he returned to Canada as chair and CEO of GE Canada.

But because the parent company had him on a promotion track that demanded international transfers, he left in 1992 to join Toronto-based Noma Industries. A family enterprise, Noma had its own challenges. Steve was the first non-family executive, aside from a president who'd been with the business for half a century. It expanded from a Canadian consumer-products manufacturer to a maker and distributor of industrial products such as auto parts. In 1995, Noma earned more than $13 million after losses during the previous five years. A year later, when the founders' daughter was being primed for the presidency, Steve decided to skedaddle.

After an Alberta friend tipped him off to the opening at TransAlta, he exercised due diligence by doing some research about the changing nature of the utility industry. He asked the headhunters to put his name in the hat—only to find out that he was already on their list. Gerry, I, and others on the search committee liked his experience with GE, which under Jack Welch had popularized many effective techniques of human resource development during the 1990s. Among them was the idea of offering people jobs in various areas early in their career—"Let them learn from their mistakes at a time when the damage is controllable," as Steve expressed it. "If you wait for twenty years to put them in a key job and they fail, it's cost them and the company big time."

What we sensed—and proved true—were his strong communications skills. His first challenge was dealing with the scars from the BDA mess, still smarting after a year. He made sure he went to every plant and met every junior employee in the office. And he held back from letting any unproductive senior people go for several months until he had a good fix on their abilities. Dealing with his directors, he worked hard at informing us with regular written updates and bringing his management team in front of the board to present a unified front and explain their collective decisions. As Steve said, "I'd rather make my stupid decisions with the board in the boardroom than in public." I tried to facilitate those appearances by putting myself in the managers' shoes, attempting to understand the logic behind their actions, and helping to translate their thought processes to my colleagues.

Steve appreciated the fact that I was a non-exec chair, which was still a rare animal in Canada. "A lot of people don't understand how different that role is than just chairman," he says. "A non-executive chairman is one of the most challenging roles because most of the people in those jobs have run companies—and when you're in that chair, you're not running anything. You are managing board dynamics and laying out a course of action. What a non-exec chair needs to do is set the tonality, help set the agenda, and engage the board and management in discussion. Create an atmosphere where the directors and managers can have a discussion together—as opposed to presentations by management, which the board then critiques, and those who yell the most get the attention of the board. Communicate to a CEO what the board issues are without telling him what to do about it. Translate concerns back to the board in a way that they understand where the CEO is coming from."

Some of the decisions Steve made in his first two years were momentous. Running out of growth opportunities in Canada, TransAlta had been expanding internationally under Ken McCready, but not always wisely. Steve explains the situation: "The theory was, I think, to spread risk. But my view was that they ended up with three countries that were successful, three that were awful—and the net effect was zero. We had people doing projects where there was no hope in heck we were ever going to succeed, yet we were tying up people and resources. I had customers in Brazil saying, 'When are you going to do this project?' I said, 'I don't think we ever will.' 'Well, why is your guy down here talking to us, then?'

"And the other thing was that the company was making about a 10 percent return and told the board it could make 15 percent by going international. Problem was, you really needed to make 30 percent for the risk you were taking in these countries. Argentina was a disaster, and we wrote off $100 million in hydro facilities there. Then the board specifically said, 'Look, we've got this little thing going on in New Zealand, we're not sure what it is.' So I went down to New Zealand, and my conclusion was this thing actually has some legs to it, this may be the one we should keep. We were very small then, just building one plant. But we did a couple of acquisitions and became effectively the largest retailer of electricity in New Zealand." Later, when the nation changed governments and decided to close the market, TransAlta sold at a peak price to locals who did poorly with the operation. The company went on to acquire and sell electricity generation and transmission resources in Western Australia while keeping a few small plants that, on a per-megawatt basis, became its best performers.

By then, I had resigned as chairman. Under deregulation, TransAlta and TransCanada Corp., where I'd also been appointed chair in 1998, would become head-to-head rivals. TransAlta asked me to stay on as a director, but after a couple of meetings where I had to excuse myself as competitive projects were being discussed, I decided to go with TransCanada.

For a time afterwards, TransAlta was stumbling. Utilities get bored doing their basic job, so they often look for bigger markets and ventures with potentially higher returns. My friend Tom d'Aquino of the Canadian Council of Chief Executives quoted Steve in *Northern Edge: How Canadians Can Triumph in the Global Economy*, a book he wrote with David Stewart-Patterson:

> The big challenge for us is growth. Provincial regulations make east-west growth extremely difficult. We're already large in our home province. We were forced to go international, but with at least one arm, if not our legs, tied behind our back.

Steve and his people bought the sizable Big Hanaford coal-fired plant in Washington and (as TransCanada did) got involved in trading power in the U.S.—all of which lost money. After I sold most of my shares in the mid- to high 20s, the stock kept falling, along with the corporate credit rating, though shareholders still got a dividend annually. At one point, TransCanada considered taking the company over on a friendly basis. The two seemed to be a natural fit, but then TransAlta got back on track. It had to decide whether it could continue investing in both the generation and transmission of energy and whether it should remain in the distribution and retail (D&R) business. In 2002 and '03, the company sold its transmission and D&R arms for $3 billion and then spent $4.5 billion to increase its electricity-producing capacity by 40 percent as it refocused as a wholesaler. It now serves only major customers in Canada (Alberta and Ontario—which are 64 percent of its total market), the U.S. (25 percent), Mexico (6 percent), and Australia (3 percent). And it's generating healthy profits ($199 million in 2005). One of the people helping to shape TransAlta was Jim Dinning, now one of the prime candidates to replace the retiring Alberta premier, Ralph Klein. Jim had been provincial treasurer when he joined the company in 1997, and he became executive vice-president responsible for sustainable development and external relations. He would concentrate on clean-coal technology and other long-term initiatives until leaving to focus on his political future in early 2005.

The corporation has a strong board now, chaired by Donna Soble Kaufman, a well-known Toronto lawyer, former head of Selkirk Communications Ltd., and director of Bell Canada, TransAlta, Telesat Canada, and the Hudson's Bay Company. Donna still sometimes calls me for a bit of private counsel on governance issues and the chair's role. "We are firmly committed to an ethical culture and good corporate governance," she says. TransAlta was named in a KPMG/Ipsos Reid poll as one of Canada's ten most respected companies, the *Globe and Mail* called it one of the country's best-governed corporations, and the Canadian Institute of Chartered Accountants has consistently honoured it for its financial and corporate reporting. Like TransCanada, it's investing in alternative-energy technology like wind farms. As the *National Post* has pointed out, "With energy prices and energy utility markets soaring in the U.S. and Canada, TransAlta Corp. is positioned for growth." My guess is that someday it might be one of the biggest power merchants on the continent—and a possible Northern Tiger.

THOUGH I LEFT TRANSALTA'S board in 1998, I was still spreading myself thin on the boards of other companies, among them Crestar Energy, operating out of the Dome Tower in Calgary. I was one of the original directors when Crestar was created six years earlier by the Canadian subsidiary of Amoco Petroleum of the U.S.—which in taking over Dome Petroleum had promised Ottawa it would let Canadian investors own 20 percent of Amoco Canada Petroleum. As things turned out, it decided to launch a domestic company instead, built on assets owned by Amoco, Dow Chemical, and Encor Inc., TransCanada's upstream oil and gas subsidiary. The promising new venture, which I felt had at least an outside chance of evolving into a Tiger one day, would survive on its own for only eight years. Its demise would have one major lesson for those who want to create Canadian corporate champions.

Crestar's founding president and chief operating officer was Murray Todd, a thirty-six-year veteran of the industry. He'd been president of Dome's offshore-exploration division, Canadian Marine Drilling, and after the takeover, became a VP of Amoco. He was now in charge of a lean, privately held operation with about three hundred employees—about two-thirds of them from Dome—and four hundred thousand hectares of decent Alberta resource leases, much of them on former Hudson's Bay Oil and Gas lands. In 1993, Crestar was being prepared for an initial public offering in which Amoco and Dow, honouring their pledge to Canadianize the company, would sell their shares to domestic investors. Murray's strength was as a driller, not as a dynamic CEO. The board asked him to take early retirement.

His replacement was Barry Jackson, president and COO of Northstar Energy Corp. and other smaller public companies. Don Stacy, Amoco's president and Crestar's chairman, had decided Barry was the best candidate. When I complained that I didn't know the guy, Don said, "For God's sake, Haskayne, he worked for you at Hudson's Bay." Unknown to me, Barry had been with HBOG as a junior engineer. He proved to be a fine choice: level headed, technically skilled, and a good public speaker. He did the

IPO and, under his leadership, a $6.9-million loss in the first ten months of Crestar's life turned into a $5.7-million profit in 1993.

We had an interesting group of directors backing him—among them, Roland Priddle, ex-chairman of the National Energy Board; Murray Fraser, president of the University of Calgary; and my suggestion, sharp-eyed Harry Schaefer, who became chair of our audit committee. But all of us—board members and management—were facing the same challenge: We had a nice enough company, but it was a Mr. In-Between. While it had some heavy-oil prospects and an okay natural-gas base, most of its assets were old ones in southeastern Alberta where production was declining rapidly. Crestar didn't have a growth story to tell. By now, it had 550 employees and a daily production of forty-three thousand barrels of oil and 351 million cubic feet of natural gas. Yet it just wasn't big enough to rank among the senior producers but was too big to be considered a junior. And many investors, especially Americans, preferred larger companies and thought that anything under $10 billion was a small-cap venture. Crestar eventually did try to expand internationally, buying $142 million worth of producing assets in Ecuador. But that wasn't enough of an attraction.

So in 2000, this mid-sized company was a ripe prospect for a takeover by a senior producer—Gulf Canada Resources. Years earlier, after the Reichmann brothers had to relinquish control of their Gulf shares to a consortium of banks, the company was sold to a consortium headed by the swashbuckling Houston entrepreneur J.P. Bryan. A classic Type-A personality, J.P. (James Perry) was a lawyer who'd studied art history and worked in the rare-book business before doing deals on Wall Street as an investment banker and then launching a company in Houston that bought and managed oil investments for institutions and corporations. Because he was a lover of all things western, we used to call him "Texas—all hat and no cattle." He was a delightful guy to chat with over dinner, but was always shooting from the lip. He once told a Canadian Senate committee that it was too bad that, under federal law, Gulf had to have so many Canadian directors, referred to corporate governance as "just a load of guacamole," and said

Canada should ship all Quebec's hardcore separatists to France—just the kind of diplomat you want running a respected Canadian business. In 1994, J.P. was among a group that paid $30 million to buy control of Gulf. He became president and CEO and soon cut 40 percent of the staff, bought a $9.3-million Challenger jet, and moved the executive office to Denver. (Meanwhile, his chairman, Earl Joudrie, was convalescing after being shot by his estranged wife, Dorothy.) All this was going on while oil prices were sinking and the corporate debt was climbing to $2.7 billion. Four years later, his board ousted Bryan.

His successor was Dick Auchinleck, a good engineer, a twenty-two-year mainstay of the company, and a hell of a lot less flamboyant than his predecessor, thank God. He sold the jet, brought the executives back to Calgary, and began retiring the debt while selling off Gulf's majority share of holdings in Indonesia. If J.P. was "the gunslinger," people called Dick "the mechanic" (and in fact, he fixed vintage cars as a hobby). In 2000, looking to grow and perhaps fend off takeover bids, he approached Barry Jackson with a friendly $2.3-billion offer in cash and Gulf stock to buy Crestar. The combined oil and gas producer would be the seventh-largest independent in North America. An analyst told Dick it was a case of two ugly ducklings turning not into a swan, exactly, but at least into a stronger duck.

For our shareholders, the deal would make a heap of sense. As petroleum prices rose, the company was stuck with a big income-tax charge and Gulf was prepared to assume Crestar's $565-million debt. The sad reality was that if our board didn't accept this amicable offer, there were some unfriendly ones very likely lurking just over the next hill. For all the reasons I've mentioned, a mid-sized company like ours with well-tapped properties was a natural target for takeover, quite possibly by a foreign acquisitor. The simple lesson: Unless you occupy a very special niche in your industry, you'd better grow big enough to be predator-proof. Our board approved the deal. A couple of our directors, including Harry Schaefer, became Gulf directors. Having had my heart bypass only a year before, I happily *didn't*.

Yet I did watch, with concern, what happened only a year later. Dick's executive VP of business development and general counsel was Henry Sykes, a long-term mergers and acquisitions lawyer with the Calgary office of Bennett Jones. So in 2001, Henry was primed to entertain a bid from the folks who once controlled Hudson's Bay Oil and Gas when I was there: U.S.–based Conoco. After selling HBOG to Dome Petroleum, Conoco had slipped back into Canada in a minor way and, frankly, what bothered me was that they were poor corporate citizens, stinting on their charitable donations and community involvement. Now, in what would be the costliest takeover of a Canadian petroleum company, Conoco was making its Canadian presence felt with a big splash. It paid $9.8 billion for Gulf and the remnants of Crestar.

Dick Auchinleck went on the board of Conoco Canada Resources Corp., and Henry Sykes, who'd fashioned the agreement, became president. But gone from the scene were two Canadian-owned petroleum producers: Crestar, a wannabe with a legacy of historic HBOG holdings, and Gulf Canada, one of the older and more storied public enterprises in the Oil Patch. And there'd be one more change of proprietorship: In 2002, Conoco Inc. and fellow American Phillips Petroleum Inc. merged to create an oil and gas leviathan that owns the renamed ConocoPhillips Canada Resources Corp.

At the time, Barry Jackson, who was on the Canadian corporation's board, was quoted as saying, "A lot of those same properties and, interestingly enough, a lot of the same people have moved right from the HBOG days through all of those companies and now back to Conoco. So, there is the circle."

True enough, I agree with my friend, but given that effective control of the company now rested with its American parent, another prospective Northern Tiger had bit the dust.

Chapter Ten

CLEAR-CUT
MacMillan Bloedel

I DIDN'T REALLY NEED OR EVEN want to become chairman of the ailing lumber giant MacMillan Bloedel. In 1996, after I'd been a director for two years, the board approached me about assuming the chair of the Vancouver-based forest-products company that had been part of British Columbia's economic history for seventy-seven years. Ced Ritchie and I had joined the board at the same time when Noranda sold its controlling interest in MacBlo. Now Ced was urging me to add another chairmanship to my lengthening string of obligations. "Ritchie," I replied, "I can't do that." Lee had just died the year before. I was already the chair of both NOVA and TransAlta as well as a director of CIBC and Manulife. Not only that, even after being on the MacBlo board for a couple of years, I knew relatively little about the wood business. And, frankly, the company was then in a financial freefall following a brief upturn in its fortunes.

Ignoring my protestations, Ced was insistent, as he had been about TransAlta: "Haskayne, this is an important company on the West Coast. It's an international company, and its lumber exports lead the country. So you have an obligation to do this."

"You know," I said, "all these obligations I'm accepting are going to kill me one of these days."

As it turned out, they almost did. Yet I capitulated to Ced's plea and accepted the chairmanship—which is how I came to play a key role in the eventual death of what was likely another logical Northern Tiger.

IF YOU LIKE YOUR STORIES to have supersized figures, you'll appreciate the first half-century of MacMillan Bloedel. Though MacBlo became its popular nickname, the company always preferred the more formal initials "MB." The two predominant figures in its early history were also known by their initials: H.R. and J.V. Harvey Reginald MacMillan was never referred to as anything else but H.R., while John Valentine Clyne was more familiarly called Jack by his friends. H.R., raised in southern Ontario by his poor widowed mother and his farming grandparents, showed his academic brilliance early on while attending the Ontario Agricultural College, where he earned nine cents an hour working on a test forest project, and Yale, where he shone as the first Canadian forestry student at the university. The big, broad-shouldered master's candidate spent a summer in British Columbia, surveying potential timberlands for private investors. After working in the forestry department of the Department of the Interior in Ottawa, he returned to B.C. to become the province's first chief forester. The federal government then made him a special trade representative to boost Canadian lumber sales in Europe, which he did with some success.

Turning his back on government in 1916, he wet his feet in business by helping manage a sawmill for a lumber company in Chemainus, B.C., where he learned how Frederick Weyerhaeuser, a nineteenth-century American lumber baron, had bought up some of the choicest local land. Near the end of the next century, Weyerhaeuser's company would loom large in the fate of MacMillan Bloedel.

H.R. briefly returned to the civil service during the First World War, overseeing the supply of B.C.'s strong, light Sitka spruce for military aircraft. But in 1919, he went out on his own to create the H.R. MacMillan Export Company, the first such private brokerage in the province. That was the start of a great Canadian success story: He bought sawmills and opened a plywood plant and a pulp mill while acquiring a competing lumber company, huge provincial timber holdings owned by the Rockefeller financial family, and the company in Chemainus where he'd once been an assistant

manager. By 1951, as the major lumber producer on the West
Coast, he merged with his only real rival, Bloedel, Stewart &
Welch, a forty-year-old sawmill and pulp-mill venture co-founded
by Julius Bloedel of Washington State. It was the biggest corporate
merger in B.C. history up to that time. Bloedel's son Prentice,
another Yale grad, was president and then went on the board of
what became MacMillan and Bloedel Ltd. Nine years later, it
merged with the Powell River Company, named for the mainland
coastal town north of Vancouver where the brothers Harold and
Joseph Foley ran the world's largest newsprint mill. The expanded
company was called MacMillan, Bloedel and Powell River Co.

By then, J.V. Clyne had become chairman and oversaw the
merger. Nearing retirement, H.R. had asked his friend to succeed
him—to which Jack Clyne had replied, "What's the end of the
joke?" He had good reason to wonder, given that he was a justice
of the B.C. Supreme Court at the time. Though the University of
British Columbia grad had studied at the London School of
Economics, his specialty was maritime law. Back home in
Vancouver, he acted for a MacMillan-owned shipping subsidiary,
the Canadian Transport Company, and became president of a
Crown corporation operating a fleet of merchant vessels. But this
larger-than-life character, who'd also grown up with a widowed
mother, was used to taking on unusual tasks: As a young man,
he'd been a deckhand on a freighter, a lumber-stacker at a local
sawmill, and a cowboy and a placer miner in the B.C. hinterland
(he'd call his memoirs *Jack of All Trades*).

Becoming chair of MacMillan, Bloedel and Powell River Co.
in 1957, he got more than he bargained for—tackling the first big
strike of pulp-and-paper workers in the province and a corporate
bloodletting over the ownership of shares in a subsidiary company. In what some say was the biggest in-house battle ever
witnessed to that point in Canadian business history, the two
Foley brothers, serving as vice-chair and president, were forced to
quit and the company became simply MacMillan Bloedel Ltd.
(During the debacle, Clyne poured a glass of scotch over Harold
Foley's head at a party.) As both chair and CEO of MacBlo, J.V.

Clyne helped turn B.C.'s biggest company into a multinational by logging in southeast Asia and even diversifying into Australian real estate, and over his sixteen years, sales rose to $966 million from $160 million. But, from many reports, he was neither a gifted leader nor businessman. His imperious style rubbed people the wrong way, and his later reign was marred by missteps of strategy and the building of a bloated executive class. In 1972, after the company was recovering from its two worst years—with a downturn in the U.S. economy and the Canadian dollar being higher than the Americans'—he announced his retirement. The new chairman was Robert Bonner, a former provincial attorney general, who'd become president and CEO a year earlier.

That was the rich, if somewhat erratic, legacy I walked into as a director in 1994. In rapid succession, there had been four more men filling the chair and CEO roles after Clyne and Bonner, until Raymond V. Smith became president in 1980. Ray was a steadying presence even though 49 percent of MacBlo's shares were about to be bought by a subsidiary of Noranda Inc., the Toronto-based mining and forestry multinational—part of the Bronfman empire, which was then Canada's largest business group. It was yet another record takeover of a Canadian company. Noranda's forestry chief, Adam Zimmerman, led the acquisition and was chair of MacMillan Bloedel from 1983 to 1991. The increasingly troubled Noranda held sway until '93, when it spun off its shares in a $932-million secondary offering. (B.C.'s NDP government paid about $40 million to become MacBlo's largest shareholder, as well as being its regulator). The savvy Adam, who was once an accountant with Clarkson, Gordon & Co., stayed on for another three years as one of thirteen directors on our eclectic board, which had traditionally included the president of the University of British Columbia—David Strangway during my time.

I'd come to know lanky, quiet-spoken Ray Smith when we were both on the board of CIBC. After Noranda sold its control block of MacBlo, two of its directors—Alf Powys and David Kerr—stepped off the lumber company's board, and in 1994, headhunters approached Ced Ritchie and me to replace them. I knew Ray as a really decent human being and, as I learned, in employees' eyes he'd been a cherished president for a decade and a well-respected chairman of the company for the past four years. (The fact that he played a mean trumpet and wound up his life in a relationship with Juliette, the songstress who starred on an early Canadian television show named after her, just added to his charm.) He was the kind of guy who on Secretaries' Day would present every administrative assistant in the place with a rose and who was the first forest executive in B.C. ever to be asked to open a convention of the International Woodworkers of America. IWA and company representatives sat on the board of MacBlo's Employee and Family Assistance Program that Ray championed even during the toughest times in the industry. He earned his reputation despite reducing the payroll to fifteen thousand from twenty-five thousand while giving managers at the mill level more authority. His other success was moving the company into higher-priced, value-added lumber products at a time when the international economy was on an upswing. But by 1988, a recession started cutting into MacBlo's record profits, and two years later, Ray kicked himself upstairs as chairman.

His successor as president was Bob Findlay, a Scot who came to New York with his family as a boy and later moved to Montreal to study mechanical engineering at McGill University. He spent summers working at MacMillan Bloedel's mill in Powell River, B.C., and wound up employed by a manufacturer that sold pulp-and-paper machines to the company. Bob joined MacBlo full-time in the mid-1960s and progressed through several mills as a manager. When Noranda took over, he became a senior VP of a region and then of the global-marketing division. A year later, he was the chief executive.

The tall, likable, low-key fifty-eight-year-old walked into a minefield of problems. Profits in 1990 had slumped to a fifth of the previous year's. By the time I showed up four years later, he'd slashed 1,400 jobs and was selling the pulp division (unfortunately, just as pulp prices started increasing) and a building-products division (even though it had been doing well).

Meanwhile, hundreds of millions of dollars were being ploughed into a packaging operation that would continue to bleed with losses. Environmental issues loomed up: Hundreds of protesters were arrested as they confronted the company over the clear-cutting of forests at Clayoquot Sound, on the west coast of Vancouver Island, in what became an international campaign. On the upside, Bob formed a senior team to initiate a wholesale strategic review— the Gap Attack—that refocused the company into three core businesses and propelled it further into value-added products.

Bob was on the cover of *Canadian Business* in 1994 under the headline "Unsung, Underpaid," the poster boy for Canadian CEOs who were supposedly being shortchanged in their salaries and bonuses. He was earning a total of $450,000 a year for running a $4-billion company. At the time, Ted Newall was making $1.5 million as CEO of NOVA Corp., where I was chair. Noranda *had* been a little tight-fisted with Bob, and our board, maybe a bit embarrassed, agreed to give him more than a 60 percent hike to $844,000—followed by another raise. (Our generosity did not go unnoticed. Peter Newman points out in *Titans: How the New Canadian Establishment Seized Power* that in 1997 we recorded a $368-million loss: "It says something about the bumbling company's view of reality that this profit slide prompted its board of directors to reward Findlay with two raises and a humongous bonus, so that his take-home pay reached nearly a million— $925,000, to be exact." Newman had a point.)

In 1996, with MacBlo's prospects not visibly improving and Bob coming up for retirement, Ray had planned to replace him as CEO with Dale Tuckey, the executive VP of operations. As it happened, major institutional stockholders with as much as 40 percent of the shares and the Vancouver brokerage firm Goepel McDermid confronted Ray to announce their disapproval of that succession plan. They were also saying that with the stock price so low—40 percent lower than its $30 peak a decade earlier— the company was easy prey to corporate vultures who could cherry-pick our various divisions. I realized that one reason for our poor stock performance was that the senior executives couldn't properly define their different businesses for analysts and potential investors.

Among the key shareholders, with a 9.5 percent holding, was an investment partnership of the oil-billionaire Bass brothers of Texas and the Ontario Teachers Pension Plan Board. Representing them as a MacBlo director was investment advisor Tommy Taylor, another Texan. They and the other investors leading the revolt demanded some new board members. Ted Newall, who was approached, wasn't available, but Ian Delaney was. Ian was the well-regarded former president and COO of Merrill Lynch Canada and now the sharp, tough-minded head of the diversified resource company Sherritt International of Vancouver. The gentlemanly Ray, meanwhile, reacted to the restless investors by resigning from the chairmanship earlier than intended.

His interim replacement was a long-time director, the Vancouver lawyer Dave Davenport. That's when I was approached by Ced Ritchie and another board member, Paul Douglas, former head of the Pittston Company, an American resource conglomerate that owned the Brink's security operation. They wanted to conscript me to become the chair. Only reluctantly, I agreed. In a hint of just how strongly the company was seen as a British Columbia icon, my buddy Don Campbell's sister, a long-time Vancouver resident, told me to my face, "I don't know why we need a guy from Alberta to run MacBlo."

Visiting corporate operations around North America with friendly Bob Findlay—a great guy to travel with—I began asking questions, observing problems, and getting the equivalent of a bachelor's degree in forestry. I found, for example, that the company had a plant built in the Ottawa Valley using new technology to make medium-density fibreboard, a reconstituted, non-structural panel product. A group of small sawmillers with an equity interest in the mill approached me, as the new chairman, to complain that costs had soared out of sight. Some of their companies had been operating in the valley for a century or so, and here they came, nice people with their hearts in their hands, fearing that they were about to go bankrupt. For MacMillan Bloedel, the project amounted to peanuts, but for them, it was their whole livelihoods at stake. And because the mill abutted a residential area, there were environmental issues, as well. Later, we did bail the sawmillers out, but we shouldn't have been in that business in the first place because the company simply didn't have expertise in that area. Only when a new broom appeared did it finally sell the operation in 1998.

MacBlo had also bought mills in northern Ontario and Minnesota from two different groups of entrepreneurial promoters. Neither of them was running well with the operators we'd inherited. There had been some fancy financing, and in one case, the contractor who'd built the plant still had a monetary interest in it. And again, the company was dealing with unproven technology. A similar situation arose with its venture to make cement shingles: A promoter pushing them as a replacement for cedar shakes in California convinced MacBlo to go into the business. Unfortunately, they leaked, so unhappy customers launched class action lawsuits against us. Another business we didn't know much about was the American containerboard industry, manufacturing solid-fibre products used to make shipping containers. Yet we were deeply into that trade, with competing mills in Alabama and Kentucky jockeying for position with no consolidated management at the top—while prices plunged as competitors flooded the market.

Over the years, MacBlo had developed its own groundbreaking technology. A decade earlier, for example, a team of its researchers was awarded the prestigious Wallenberg prize, presented by the king of Sweden, for inventing Parallam, a lumber made from plywood-mill waste products that are reduced to parallel strands bound by glue to become strong, attractive, and endlessly long extruded beams. A great product, but the company didn't know how to promote it and had to hive their invention off as a minority partner in a small company in Boise, Idaho, that produced and marketed Parallam on MacBlo's behalf.

In 1997, the stagnant B.C. economy, based heavily on forestry, stood second-last among all other provinces in employment growth. Our earnings the previous year had been only $51 million on sales of $5 billion. All in all, the situation was shaky, and there was a firm consensus on the board that a new hand was needed at the helm. We asked Bob to retire early, offering him a couple of hundred thousand share options to see him on his way. In my farewell speech, I commended him for fostering a collegial culture and said, with heartfelt feeling, that "we are grateful for his dedication, leadership, and loyalty through the good times and the bad."

As chair, I'd led the search committee to find a new CEO. Though I would have preferred a Canadian, the company was in deep enough trouble to need the best possible person, regardless of nationality. We finally narrowed our list to three strong candidates, with only one having any experience in Canada, and he was now resident in Europe. A second fellow was working in Australia for a U.S. paper company, and the third was W. Thomas Stephens, the former chair, president, and CEO of Manville Corporation of Denver.

Tom grew up in the forest industry. He'd driven a truck for his father's logging business in his hometown of Crossett, Arkansas. With an industrial-engineering master's degree from the University of Arkansas, he joined and later became president of Olinkraft, a forest-products company operating in the southern U.S. Olinkraft had been acquired for half a billion dollars in 1979 by Johns-Manville, the global forest-products and building-materials manufacturer and mining company. Tom moved as chief financial officer to what became the Manville Corporation and was named president and CEO in 1986. It was a troubled company in bankruptcy protection, facing billions of dollars in decade-old lawsuits that charged asbestos building materials used in Manville-made insulating fibre had caused several serious illnesses.

But a year after his arrival, profits had doubled to a record $164 million, and Manville emerged from bankruptcy, a healthy enterprise again with fresh product lines and annual sales of $3 billion (compared to MacBlo's $5 billion). He turned platinum-mining and forestry divisions into public stand-alones while concentrating on the (non-asbestos) insulation business. Among many rebuilding initiatives over his ten years were the meetings he held with small groups of employees to re-establish their trust in the once-crippled company. Not only that, he later taught economics at inner-city schools in Denver.

We needed someone with excellent communication skills and extensive experience in the restructuring and strategic growth of a major company (and maybe even someone who could handle the class action suits we were fielding over those leaky cement shingles). This guy had those capabilities in spades. That pivotal shareholder and director, Tom Taylor, was impressed by Tom Stephens' "level of energy." But it wasn't easy to convince the fifty-five-year-old to come north, as he confessed later: "Are you kidding? Go up there in that strange part of the world with the environmentalists and the unions and the cost problems?" The only reason he interviewed with us was because of the encouragement from Tom Neff, a legendary director of the Spencer Stuart executive-search firm in Chicago.

Tom Stephens played his cards close to his chest during our interview, insisting he wanted to keep his home in Denver and didn't intend to move to Vancouver. We said, "If you don't have a permanent residence here, you're not welcome to the job." In the end, he and his wife rented and later bought a fancy three-storey apartment on downtown False Creek, where he could moor his pleasure boat.

Tom hit the deck galloping. After a ninety-day strategy review mucking through what he called the "swamp" of the company, he weeded out 14 percent of the workforce—2,700 employees—but accomplished it in a sensitive manner by offering early retirements and hefty severance packages. He didn't want to be compared to the American Al Dunlap, who earned the nickname "Chainsaw" for his policy of brutal layoffs at Scott Paper, where Tom worked for a long six months. At MacBlo, Tom got union and management staff collaborating to reduce costs by redesigning the solid-wood division (which generated sawn timber and its products). He reshaped the North American distribution business to stress the importance of high-margin products that boost profits. Narrowing our focus to lumber and packaging, he closed the research centre and sold the money-losing medium-density fibreboard division and the under-achieving paper-products division to pay down debt.

Though a consortium eventually bought the paper operation, the most logical buyer had been Fletcher Challenge Canada, which was 50 percent owned by its New Zealand parent. We got very close to making a deal that would put their pulp mills together efficiently with our two at Powell River and Port Alberni, B.C., but then some complicated accounting issues reared up on their side. After I approached my friend Ron Southern, who was on both Fletcher boards, we met in Washington, D.C., with Global CEO Hugh Fletcher, who seriously entertained the possibility of a deal. When he later retired after a boardroom battle, I was in New Zealand on TransAlta business and met with Fletcher's top brass—who were more interested in buying American assets. Ken Shields of Goepel McDermid, the investment firm, came to see Tom and me about a group of institutional shareholders with ready money to buy MacBlo's pair of pulp mills. They were offering $600 million, but not a penny more.

"We'd consider that," Tom said, "but you have to show us where the money's coming from."

It was a new company to be called Pacifica Papers Inc., whose investors were mainly pension funds, Ken explained, giving us a few details. Taking his leave, he asked, "When can I hear from you?"

Tom replied, in his wry Arkansas way, "Well, as my old dad used to say, 'We're interested, but don't let the doorknob hit you in the ass on the way out.'"

We were interested enough to complete the deal to sell MB Paper's North American assets—the mills, sales and marketing offices in Washington State and Tokyo, and two power dams—for $850 million, not a penny less. And when I saw Ken recently, he admitted, "Dick, quite frankly, on that deal you got the better of us because we did not do well with Pacifica."

MacBlo, meanwhile, began doing well. In 1997, it had taken a $340-million after-tax charge against the year's results to reflect all the restructuring, resulting in a $368-million loss. In 1998, the overall profit was $42 million. That year, Tom surprised the industry by announcing that the company would be phasing out its controversial clear-cut logging over the next half-decade. Tom had tasked company people and outside consultants to determine what were the best alternative logging practices, without trying to justify the current ones—the world wouldn't stand for that. The solution was to introduce "variable retention logging" in three "stewardship zones" to protect old-growth trees and wildlife habitats on the 1.1 million hectares it managed along the B.C. coast and on Vancouver Island. He argued that the end of clear-cutting would stop the downward spiral of the company's annual cut and create a sustainable supply of timber. The news had the happy effect of getting the environmentalists off MacBlo's back. A die-hard campaigner for the Greenpeace movement—which had been effectively convincing customers around the world to boycott our forest products—even shared a bottle of Dom Pérignon champagne with Tom.

I travelled with him the first time he met with labour leaders at the big but idled Somass sawmill in Port Alberni. One union executive read a letter written long ago from MacBlo officials who had made promises that weren't kept. Tom said he couldn't do anything about the past or affect the world price for lumber. But if the workers could reduce production expenses—and he gave them precise targets expressed in the cost per linear board feet— the mill would go back into production. They accepted the challenge, and a year or so later, they appeared in our boardroom to tell us proudly what they'd accomplished. They had focused on the issue of safety in the woods as well as cutting costs. Among other stories, they told of scalemen who no longer refused to weigh a truckload of logs because it was too close to quitting time. After hearing such simple yet cost-effective examples of initiative, I thought, *B.C. is turning around!*

IN APRIL OF 1999, AS MACMILLAN BLOEDEL continued its recuperation under Tom Stephens, I unexpectedly needed a heart-bypass operation. After several hectic years of being chairman of three companies and director of two others at the same time, it was my turn to recover. The surgery took place just two weeks before MacBlo's annual meeting, which I didn't make for the first time since becoming a director. But at least I could read the newspapers by then. They quoted Tom as telling shareholders that if MacBlo had been lean enough to earn a decent profit at the bottom of the commodities cycle, as it happened, the company could "take it to the bank by the truckload" as things improved.

I read about it at home, trying to relax while Lois made sure to keep me away from the phone. Just one day after the meeting, Tom called and told her, "I *really* need to talk to Dick." She relented. I thought he simply wanted to let me know how things had gone. It was more than that: "I have to tell you that I just got a call from this guy, Steve Rogel." Rogel, I knew, was the chairman, president, and CEO of Weyerhaeuser of Federal Way, Washington. One of our competitors, with assets nearly quadruple ours, the forest-products corporation operated in a dozen countries, including Canada, where it had both major manufacturing facilities and timber assets. It traced its lineage north of the border to the nineteenth century, of course, when the founder—the American lumberman Frederick Weyerhaeuser—was buying up timberland around Chemainus. Tom went on, "They want to make a friendly offer for our company."

Oh, hell. And I was supposed to be recovering. The background to the Weyerhaeuser offer, as it transpired, was that they'd been looking at us for some time. At first, they were interested primarily in our packaging assets in the U.S., which we were hoping to sell to consolidate and, in Tom's words, become more of "a bull of the woods." The more the Americans saw, the more they liked the potential for the whole damn company. Now Steve Rogel—a fifty-six-year-old chemical-engineering grad from a small wheat-farming town in Washington—was suggesting a no-cash, share-for-share merger of the American and Canadian corporations. We weren't exactly an even match: Weyerhaeuser's most recent net annual earnings of $294 million were exactly seven times higher than ours.

Where was I in all this? Like other directors and Tom himself, I was concerned that we'd be a target for predators simply because of our low share value. As he told *Report on Business* magazine later, "What worried us was we were worth more dead than alive. With a cheap stock price, somebody could buy us and sell off the pieces, which would be worth more than the whole." As for Weyerhaeuser wanting MacBlo because it was actually successful now, "We didn't anticipate that." The fact that the possible buyer was American became a whole other issue that I, a proud Canadian, would be wrestling with over the next few months.

Tom had got on the phone immediately to brief all the directors and then contact our financial advisors, RBC Dominion Securities, J.P. Morgan, and Salomon Smith Barney. Four days later, our board reviewed all the publicly available material on Weyerhaeuser. The biggest problem would be evaluating their widely held stock, which was at an all-time high, and determining whether it would be heading up or down. Our directors gave management the go-ahead to discuss a possible transaction.

The initial discussions went on and off throughout May as the two sides did some limited due diligence. After each session, we directors met by phone for briefings by Tom and others, and on each occasion, we gave them the go-ahead to keep talking. There was plenty of time for other bids, but we couldn't identify any other buyers that would pay more. On June 1, Weyerhaeuser made an enhanced proposal and, over the next week, met with our RBC Dominion advisors to improve on the offer. The board had a couple more meetings with management to review the revisions, and by mid-month, Tom and Steve and their colleagues were gathering in secret at a hotel near the Vancouver airport. Booking rooms for "the Robinson family reunion," they showed up in their pinstripe suits and hashed out the unsettled issues over one weekend.

On June 21, Weyerhaeuser announced its intention to merge with MacBlo in a $3.59-billion stock swap that would create North America's third-largest forest-products corporation. After eight decades, MacMillan Bloedel would disappear as a corporate entity. B.C.'s *Logging and Sawmilling Journal* called it "a block-buster move that surprised most people in the forestry industry." Our team had phoned about eighty key managers about the impending sale. Tom had met in advance with NDP Premier Glen Clark and his forest minister, Dave Zirnhelt, to present the case for the merger. A little astonishingly, the two politicians accepted the idea with none of the knee-jerk ideological bluster you might have expected. "This is just another chapter in the evolution of the forest business in B.C.," the minister said. It was "an incredible vote of confidence" in the provincial economy, the premier said. Some observers suggested that British Columbians were probably just happy that this icon of B.C. had been acquired by a west-coast company, even if it was American, rather than one from eastern Canada. A few people may have recalled that the "Bloedel" in MacMillan Bloedel had also been an American from Washington State.

Why did the board of directors and a big majority of investors accept the deal, which was completed at the end of October? Well, the final offer amounted to a premium of 50 percent for MacBlo's shares. As Tom was quoted as saying, "A board is compelled by those kinds of premiums." And the combined new company promised to be less vulnerable and more valuable than its separate parts. Weyerhaeuser was already the world's largest producer of softwood lumber and market pulp and the second-largest manufacturer of oriented strand board (OSB, a popular panel-type product made from narrow strands of wood laid lengthwise and crosswise and then bonded with resin). Its Canadian manufacturing accounted for about a third of its softwood lumber capacity, nearly 60 percent of its OSB production, and about 17 percent of its pulp-and-paper output. The deal would make it Canada's largest lumber producer, bar none.

Yet when it came to a shareholders' ballot on the merger, the Ontario Teachers' Pension Plan Board voted against it. No longer part of the Tommy Taylor investment group, Teachers' now held the largest single block of stock—8 percent. Freed from that alliance, it argued that the deal was no longer lucrative enough. Originally, the offer was to swap 0.28 of a Weyerhaeuser share for each MacBlo one. When Weyerhaeuser shares were trading at more than $67 U.S., MacBlo's were valued at about $28. Since then, Weyerhaeuser's had slipped to less than $56 and MacBlo's to under $23. But this lone dissenting voice was lost in a clamour of approval: Well over the required two-thirds of shareholders accepted the deal happily.

His job done, Tom Stephens departed with about $13 million worth of severance—yet with tears welling in his eyes as he packed up his office. In a farewell speech, he said I'd been "a shoulder to cry on, a friend, and a fellow board member here and at TransCanada [Corporation]. Most American CEOs think that the idea of a non-employee chairman is a bad idea. I'm here to tell you they are wrong..."

The benefits and the disadvantages of the takeover have never been absolutely clear-cut for me. My initial hesitation was less about money—I eventually did fine with my shares—and more about the loss of a venerable corporation with its head office in Canada, responding primarily to Canadian needs and desires, supporting Canadian charities and cultural institutions, and reflecting Canadian values. Not that long ago, I met a friend, Doug Whitehead, the CEO of Finning International Inc., who said, "Dick, you guys did a great job in selling MacBlo." And I said, "Jeez, I still feel badly about it"—as I have ever since the merger. In his eyes, domestic stockholders had done very well out of the deal, which was true. But as the MacMillan Bloedel chairman and as a shareholder, I would have much rather had a Canadian company that we could build into a Northern Tiger. "Rueful" isn't a word I use very often, but in this case, it fit. Should we blame the Americans for their acquisitive, opportunistic ways? Maybe we should blame ourselves for our inability to explain our various businesses to investors, our lack of initiative in marketing our wares, and our failure to equal the vision that H.R. had in his day.

AFTER ADMITTING THAT, I have to say that Weyerhaeuser has worked hard, with some success, at being a good corporate citizen while operating in Canada. I know this from the inside because the company invited me on to its board after the takeover. I joined a pretty distinguished slate of directors. Martha Ingram, a genteel and astute Vassar College grad, chaired Ingram Industries, her family's $11-billion distribution conglomerate based in Nashville (where she also chaired the Tennessee Performing Arts Center she helped create). Martha always gave me a big kiss or hug when we met as two of the three members of Weyerhaeuser's executive committee. Other directors have included Jim Sullivan, the retired vice-chair of Chevron Corporation; Mike Steuert, senior VP and CFO of Fluor Corporation, the massive global contractor; and fellow Albertan Don Mazankowski, who was a member of Parliament, deputy prime minister, and federal minister of finance. While I've had some minor issues with the overall company about its corporate governance (which I discuss in chapter 14), it has tried to be sensitive to Canadian concerns.

Early in his career, chair and CEO Steve Rogel was an assistant manager at a pulp-and-paper mill in Nackawic, New Brunswick. At Weyerhaeuser, he's running a company with firm, four-decade-old roots in Canada. From one pulp mill in Kamloops, it grew to seven thousand employees working in Canadian timberlands, cellulose-fibre and paper mills, engineered-wood plants, OSB mills, softwood and hardwood lumber mills, a plywood facility, and a cross-country network of distribution centres.

Those working in the forests along the West Coast appreciated the fact that Weyerhaeuser focused on their safety. In 1998, MacBlo had a recordable incident rate—RIR, the measure of forestry accidents—of 12.3, or 410 loggers and others a year who were injured seriously enough to require medical treatment. With Weyerhaeuser's new "Personal Accountability Policy" aimed at its dangerous coastal operations, the RIR dropped steadily to below 2, or 36 injuries a year.

Another Canadian sensitivity has been the company's ongoing dealings with the First Nations. The Haida people of Haida Gwaii (the Queen Charlotte Islands) have included Weyerhaeuser among the offenders in their negotiations over land claims with the B.C. government. On the positive side, until 2005, the corporation was a partner in a unique joint venture that MacBlo had begun with the Nuu-chah-nulth people in the controversial Clayoquot Sound area. Iisaak Forest Resource Ltd.—*iisaak* means "respect"—is a small company (in which Weyerhaeuser had 49 percent) that practises sustainable eco-logging on Vancouver Island. While some of Weyerhaeuser's operations managers were skeptical of the business, the head-office environmental staff was strongly supportive.

And Weyerhaeuser also continued to pursue and enhance those responsible silviculture practices that Tom Stephens initiated on the coast with variable retention logging rather than clear-cutting.

All these initiatives, admirable as they were, ended in 2005 when the company sold off all its coastal forestry operations, which employed 2,300 people, for $1.2 billion. Included in the deal were 258,000 hectares of private timberlands, annual harvesting rights to 3.6 million cubic metres of Crown timber, two Port Alberni sawmills, and three other softwood mills. None of these had ever formed part of its core softwood business and long-term strategy because of the Coast's specialized timber species and much-more-complex logging procedures. Our board agreed that it was a very timely transaction: Weyerhaeuser had bought the assets with a sixty-six-cent U.S. dollar and was now selling it for an eighty-cent greenback. And at this point, it could sure use the money, given its $10.6-billion (U.S.) debt burden.

The good news in all this? The buyer of the coastal assets was Brascan Corporation—now Brookfield Asset Management, which invests in big-ticket industries such as real estate (Royal LePage), natural resources (Noranda), energy (Great Lakes Power), and financial services (various investment funds). For me, the most important factor is that Brookfield remains a resolutely Canadian company, based in Toronto and under domestic control. This was a win-win situation for both Brookfield and Weyerhaeuser.

A former Weyerhaeuser VP in Canada, Reynold Hert is now running Brookfield's Western Forest Products operations, which controls nearly 40 percent of the West Coast's Crown timber. As Hert recently told the *Vancouver Sun*'s veteran forestry reporter, Gordon Hamilton, "Our goal is to create superior value for shareholders by building a margin-focused lumber business on the B.C. coast of sufficient size and scale to compete in global softwood markets."

I was damn pleased with this turn of events—and suspected that old H.R. would have been, too.

Chapter Eleven

THE BEST OF SHOW
Alberta Energy, PanCanadian Energy, and EnCana

IN 2005, ENCANA CORP. surpassed the Royal Bank as the leading company on the benchmark Canadian stock index. Not long after, its president and chief executive officer, Gwyn Morgan, was named "Canada's Outstanding CEO of the Year," chosen by his peers for an award sponsored by The Caldwell Partners, a major national executive search firm. Hearing all this news, I couldn't help thinking back to how we just might have lost this mighty Northern Tiger of an energy company.

North America's largest independent gas producer was born only three years earlier in a brilliant cloak-and-dagger merger of PanCanadian Energy and the Alberta Energy Company (AEC). PanCanadian began as a subsidiary of Canadian Pacific Ltd., which had recently cut it loose to operate on its own. Peter Lougheed's Conservatives created AEC as an all-Canadian, fifty-fifty public-private enterprise in 1974, and then Ralph Klein's government finally privatized it in 1993, a year after I joined its board. That's when Gwyn and I got to know one another well. He'd been with the company almost since its inception and was now one of two candidates vying to be its president. Within two years of my arrival, he did land the top job—in a company that had become a sitting duck for a takeover, especially by hungry foreign hunters of prime Canadian prey.

AEC had spread itself thin with investments in natural gas, oil, pipelines, forest products, and petrochemicals, among other businesses. As Gwyn himself recalls, "When I was handed the reins of the new company, we had a lot of highly valuable assets that were worth a lot more than the stock price was reflecting. Nobody knew what this guy was going to do with this company. And so we were totally open to takeovers. I sometimes look back and wonder how we ever lived through that period. We were highly vulnerable. There were all kinds of rumours, and I know now, talking to investment bankers, that there were a number of companies working on takeover bids."

If an outside buyer had acquired AEC, there would likely never have been a merger with PanCanadian, and EnCana would never have existed. Luckily, Gwyn Morgan was at AEC's helm during that tricky period and, like me, has always been a diehard nationalist, determined to build companies that are controlled by Canadians and reflect our values. There was a Canada-first champion at PanCanadian Energy, too: the chairman, David O'Brien. And because he and Gwyn were both friends of mine, I was helpful in the process of bringing the two companies together in a deal that was not only good for shareholders and employees but also equally good for the country.

Of course, David O'Brien was the guy who'd once, as president of what was then called PanCanadian Petroleum, disdained my offer to sell him Husky Oil. And who, while I was CEO of Interhome Energy, had also turned down the Reichmann brothers' proposition to sell him the company. He had left PanCanadian in 1995 to become president of its parent, Canadian Pacific, the country's second-biggest corporation. At that time, it also had CP Rail, CP Ships, CP Hotels, Marathon Realty, Laidlaw Inc. (the Canadian health-services, transportation, and waste-disposal group), and Fording Coal—where I'd been on the board since 1986, and David, more recently. Combined, the CP companies generated $15 billion a year in revenues. But many people had the idea that all these enterprises could do better—be much more attractive to investors—if they were cut loose from the mother ship and sent out on their own as public companies. David rejected that possibility until he'd had the chance to strengthen the subsidiaries over several tough years.

This genial yet competitive Irish-Canadian (as a promising eleven-year-old boxer, he'd had his picture on the front page of the Montreal *Gazette*) was CP's first non-railway president. He came in under chair and CEO Bill Stinson, a fourth-generation railroader trying to bring the conglomerate back to its basics. "Bill had sold off a number of things, including CP Air," David recalls, "but the railway was still down in the dumps." Even before officially becoming CEO, he told Stinson that CP Rail should move from its ancient rut in Montreal to western Canada, where most of its business and history was. And in 1996, he brought CP Ltd.'s head office along with the rail company to Calgary, where David hadn't bothered to sell his home.

"Quite apart from the move," David says, "I sold off Marathon Realty, then Laidlaw at the top of the market for $1 billion (I was very fortunate to get out of that), and sold the city-centre hotels [The Empress in Victoria and the Château Frontenac in Quebec City] for $305 million to the Legacy Hotels Real Estate Investment Trust. In 1995, CP had lost about $300 million, and by 2000, we were making over $1 billion.

"But as I told my CFO, Mike Grandin, back in '97, it was only a question of time before we'd have to break this thing up. Because the stock market would never pay you for the value of an overly complex, overly diversified company like ours. And the analysts don't like it because it doesn't fit into their nice little boxes, so you always suffer a big discount."

The opportune time came in February 2001, when CP announced its intention to spin off its five remaining pieces: PanCanadian, Fording, CP Rail, CP Ships, and Fairmont Hotels & Resorts (which had seventy-seven deluxe properties in North America, Mexico, Bermuda, and Barbados). It was a brilliant decision that benefited almost all of the divisions, as their collective market capitalization of $13 billion before the breakup grew to $23 billion within two years. Two of them, especially, would prosper—Fording and PanCanadian, which evolved into EnCana—and would have a powerful and important impact on me, personally, as well as on the Canadian economy. Of these, EnCana today has the higher profile, in large part because of the leadership of Gwyn Morgan and the chairmanship of David O'Brien.

FROM MY PERCH ON THE BOARD of the Alberta Energy Company, I'd watched Gwyn drive the business into becoming Canada's largest natural-gas producer and second-largest overall petroleum producer, after PanCanadian. Not bad for the youngest of four farmer's kids who grew up on a "godforsaken homestead" near Carstairs, north of Calgary. His father, born in Wales (which accounts for Gwyn's name), cultivated grain and raised livestock, which his only son fed before and after school. There was no running water until he was twelve, when he and his dad dug the ditch from the well to the house—"We were both tough as nails," he remembers. By his mid-teens, the family moved to Carstairs where Morgan Senior was selling farm implements, which Gwyn helped repair. Good in math and science, he took mechanical engineering at the University of Alberta, working for Imperial Oil in the summers. Turning down an offer to design aircraft for Boeing in Seattle, he became a petroleum reservoir engineer for the Alberta Oil and Gas Conservation Board, the industry's government regulator headed by the highly respected George Govier. With that solid foundation of learning, Gwyn went to work for the Consolidated Companies—which had gas and pipeline subsidiaries and Norlands Petroleum—exploring the Arctic. There he was, this intense, feisty twenty-four-year-old, only three years out of college, and managing the engineering operations of all three companies. But, like Imperial, Consolidated was a branch plant of an American company, and his nationalistic mindset was starting to gel.

With the provincial government's launch of AEC in 1974, financed in part by the Alberta Heritage Fund, he was attracted by the idea of a company headquartered in Canada that would sell its shares to Canadians. "When I graduated in engineering, there were very few options at Canadian companies. With AEC, there would be a lot of ownership by the people of Alberta and other parts of the country—some of whom had never owned a share in a company. Even at that time, I was quite keen on the free-enterprise system, the idea that we could create something where people would learn how to invest in shares—other than just putting their money into bonds and banks—and we'd actually be developing a Canadian-owned industry. That was number one for me, actually, for a number of reasons. One is that I felt that people needed to have positive experiences around investing and equity. And another is just the fact that we were going to be making decisions in Canada, and Canadians would get the top jobs and be the leaders rather than always reporting to somebody."

Leading the new Crown corporation was Dave Mitchell, the ex-president of Great Plains Development Company, which had been a subsidiary of Burmah Oil (where Dave Powell had worked). I knew Mitchell as a meticulous engineer when I did audits at Great Plains in the 1950s. At AEC, he was uneasy about its public ownership, though the company had a couple of government-generated strengths to kick-start its success. The first was an option for up to 20 percent ownership of the Syncrude oil-sands project in Fort McMurray and the rights to build two-thirds of the power plant there as well as the entire pipeline to bring the oil to Edmonton. The second was an exclusive lease to explore for petroleum using Alberta's subsurface mineral rights to the 2,600 square kilometres of the Suffield Military Block, northwest of Medicine Hat, where soldiers from around the world had trained since the Second World War.

"I joined the company in 1975," Gwyn says, "and my job was to get the first production organized from scratch at Suffield. So I had to hire people and build a team—rented an empty office and went from there. On April 22nd, 1976, we had a spudding ceremony and had this huge Canadian flag on top of the drilling rig, blowing in the wind. And I guess it was a bit symbolic of my feelings. Running through my whole career from graduation, I didn't like the idea of having to work for American companies. Nothing against Americans—I love them. Just that my passion was for things controlled in Canada."

Gwyn built the profitable oil and gas division, and in 1992, Dave Mitchell asked him to oversee most of AEC's other businesses, which included forest products, petrochemicals, coal mining, and fertilizer plants. We on the board of directors were considering both Gwyn and Frank Proto, a senior VP, to replace Mitchell, who announced his retirement the following year. I'd had my own dealings with a combative Gwyn during the Alliance pipeline dispute between AEC and NOVA. Watching him now at work in his new job, I welcomed him as CEO as heartily as the other directors did. As we became friends as well as corporate colleagues, he tolerated, and sometimes even appreciated, my counsel based on a long career involving so many boardroom dramas.

For a guy with a reputation for shrewd dealmaking, Gwyn, with his sober manner and spectacles framing his lean face, appears deceptively mild. Thin as a blade of wheat, he works out for ninety minutes a day. In the words of columnist Diane Francis, he looks less "like central casting's version of a self-made tycoon" and "more like a school teacher." He's a surprise in his philosophical approach to life, too. Not many people know that he and his wife embrace the tenets of Buddhism and he's visited the Dalai Lama's birthplace in Nepal.

Gwyn quickly realized that the company was over-diversified and in 1993, when the Klein government pulled out of AEC, began selling the non-core operations. "I became a zealot about this," he'll tell you today. "And then we had to build the business we wanted, which was oil and gas." That's when he felt the company was highly vulnerable because the stock price wasn't reflecting the excellent balance sheet on the remaining petroleum assets.

In 1996, Gwyn increased the company's crude-oil, natural-gas, and natural-gas liquid reserves in a friendly $1.1-billion stock swap with Toronto-based Conwest Exploration Company. The merger effectively doubled AEC's portfolio, trailing only PanCanadian in size. Harley Hotchkiss joined the board just after the alliance and observed, "I think history will look back on that as the merger that gave Gwyn Morgan the confidence and the foundation to do a lot of other things. It was hard bargaining, but it was a friendly merger, and it was handled efficiently and smoothly from a people standpoint, from an asset standpoint. It made all kinds of sense for both sides. But perhaps particularly for Alberta Energy because Gwyn was early in his career there as leader and it gave him and the team around him the courage to do what they've done since."

Over the next three years, Gwyn also acquired Amber Energy Inc. and PacAlta Resources Ltd. on a so-called "unsolicited friendly basis" (not quite hostile, but not entirely appreciated). Amber, especially, was a steal: AEC had been offered Amber at $27 a share the year before but, when petroleum prices fell to less than $10 a barrel, paid only $7.50 in a deal that gave it Canada's largest gas reserves. One bonus was acquiring a well-respected former AEC employee, Mike Graham, then with Amber and now an executive VP responsible for all of EnCana's upstream operations in Alberta. (Gwyn placed one of his own people as Amber's CEO: Randy Eresman, who was to play a prominent part in the evolution of AEC into EnCana.) The PacAlta purchase put Alberta Energy well into the global market with 180 million barrels of oil reserves in Ecuador.

Even then, in his zeal to create what he called a world-beating "super-independent" petroleum company, Gwyn's eye was always on North America. He got a foothold on Alaska's North Slope, signed a farm-in deal with Conoco to explore in the Gulf of Mexico, and took over two key petroleum companies in the U.S. Rockies. By 2000, AEC earned a record $950 million, and the following year, its cash reserves and unused lines of credit totalled $2.7 billion, prompting industry analysts to suggest it was on the prowl for a major acquisition.

Over at PanCanadian Energy, meanwhile, things were changing after the breakup of Canadian Pacific Ltd. David O'Brien decided to stay on as chair of the petroleum company (as well as a director of Fairmont Hotels). PanCanadian had solid properties in both Western and Eastern Canada, the North Sea, and the Gulf of Mexico. At that time, its president was David Tuer, a former assistant deputy energy minister in Alberta who, at fifty-two, had been running the company for eight years. In mid-October 2001, Tuer was publicly extolling the strengths of PanCanadian and pooh-poohing any possibility that it would be taken over. And then just two days later, he resigned, citing "personal reasons." He has never explained his decision on the record since: "I've talked about it; I've said as much as I have to say," he tells most people. "It's behind me." (He went on become part of Matco Investments, a private investment company led by Ron Mathison, the very successful son of a family friend of mine from Gleichen.) As David O'Brien says today of Tuer's mysterious departure, "I don't know if it was pressure, or what."

Whatever the reasons, it sent the industry into overdrive. The next day, I was among the directors of AEC having a board meeting in Houston. On a break after visiting the oil-drilling platform of a well in the Gulf of Mexico, one of us—I think it was Dale Lucas—read in the electronic version of the *Globe* about the sudden resignation. With PanCanadian now out on its own, and without a president, the possibility arose for a renewed attempt to make a deal to merge.

Renewed, because Gwyn had already made such an approach about eighteen months earlier. David O'Brien was then still head of CP Ltd., which had not yet divested itself of PanCanadian. But hearing the proposal for a merger with AEC, he replied, "You know, Gwyn, there's merit to putting those two companies together, but the structure just won't work. Here I am sitting at CP, and if I [meaning his company, CP Ltd.] go from owning 90 percent of PanCanadian to 50 percent of a combined company, I'll get a further discount in my stock price because I don't own the whole thing. And you've said you don't want me to have voting control [of the merged company], even though I'll have my investment there. So we just can't do it, the way things are now."

And now, as the board discussed the developments in Houston, Gwyn said, "As you can see, we've got this tremendously strong company, and we don't need to do anything. Our future is that we'll become the strongest independent, no matter what. I'm ambivalent about doing a big acquisition or merger."

Yet after a couple of hours' discussion, we said, "Gwyn, you have the authority to call David O'Brien."

He did, but David didn't call back. So then I got on the phone to Calgary because I had to talk to David about getting him on the board of TransCanada Corporation. "Haskayne," he said, "I got a call here yesterday from Gwyn Morgan. Should I call him back?"

"You'd *better* call him back." Many a deal is done because of strong personal relationships—and David O'Brien and I had become great friends.

Very quickly, David had stepped in to become the interim CEO as well as the chair of the rudderless PanCanadian. He'd named his former chief financial officer at CP Ltd., Mike Grandin, as the pro-tem president (Mike would later have a more prominent part in the future of Fording Coal). When he and Gwyn did connect by phone, David suggested getting together in about ten days: "I wasn't feeling any urgency, I'd just come through the CP divestiture, so I wasn't rushing into anything. I said, 'Come on over and we'll have a chat.' And we started chatting. I had the advantage, in a sense, since I wasn't running PanCanadian on a day-to-day basis and had the time to focus and have a good hard look at whether the combination of companies would be well received in the market. I retained RBC Dominion Securities to do some analysis for us, and Gwyn had some work done on his side by CIBC World Markets."

The two men began meeting—as secretly as possible, to avoid any industry gossip about a potential merger that would affect share prices—at the luxurious former CP Ltd. suite in Bankers Hall. It was two floors below my office, where Gwyn used to regularly visit me. Recounting those sessions now, Gwyn says, "So it was okay for me to go up and down in the elevator there. If anybody was on the elevator, I'd push '20,' and if not, I'd push '18.' And at that time, this big space on [floor] 18 was totally unoccupied except for two people, David O'Brien and his assistant,

Marilyn. The first time I arrived, she meets me, and I'm walking down this hallway, and there's a bunch of display cabinets that were like the archives of CP—some of the famous artifacts of the original railway company. It was like walking into this big, beautiful museum with nobody around.

"AEC was driving the deal, obviously, and we'd done all the analysis of PanCanadian. My executive team and my key legal people and others in AEC knew about the deal because we were doing as much analysis prior to Christmas as we could, but only involving a very few people over at PanCanadian. Whereas at AEC, it was a much larger group. We drafted the purchase-sale agreement, put together what would be the due-diligence program, and so on. And we agreed that once we got back from Christmas holidays—basically January 2—that David O'Brien would expand the net inside PanCanadian, get people fully engaged, and that we'd have twenty-five days to get all the work done."

As their talks became more serious, they no longer met at David's office. Now the pivotal players gathered in rooms at the Hyatt Regency downtown. Again, the watchwords were confidentiality and stealth. Nobody wanted to torpedo what could be the biggest all-Canadian industrial merger on record. Gwyn showed up at the hotel in a sort of disguise, wearing jeans and a backpack. "He looked like he was about to go duck-hunting," David recalls, chuckling. "The first time, I was given a key card for the room where we were meeting, and I got there first, and the card didn't work. I banged at the door, and there was no answer. I didn't want to be loitering there, so I went down to the ground floor and into one of the stalls in the men's room and just hung out for about fifteen minutes, figuring Gwyn would come and his card would work. Well, it turned out his card didn't work either, and he couldn't remember the name of the lawyer in whose name the room had been booked. But somehow, he went to the front desk and managed to get a proper key card."

After seeing Gwyn up close, David describes him as "a very focused, smart, hard-working, disciplined, and driven guy. He and I have very different political philosophies. I tend to be more of a

worth—of more than $27 billion. It had one of the strongest balance sheets of all the continent's independents and one of the largest capital-investment programs of any company based in Canada. Overseas, in the United Kingdom, it had made the most major oil discovery in the central North Sea during the past decade—the Buzzard find—and in Ecuador, it was the major private-sector oil producer. While we didn't call EnCana a Northern Tiger then, we knew it was a flagship corporation of those proportions. The press had no trouble recognizing the enormity of the enterprise, reflected in headlines such as "Globe's Largest Independent" and "EnCana's Energy Bonanza."

Shareholders of the two companies gladly approved the deal that spring. EnCana set up shop in the old CP Ltd. suite, with David O'Brien the non-executive chairman and Gwyn Morgan the president and CEO. Mike Grandin stepped aside but stayed on as a director. I went on the new sixteen-person board, with eight people from each company. Gwyn had wanted me on the board especially to chair the human resources committee that oversaw the complications that arose with the marriage of two companies. When David O'Brien called me down in Palm Desert, I said, "It'll be time for me to go in a couple of years. I don't want to be the chairman of any committees. I'm tired of working, David."

"Haskayne," he said, "I need help here because this is a critical issue." Because of my experience on the HR committee of AEC, Gwyn insisted on having me head EnCana's committee. Oh, and then there was also the corporate-governance committee that wanted me as vice-chair, working with David. In the end, I couldn't say no to him.

On the human resources front, one issue was that senior managers had contracts in place from their former employers, some of them allowing PanCanadian people to walk off with good severance packages. Some weren't needed in the new organizational structure, while others were critical to EnCana's success. But in any merger, one side has to take charge, and in this case, it was the Alberta Energy group whose well-defined culture—which became the EnCana culture—may not have melded smoothly with

PanCanadian's. In terms of corporate governance, we were soon dealing with the rigorous dictates of the *Sarbanes-Oxley Act* in the U.S. and similar regulations introduced in Canada by the Canadian Securities Administration. As our chief financial officer John Watson put it, "For the first time, CEOs and CFOs are now personally at risk, in a very significant way, if the financial statements and related disclosures do not meet the standards set forth. I find that extremely motivating in terms of setting priorities." So did I, as Enron and other scandals had swung the pendulum from internal to legislated standards. Fortunately, the environment at EnCana was summed up by a corporate constitution the board approved, which began as follows:

> Our vision is to create a truly great company—one where quality work is the norm, where we stretch and strive to be the best we can be, and where great things are accomplished. Principles grace every decision and punctuate every interaction along our journey. Shareholders and other stakeholders support our endeavours because we have earned their trust and respect.

In the first year, there was one unwelcome surprise. At AEC, we'd always had our reserves of oil and gas evaluated by independent engineers. PanCanadian, though conservatively run in most of its operations, never did have such arm's-length evaluations. So in doing due diligence before the merger, AEC had relied on its own in-house people to audit the PanCanadian reserves and finally had to suck up its guts and accept that the estimates were probably accurate. As it turned out, they weren't. After the deal, EnCana hired outside consultants to judge just how much proved petroleum reserves both companies really had. (An independent evaluator has to determine there's at least a 90 percent probability that reserves will be recovered to declare them "proved.") While AEC's had been understated, PanCanadian's had been overstated— not deliberately, but through poor evaluation processes, including (as Gwyn says) "just some plain bloody errors."

As a result, we had to take a huge writedown on the PanCanadian reserves and, of course, report it publicly. I was in Hawaii at the time and had a conference call with the board's distraught audit and reserve committees—after which Ian Delaney phoned to say, "Haskayne, I am sitting here with my fingers in my ears waiting for the explosion to happen." Fortunately, the big bang never occurred: Because of AEC's improved reserve picture, which more than offset the PanCanadian loss, the stock market accepted the writedown with barely a murmur.

Over the next three years, the rest of the surprises were mostly happy ones, even though I questioned some of Gwyn's strategy. In early 2003, EnCana sold most of its stake in the Syncrude oil-sands project in northern Alberta to the Canadian Oil Sands Trust for what was seen as being a top price: $1.1 billion. While I voted for the transaction, I liked the solid underpinning of Syncrude—an asset we didn't even have to manage. In my HBOG days, we'd bought an interest in Syncrude from AEC because we felt it provided stability.

Their sale left us as primarily a natural-gas company (though we did retain some of the best leases in the in-situ oil sands that require steam injection, rather than surface mining, to release the bitumen to produce high-sulphur oil). Gwyn had more guts than I would have shown in transforming the company and selling his vision to the world. While I worried that we were turning into a one-trick pony, he was determined to shed more of what he considered to be the non-core assets the new company had inherited. He got rid of EnCana's holdings in the Gulf of Mexico for $2.5 billion, those in Ecuador for $1.5 billion, and its North Sea oil field for $2.1 billion (all figures in U.S. dollars), which was bought by Nexen Inc., another Canadian company.

Even before Gwyn sold the North Sea assets—and just when I thought he was all sale and no buy—he capitalized on the increasing value of the Canadian dollar to acquire Tom Brown Inc. of Denver for $2.7 billion (U.S.). That purchase more than tripled EnCana's natural-gas production down south to about one billion cubic feet per day. "We realized the huge opportunity we had in

North America with our special knowledge and the fact that we were going to have more cash," Gwyn says. "The company was a hand-in-glove fit for our assets. And we actually did it about six months before we really had the balance sheet to do it."

The Tom Brown deal was another signal that Gwyn was pursuing a shift in emphasis from mature, conventional gas fields to deeper, multi-zone deposits. These "tight" fields use more sophisticated technology to extract small amounts of gas from each of thousands of wells and usually yield a more predictable production over a longer period. Piloting this program was Randy Eresman, who'd joined AEC as a technologist five years after Gwyn but left for a while in 1980, when the National Energy Program slowed the industry down, to get his engineering degree. "I like to say he's the only good thing that came out of the NEP," Gwyn says. "We were really good at getting the most out of difficult reservoirs. That was always Randy's forte."

Randy became executive VP responsible for the onshore North America division and then chief operating officer. He and Gwyn continued to build the company by developing resource plays, a tight-field strategy. The company also spent about $350 million in a single day in a British Columbia land sale to exploit what Gwyn calls "a big new resource, the biggest in the history of the country, by far." These gambles were paying off handsomely. By 2005, with the price of natural gas rising by a factor of six since the 1990s, EnCana's market value had doubled.

And in October of that year, coming up to age sixty, after thirty years in the industry, the always-surprising Gwyn Morgan announced he was ceding the CEO's position to Randy, his heir apparent. Gwyn consulted in advance with three people: his wife; Dave Mitchell, AEC's founder; and me. He'd step back and become executive vice-chairman in an advisory role for at least a year, leaving himself free to pursue other passions.

Through all of this, Gwyn has been true to himself. Even at the press conference to announce his decision, he was dismissing widespread speculation that Royal Dutch Shell PLC was bidding for EnCana—*his* company would remain Canadian-controlled. Ever since I've known him, he's always been fearlessly outspoken, saying out loud what may be on other people's minds. The Kyoto environmental accord wasn't working, he said, and Canada needed a viable alternative. To cure our ailing health care system, the nation must adopt world-class quality standards and reporting systems. Other Canadian companies—and governments—should adopt an ethical stance similar to the one enshrined in EnCana's corporate constitution, which sets out standards of behaviour and expectations of performance. While knowing that many Canadians would dispute his arguments as self-serving, he obviously felt duty-bound to discuss them in public, and damn the torpedoes.

He suffered some cheap shots after a parliamentary committee rejected him as Prime Minister Harper's handpicked chair of the Public Appointments Commission, the federal patronage watchdog. The politicians lambasted him for a speech in which he'd linked Canada's problems of gang violence to immigrants from places such as Jamaica and Indochina, "where culture is dominated by violence and lawlessness." I was at that event and winced inwardly at his words, wondering about the wisdom of identifying ethnic groups by name and the effect this might have if he ever wanted to go into politics or serve Canada in any public capacity. Yet he *was* articulating a truth: There *are* a tiny minority of bad apples in those two groups—where the vast majority are decent and loyal Canadians.

While Gwyn didn't get to take the $1-a-year post with the accountability commission, there was no doubt he would find other ways to volunteer his leadership talents, three decades' worth of business experience, and innate sense of ethics to the community at large. And whatever else he does in future, his legacy will always be the masterminding of the esteemed company that EnCana became, one that meets the challenging standards for social responsibility and sustainability set by investment-fund managers such as Vancouver's Ethical Funds Co. No wonder the University of Victoria's Faculty of Business's board of advisors presented him with the 2006 Distinguished

Entrepreneur of the Year Award at a ceremony that Lois and I were pleased to witness.

Is EnCana a Tiger today? Without a doubt. In sheer size, of course, as the global industry's largest independent. In residency, with its head office in Calgary. In nationality, with all its major strategizing and decision-making done in Canada. In perfecting an extremely profitable niche, by focusing on resource plays. And in a Canadian brand of assertive behaviour, by acquiring a corporation across the border in a friendly takeover and teaming up with ConocoPhillips in an $11-billion (U.S.) deal to ship bitumen from its Alberta oil sands to Conoco's refineries in Illinois and Texas for upgrading into synthetic oil to make gasoline.

I know all this from being on the board from the birth of the company until my retirement as a director in 2005. It had been an absorbing journey—interrupted only occasionally by the times I had to excuse myself from board meetings to deal with a developing crisis as I was trying to help transform Fording into the EnCana of the coal industry.

Chapter Twelve

DIGGING FOR A DEAL
Fording Canadian Coal Trust

THE MEDIA QUOTED ME AS CALLING the proposed deal an "elegant solution"—that's a phrase I've never used in my life, though I guess it did describe the agreement I was helping to broker with four warring parties. The *Globe and Mail*'s savvy Alberta columnist, Deborah Yedlin, said I'd been displaying "King Solomon–like skills," which seems overly generous: I never threatened to divide any company in two, like old Solomon suggesting he'd split a baby between a couple of women claiming to be its mother. Actually, my colleagues and I were trying to make one big happy family by combining three medium-sized companies into a single Tiger with strong Canadian bloodlines. It would take us four months, and ninety thousand copies of each of seven offers and counter-offers to shareholders, and bitter negotiations with a friend—with me exploding in anger during last-ditch negotiations in the middle of the night. It involved the launch of one of Canada's first major income trusts, then a hostile-takeover bid, a pitched battle of press releases, and a flood of disclosure documents throughout the Christmas season of 2002. The collective cost of just putting the deal together was about $100 million. Our goal was to consolidate the national coal industry to create the world's second-largest metallurgical coal company, Fording Canadian Coal Trust.

You learn a lot in dealing with a hostile bid. As Stan Magidson says, "It requires critical decision-making by board members in a compressed time frame." Stan, who heads up the business law practice in Western Canada for Osler, Hoskin & Harcourt LLP, had acted in the merger of NOVA and TransCanada PipeLines and represented the Fording board in our fight with Sherritt International Corp. and the Ontario Teachers' Pension Plan Board. "These are real-time decisions," he pointed out later when we were on a panel together at the University of Calgary. "They're highly visible, and people read about them. And there's a real possibility that the proponents of the transaction, if they don't like what you're doing, will sue you. So your judgment calls are subject to a lot of scrutiny and second-guessing." All those pressures sure came into play during the war games we waged to determine the fate of Fording.

I'd got to know the company in the mid-1980s while I was president of Home Oil. Through its subsidiary Scurry-Rainbow, Home had a minority interest in a potentially huge coal development on the B.C. side of the Crowsnest Pass region of the Rocky Mountains. The other partners were Canada's Stelco and several European steel companies. As we were contemplating the future of the project, I flew to Germany to visit the giant ThyssenKrupp steel operations and began to develop a relationship with some senior guys there. After due deliberation, the consortium decided not to proceed with the mining. My main ThyssenKrupp contact said his company wanted to sell its interest in the Crowsnest property and, because Scurry-Rainbow had the right of first refusal, was offering it to us. We didn't want it, but we worried about who might acquire the interest. I said if ThyssenKrupp could find an acceptable buyer with mining experience and financial credibility, we wouldn't stand in the way of any deal. They found this company called Fording Coal that was barely on my radar screen.

Enormous reserves of coal had been found in the Elk Valley region of southeastern B.C. in the late 1880s. It was only in 1967, after detailed exploration, that the area around the Fording River got serious attention. A year later, Canadian Pacific and Cominco incorporated Fording Coal, opening a mine there in 1972. And in '86, CP took full ownership of what was becoming a major source of metallurgical (or coking) coal for export to steelmakers overseas, especially in Japan. CP was in the business because Fording, the biggest shipper of coal in Canada, was its biggest railway customer.

At the same time the Germans were unloading their share of the Crowsnest lands to Fording, we at Home decided to sell ours, too. That's when I met Jack Morrish, an engineering grad who'd been a marketing vice-president at CP Rail. He became chairman and CEO at Fording and turned into a hard-rock negotiator with the miners' unions. But he was an outgoing guy with a great sense of humour to go with his bold approach to the coal business. Once, when I asked him how Fording had succeeded, he said, "We knocked the top off Eagle Mountain"—the peak above Fording River where the company had its original open-pit mine. (Yes, I know, environmentalists will wince at his remark.) The day we were to meet in Home's fancy dining room to close our sale to Fording, Jack arrived early and asked if I'd become one of three independent directors, complementing the CP appointees, on Fording's board. Given that I had little knowledge of the coal industry, I was flattered, and I accepted in the spring of 1986.

Bill Stinson, CP's chief executive, sent a nice letter welcoming me: "Over the past few years, Fording has been one of the stellar performers in the Canadian Pacific group of companies. Now that the ownership of the company resides solely with Canadian Pacific, we look forward to Jack Morrish and his management team producing even better results as they expand and diversify their operations. The background and experience you bring to the Fording board will significantly assist Jack in these endeavours."

Among Jack's team was Jim Gardiner, a fellow engineer who was just as hard-nosed as Jack. Jim, bred in Saskatchewan, started as a construction engineer at a Cominco potash mine in his home province and at a coal mine in Alberta. In 1970, he joined Fording in the same role to help build its first mine near Elkford in B.C.'s Elk Valley. After going back home for a while to deal with a problem potash mine, he returned to the Fording coal operation in the mid-'70s as operating superintendent. Jim was on a fast track, moving from general manager of the mine to GM and vice-president and, in '86, VP of all of the company's operations from its Calgary headquarters.

By then, Fording was running the Whitewood mine in west-central Alberta under contract from TransAlta, supplying the electrical utility with thermal coal to fuel power-generating stations. Fording soon had a similar arrangement with EPCOR Utilities in the nearby Genesee mine. It would also have mines in New York State and Mexico that made it the world's largest producer of wollastonite, an industrial mineral used in ceramics, plastics, and paint applications and as a substitute for asbestos.

At the time, it wasn't a publicly owned enterprise and had only a single shareholder: CP Ltd. I became chair of Fording's audit committee and, over the next decade, observed the major financial ups and downs as coal prices ebbed and flowed from less than $40 (U.S.) per metric tonne to a high of $53. All this while, Jim was pushing the unions to improve productivity, and near the end of the 1990s, the so-called "Asian Economic Flu" slammed the economy of Fording's customers in Japan, Taiwan, and other countries. Yet as the millennium dawned, Canada's largest export-coal producer was positioned for growth. With a capacity of more than twenty million tonnes of metallurgical and thermal coal, it employed 1,900-plus people and its revenues exceeded $890 million. Jim Gardiner, as chief operating officer, had some good people working with him. Jim Popowich, who'd been a planning engineer and shift supervisor in Cominco's potash mines, was now Fording's VP of development and Alberta operations. And Allen Hagerman, my young colleague from HBOG, Home, and Interhome Energy, had arrived in 1996 to find a company that was surprisingly sound despite the horrendous challenges of its industry.

"Mining companies in Canada don't make money, and Fording made money," Allen reminisces about his time as chief financial officer there. "Probably the best-run mining company in North America anyway, and they were producing metallurgical coal with mountaintop mining. Which is a gutsy thing to do—to take the top of the mountain off and deal with it once. This is a company that has productivities that are twice as good as their next-door neighbours, using the same equipment and with the same geological conditions. And on a par with the Australians, who are flatland miners who just get to roll their coal down to the ocean.

"This is a company that had taken a three-million-tonne mine and turned it into a ten-million-tonne mine—at the time, the largest metallurgical coal mine in the world. It bought a couple of other mines out of bankruptcy and, by sheer will and expertise and focus on cost and profitability, managed to eke out small profits in bad times and great profits in good times. Mining is an operating-cost business, not really all that capital-intensive, and you have to have that focus on it.

"When I joined in 1996, there were pretty good times, and then we went into some lower prices and things got pretty difficult there in '98 and '99. They started to get a little better in '99 and really turned around in 2000 and 2001.

"As CEO, Jim Gardiner was not laid back. He's tough and opinionated. He runs the show. But Jim does listen and is very, very smart. He's a brilliant mining engineer, a linear thinker, and a very good financial person, too. He was the guy who made Fording so profitable—but he is not an easy man to work for. He is detail-oriented and wants to control all the decision-making."

Bill Stinson once told me that Fording was the best-managed company in the Canadian Pacific conglomerate. So when his successor, David O'Brien, decided to spin off the member companies of the CP group as publicly traded independents in early 2001, the coal operation was considered plum pickings for a takeover.

A year earlier, David had asked me to be chairman of Fording's eight-member board—"this sleepy little company," as he then described it. Now, heading out on our own as a stand-alone venture, we replaced four directors with Jim Popowich, who had become the executive VP; Roger Phillips, who'd been on the CP board and was the about-to-retire head of Regina-based Ipsco, a leading North American steel producer; and two fellows, Harry

Schaefer and Mike Grandin, whom I knew from my previous involvements with other companies.

Harry Schaefer had been CFO of TransAlta, a director of Crestar Energy, and then a director of Gulf Canada Resources when it acquired Crestar and was now vice-chair of TransCanada Corporation. Heavyset, with a high forehead and a deep voice booming from a barrel chest, he was probably the strongest audit-committee chairman in the country, a role he'd play with distinction at Fording during the drama that was soon to unfold.

Mike Grandin, raised in Calgary, is an accountant's son ("That's a frightening thought, eh?" he would ask with a laugh) who's had a pretty checkered career. After studying structural engineering at the University of Alberta and working for Dome Petroleum as a summer student, he designed dams and other large projects for Montreal Engineering and partnered in a small pre-stressed concrete company. He got his MBA at Harvard at age thirty-two and, for a couple of years, worked for the management consulting firm Arthur D. Little in Boston on petroleum projects in Saudi Arabia and New Zealand.

Returning to Canada in 1979, Mike joined the corporate planning and economics group at Dome just as Jack Gallagher and Bill Richards were evaluating Hudson's Bay Oil and Gas. As HBOG's president, I met Mike briefly (and uneventfully) during that traumatic time. He wound up as the first general manager of the subsidiary Dome Canada and then as VP of land for the parent company. Fleeing that crumbling empire in 1986, he ran the Calgary investment banking practice of McLeod, Young & Weir & Co (now Scotia Capital), followed by stints as CEO of Calgary's troubled Sceptre Resources (until it was bought by Canadian Natural Resources) and as vice-chair of investment advisors Midland Walwyn. In 1998, David O'Brien hired him as CFO of Canadian Pacific—where Mike helped unlock the conglomerate's value into spin-off companies—and had recently brought him over to preside briefly at PanCanadian, just as Alberta Energy's Gwyn Morgan came courting and was leading the merger to create EnCana.

These newcomers joined Fording's current directors who, along with me and Jim Gardiner, were ex-chairman Jack Morrish, now chair of Westshore Terminals Income Fund, which operated a major coal terminal near Vancouver, and John Zaozirny, a lawyer with McCarthy Tétrault in Calgary, vice-chair of Canaccord Capital Corporation of Vancouver, and a former minister of energy and natural resources for Alberta. Within a year, we'd bring on Bob Peterson, the long-time chair and CEO of Imperial Oil. Bob is a great friend of mine, a tough little bugger, and one of the smartest guys I've worked with— ever since the time we were on the Interprovincial Pipe Line board and the joint-venture Syncrude board in its early years. And he served as a Petroleum Club director during the time it voted to admit women.

THOSE WERE THE PLAYERS at Fording in late 2002 when we decided to try to protect ourselves from possible corporate marauders. Only a year before, under a headline reading "Fording isn't a lump of coal—it's a keeper," *Globe and Mail* business columnist Brent Jang had neatly summed up the state of the Canadian coal scene and Fording's part in it:

> [A]lthough Canada's coal industry has gone through plenty of tough times since the Asian economic flu of late 1997 reduced demand, Fording's low-cost operations coupled with improved commodity prices are fuelling a rebound.
>
> In mid-1996, the Mitchell family, formerly of Edmonton, sold Luscar to create a publicly traded coal income fund. And in the fall of 1997, Calgary's Mannix family had the Midas touch when it unloaded Manalta Coal, just before the Asian economic flu spread. Manalta also became an income trust fund.
>
> In 1998, Luscar succeeded in its hostile takeover of Manalta. Then earlier this year [2001] Sherritt International

teamed up with the Ontario Teachers' Pension Plan Board in a hostile takeover of Luscar.

Manalta and Luscar were victims of slumping markets for thermal coal, which is used to fuel plants that generate electricity.

Our board was looking at ways to shield Fording from the vultures circling out there—among them, the London-based Rio Tinto Group and heavyweight Australian steelmaker BHP Billiton Ltd., the world's largest diversified resources company. We believed that putting the company into an income trust might be the answer. At the time, the Ontario Securities Commission defined such trusts as follows:

> An income trust is an entity that holds an underlying asset or group of assets. Most of the income these assets generate is distributed to unitholders. In contrast, publicly listed companies usually retain and re-invest their earnings, and sometimes pay out a small portion of earnings to their shareholders as dividends. An income trust structure is formed when, instead of offering its securities directly to the public, an operating entity creates a trust. The trust offers units to the public and uses the proceeds to purchase the common shares and high-yield debt of the operating entity. The combination of the trust's equity and debt holdings allows the income to flow through to unitholders essentially tax-free.... The trust structure avoids the double taxation that comes from combining corporate income tax with shareholders' dividend tax.

In other words, the corporate entity in the trust doesn't pay taxes on its income—the investors do. As a result, the value of the company's shares is inflated and it's therefore much less attractive as a takeover target.

Royalty trusts in the oil and gas sector and real estate investment trusts had first shown up in the 1980s. Income trusts, or "income funds" as they're sometimes called, were relatively new instruments in Canada, and ours would be one of the earliest and biggest. Since the spring of 2002, we'd discussed the idea of creating a trust, consulting with the people at RBC Dominion Securities and Osler, the business-law firm. We figured Fording was a natural for this financial vehicle because it had long-life reserves of coal, was well managed, and, being virtually debt-free, didn't require any financing. At first, Jim Gardiner didn't agree, pointing to our coal competitor Luscar, which had been a limping income fund when Sherritt took it over. (He wasn't alone: In the view of his CFO, Allen Hagerman, "Manalta became a basket case and was bought out by Luscar, who then became a basket case because of the debt they took on. And we had a concern that being a trust contributed to their debt.")

"Jim," I said rather forcefully, "you don't understand it. Luscar had a lot of debt. We have no debt. The board is telling you that this has got to be done—whether you like it or not."

As Harry Schaefer says, "The board was concerned that this [trust concept] hadn't been looked at with some seriousness. In a June meeting, there were very strong marching orders from the board to review this and get the investment bankers to help show it to the management team. It took till the fall before it clicked for them. If you have a management that comes from an operating scenario, in an environment where two other coal trusts have got into financial difficulty, they're not going to destroy their well-oiled machine getting into this funny financial thing. And if they're more *operating* mentality, they don't necessarily understand the financial arithmetic of the trust and its implications. So you have to get them there."

Jim's memory is that John Zaozirny had first started pushing the concept on him, "and we had a mindset that this was not such a good thing. But we realized that circumstances change, and the company was becoming so highly taxable that it looked like a really good model for us." Like me, Jim was also a strong nationalist and wanted to keep the company Canadian at all costs. I was concerned that, unless Fording became a trust, we'd someday get a blowout offer from BHP or Rio Tinto that our shareholders couldn't refuse. And that would leave the Canadian coal industry as a lackey to overseas interests. Yet even then (as I'll explain in the next chapter), I had reservations about the many ramifications of such trusts and their general application to individual companies in various industries.

We code-named the trust scheme "Project Willow," which suggested waving wheat fields and a gentle environment. RBC, our investment bankers, designated their role in it "Project Desert Storm," as if it would be a battleground with all guns blazing. That fall, our plans were proceeding well when suddenly—seemingly out of nowhere—an old buddy and fellow director blindsided us.

Sitting with me on the boards of both MacMillan Bloedel and EnCana, Ian Delaney, the CEO of Sherritt International, had told me, "Despite what people think, coal is the future." And he also remarked that Fording wasn't likely to last long on its own because there were bigger corporations considering it for a takeover—whether friendly or hostile. Mike Grandin remembers that Sherritt had once talked to Canadian Pacific, when it still owned Fording, about acquiring some of its thermal-coal properties. At that point, however, CP was trying to strengthen the coal company before shedding it as an independent and just wasn't interested in doing any such deal. Yet interestingly enough, Jim Gardiner recalls, "Until Sherritt took over Luscar, I had never heard of Sherritt and Delaney and company before." Then in 2001, Sherritt had approached Jim's people about swapping Luscar's metallurgical-coal operations for our thermal-coal holdings but couldn't agree on a deal.

So there was a bit of history between them and us. And I had considered Ian Delaney to be a pal, someone I'd originally got on to the board of EnCana's predecessor Alberta Energy Company. I knew the tall and intense fifty-nine-year-old as a relentlessly independent-minded character—a shrewd financial whiz who'd dropped out of college yet became president of Merrill Lynch Canada (where he was dubbed the "Smiling Barracuda of Bay

Street"). His wife, Kiki, ran Delaney Capital Management, which handled billions of dollars of mutual funds, and some observers (Peter Newman among them) called her and Ian "Toronto's Power Couple," whatever that meant in that town.

This was a guy who went on to work for Peter Munk, the charismatic Canadian who turned the Barrick gold-mining operation into such a bonanza and built his own real estate colossus, TrizecHahn, out of the ashes of the Bronfman family's failed Trizec Corp. Ian was CEO of Munk's holding company, Horsham Corp., and even when the boss he'd idolized actually fired him, allowed graciously that the move was long overdue. Ian had held shares in an old established nickel and copper producer, Sherritt Gordon of Toronto. In 1990, he and a partner from Horsham seized control of the mining company in a bitter proxy battle ("I want your job and I want your company," Ian had told the current president). Their first major move as Sherritt International was to get into bed with Fidel Castro, and over the years, they began nickel and cobalt mining in Cuba as well as investing in petroleum, agriculture, electricity, cellphone operations, and hotels in one of the world's few lingering Communist regimes. They didn't endear themselves to the American government, which forbade trading with Cuba and, therefore, barred Ian and his colleagues from entering the U.S. Of course, that didn't faze him. I liked Ian and all the interesting baggage he brought along with him. And I was pretty sure he liked me.

Why in the hell, then, he ever decided to have Sherritt and the Ontario Teachers' Pension Plan Board launch an unfriendly bid for Fording, I'll never know. (Well, I might eventually: Ian has since said he'll tell me someday over a beer.) For whatever reason, on October 21, 2002, Ian and Teachers' vice-president Brian Gibson collaborated as the Sherritt Coal Partnership II to make an unsolicited all-cash offer of $1.5 billion, or $29 a share, for our company. They were deliberately lowballing us, given that our shares closed on the stock market that day at $31.65 and analysts were saying that our stock should be worth closer to $34—it never did go below $30 after that. At the time, Teachers' had been buying our stock and held about 6 percent of the shares.

That Monday morning, I was at home getting ready to fly to a Fording board meeting in Mexico, where we'd be inspecting a local wollastonite mine. In only a couple of days, we expected to make public our scheme to become an income trust. At 7:30 a.m., Ian and Brian called me to say, "Haskayne, we hate to tell you, old buddy, but later this morning, we're going to make this takeover bid"—and spelled out their plan to announce the hostile tender at what I considered to be a very chintzy price.

"What's your reaction?" they wanted to know.

"It's going to be pretty damn negative," I replied. "If the number even started with a 3 rather than a 2, you might be a helluva lot better off. You're going to have an awful time with us, I can tell you right off the bat."

And that's where the game started. Perhaps Sherritt/Teachers' got word that we were about to do our own trust and wanted to make a pre-emptive strike. Harry Schaefer has also speculated that their opportunistic offer might have come that day because "they had knowledge we were going to have the trust, which would have popped the stock, and they would have had trouble competing against it."

Speaking to reporters later about the aggressively presented bid, Ian said, "There's no particular magic to it—it's certainly a way of forcing a discussion." Upset as hell, I got on the phone to my directors, including Bob Peterson, who'd already flown from Toronto to Los Angeles en route to Mexico.

We cancelled our own flight south and immediately held a board meeting by telephone. After an information session, we gave everyone time to let the details soak in before making a decision. Stan Magidson, our legal counsel, asked us: "What are you going to do?"

Harry Schaefer reminisces, "All our directors are set to go to Mexico that morning to inspect the properties and come back on Wednesday to announce the conversion to an income trust. Then you get this release [from Sherritt/Teachers'] heaved over the gunwales. Our stock had been down at the $21 or $22 level, and we knew that the income trust would probably bring it through $30.

A number of us thought that Sherritt had got wind of what we were doing and wanted to get their offer in before we announced. So we then sat back, being careful to move into the mentality of a special committee of the whole board about how to respond. It's not just saying no. Your job is to make sure you understand the value, where you sit on the offer, make sure you don't eliminate alternatives, and think the course forward. So you had to put aside where you were going, for the moment, and re-evaluate your responsibilities and put this new bid into context: Do we just abandon the income-trust avenue, or is that still a viable alternative? We had to reassess from square one our due diligence."

We decided to announce the creation of Fording Trust in the next few hours and to ask our shareholders to exchange their stock on a one-for-one basis. Once we did, some analysts decided our shares could be worth up to $40, which made Ian's offer look even paltrier. As Stan says, "We went out with a strong press release. We know that it was a great surprise to the other side. Nobody could believe you would have an income-trust announcement the same day the offer was made. I'll call it good luck, and fortuitous, but maybe there was an element of being prepared, as well."

Immodest as it sounds, we'd deliberately put into place a strong slate of directors, and I considered myself a strong, independent chairman—together, we felt highly capable of handling any kind of takeover attempt, even one from the combative Ian Delaney. We delegated assignments to different board members with special expertise. At every meeting, we'd have in-camera sessions without senior executives present to deal with the inevitable tensions that arise between board and management during a takeover attempt. Our skills and resolve would get tested over the next four months. Looking back on what we had to face, Stan recollects, "There were seven value-enhancing propositions from bidders to consider, numerous disclosure documents, and I recall twenty-two board meetings. One meeting went about twelve hours with an open telephone line because there were negotiations occurring in Toronto and we had people on standby—it was that dynamic."

Ian and his colleagues soon came to meet me in Calgary to discuss their offer. But at first they were maddeningly fuzzy about the details. "Lookit, you guys," I said, "let us know exactly what the hell it is, because we're about to create our own trust."

In early November, our board made it known that the company was looking for alternatives to Sherritt's initial cash offer. As the *National Post* reported, "Fording executives had come under fire from investors for standing by a plan to reorganize the firm into an income trust, rather than seek a friendly bid to combat the hostile offer." But, as the *Edmonton Journal* commented, "if the takeover battle for Fording heats up, it's clear that the big foreign players hold all the aces. Their deep pockets and lower cost of capital are huge advantages in any bidding war. That's bad news for Canada's struggling mining sector, which over the past two decades has been relegated to second-tier status on the world stage."

Not long after, I got a call from Norman Keevil, chairman and controlling shareholder of Teck Cominco Ltd. of Vancouver, formed from the recent merger of the two companies to become the world's biggest producer of zinc. Among its $5 billion in assets, it also had copper and gold mines as well as metallurgical-coal operations near ours—the Bullmoose and the big Elkview mine, the fifth-largest in the world. The son of a geophysics professor-turned-tycoon, Norman Jr. was a geophysicist, too, and inherited his father's company, stage-managing Teck's mightily profitable investment in the Voisey's Bay nickel discovery in Labrador. I was aware of Norm's reputation as a gentleman in an ungentle industry. He'd recently been honoured by five hundred guests at a gala dinner with eight speakers, including B.C. Premier Gordon Campbell and Canaccord Capital's Peter Brown.

Now he was saying that while we didn't really know one another, "You're hanging in my boardroom."

"What does that mean?" I asked.

It turned out that he had a *Canadian Business* chart rating various boards of directors of Canadian companies. I was on three of the best twenty-five boards—Manulife, CIBC, and TransCanada

Corp.—and Teck Cominco ranked among the worst (likely because of its structure of multiple voting shares that gave their holders the right to more votes than warranted by the amount of capital the stock represented).

My recollection is that there was another voice on the phone that day, a power hitter by the name of Jim Pattison. I'd got to know this compact dynamo while serving on the MacMillan Bloedel board in Vancouver, where The Jim Pattison Group has its headquarters. Of course, Jimmy's reputation was well known to me: one of North America's wealthiest entrepreneurs, owning everything from supermarkets, car dealerships, and radio and TV stations to packaging, sign, and news-distribution companies (and even the Ripley's Believe It or Not! chain of tourist attractions). But his most relevant connection to the matter at hand was his controlling share of Westshore Terminals in Delta, B.C., which shipped out nearly three-quarters of Canada's seaborne coal exports—Fording's among them. And the head of Westshore now was Bill Stinson, the boss of Canadian Pacific who'd welcomed me so warmly to the Fording board all those years ago.

They had my attention.

"Dick," Norm continued, "I think we might have a proposal that might help out." He wanted me to meet him and his new CEO, David Thompson, whom I didn't know.

Were these our white knights? And *Canadian* ones, at that? At that point, our backs were to the wall as the Sherritt/Teachers' offer seemed to be winning the war of public perception, appearing to be the best possible deal for our shareholders. "Well," I told him, "we have a critical meeting at 10:00 a.m. tomorrow, and if you have something better, let me know because we don't have much time. Make a counter-offer, or do something."

So, if memory serves me, Norm, Jimmy, and David all flew from Vancouver that very day in the Pattison jet and came to my office. David proved to be a solid guy with a chartered-accountancy background, reputed in Canadian mining circles to have "the sharpest pencil in the business." As a former senior VP and CFO at Teck, he was Norm's closest advisor ("Keevil doesn't breathe without talking to

Thompson," people observed). All in all, a pretty impressive bunch—who were about to change the dynamics of the deal in the making.

When we began formal talks on November 27, things got off to a bumpy start. They wanted to do a partnership with Fording, which made no sense to me: "Why don't you just take shares in the trust? We'll put a fair value on your big [Elkview] coal mine, and you'll end up with a very big interest in Fording." The problem for them was that sort of an arrangement would have meant paying taxes because they'd be taking liquid securities. And, as Harry points out, "Under the pressure of the bid, Teck Cominco talked to Fording about consolidating all their mines in the valley—and there was a tussle as to who'd operate those mines." Another sticking point was that the companies were competitors, and at times, in certain areas and with certain people, there was a lack of respect between them that had to get resolved. So the proposed deal was complicated from day one. We all decided to consider our options and reconvene as soon as possible.

The following day, Jim Gardiner, Allen Hagerman, and I met in my office with Ian Delaney and his CFO, Jowdat Waheed, to present what was supposed to be a more acceptable bid for Fording than their original one. I basically booted them out, saying, "Delaney, it is *un*acceptable." During the negotiations that followed, Gwyn Morgan recalls how Ian and I would excuse ourselves at different times from our directors' chairs during EnCana board meetings to take telephone calls about the progress of the deal-making. "It was like *The Gong Show*," Gwyn says.

By December 4, after much back-and-forthing, Fording had arrived at a complex agreement with Teck Cominco and the Westshore Terminals Income Fund. It was valued at $1.7 billion and $34 a Fording share—$5 more than Ian's group had been offering. We'd combine our coal businesses in a new income trust that would give Fording shareholders a maximum payout of $795 million, or a combination of cash and trust units if all shareholders elected to receive cash, and more than 70 percent of the units. Teck and Westshore would contribute $540 million in cash to the trust, while we would remove Fording debt of $255 million from the trust. We now called this an enhanced income trust because it included Teck's terrific Elkview mine as part of the package.

But in this hectic corporate tennis game, Ian Delaney kept the ball in the air during the walkup to the Christmas season. At his urging, we agreed to host a meeting of all the major players with Jim and me: Ian, Brian Gibson, Norm Keevil, and David Thompson. When we gathered across the hall from my office in Ted Newall's larger boardroom, they were soon asking Jim to take his leave. I wasn't happy with this request, and Jim was insulted, but they all insisted. The rest of us then met for several hours— and the reason for the absence of Fording's CEO at the session was quickly apparent. Ian had been buttering up Norm and David and supporting their idea of having Teck Cominco as the management of a merged company. At one stage, even David got embarrassed about Ian's smooth talk and said something like, "It's nice of you to say all this, but I can't accept any more compliments."

Nothing concrete emerged from that sixteen-hour session. On December 17, we put out a release advising Fording shareholders not to give their proxy votes to Sherritt/Teachers'. "We don't have a formal offer from Sherritt," I said. "We have only the information in their announcement, which leaves a number of important questions unanswered."

The next day, their offer finally surfaced as a 340-page document. The bid, worth an estimated $1.8 billion by their reckoning, at first glance seemed a better deal. Until you read the fine print, as Stan explains: "The $34 offer [of the proposed Fording/Teck/Westshore trust] did have the desired effect: Sherritt/Teachers' then announced their new deal, bumping up from $29 to a $35 cash offer with a unit of an income trust—but which didn't have the Elkview mine from Teck and did have the thermal-coal properties of Fording being sold to Sherritt/Teachers' and not being available to the Fording shareholders. There was a lot of dispute about the value of that trust unit."

In an initial release to the media, which was heavily lawyered and contained language Richard Francis Haskayne has hardly ever used in public, I was properly scathing: "Shareholders should not be fooled by the new offer. Its bulk does not hide the fact that the offer is based on questionable assumptions and is inaccurate in a number of areas.... In my twenty-five years as a corporate director in Canada, I have never been presented with a more questionable document than the new Sherritt offer. It is a 'smoke-and-mirrors offer' that provides a little more cash offset by a lot less unit value."

Among other things, it would transfer $210 million in value from Fording shareholders. Two days before Christmas, we sent a mail-out asking them to reject the bid, and a week later, gave them a more formal response in a circular. Harry was the board's quality-control guy, acting almost like a member of the management team during the negotiations: "We were quite offended by what Sherritt/Teachers' had in the store window and what the reality was. They said they were buying at $35, but on page 89 of the trust deed, they were issuing shares to themselves at $28.41. In addition, they were swapping out our thermal coals at the same price as their metallurgical coals—and ours had earnings, and theirs didn't. Our circular to them pointed all this out."

In another news release I'd taken a shot at Teachers': "Given the strong stand the Ontario Teachers' Pension Plan Board has taken on governance issues in the past, we were surprised to see the approach they are supporting. In particular, their refusal to provide an appropriate amount of time for our shareholders to consider their offer." Just a day before Christmas, Justice Sal LoVecchio of the Alberta Court of Queen's Bench had embarrassed Sherritt/Teachers' into extending their January 6 deadline for the takeover offer.

Throughout all this, as we were to discover later, Teachers' really hadn't wanted to steal Fording at a bargain-basement price. Its vision, under the leadership of Brian Gibson, was to do a deal that would consolidate and strengthen the Canadian coal industry. I wrote a letter to Brian that expressed surprise at the terms of the counter-offer and what we considered its lack of proper disclosure. As Stan says, "We were going into a board meeting about January 2 with legal papers ready to go that would have blown the

Sherritt/Teachers' proposal out of the water as being illegal in structure from the perspective of the SEC [the U.S. Securities and Exchange Commission, which administers federal securities laws for companies operating in the U.S.]." One concern was that American shareholders might get all the cash being offered because the trust units that were part of the deal might not be issued in the U.S. for several months—which would leave Canadian investors holding only those units but no cash.

We didn't have to take any legal action. Harry says, "People might say our letter to Teachers' had no effect, but piecing things together, we discovered that they hadn't known about some of the things in the earlier offer. So they were coming apart from their partners 'cause that's not the way they wanted to play. Brian Gibson now became clear about what Sherritt was doing—and their interests were not the same.

"Then over the transom on January 6 [2003] came a very good counter-proposal from Sherritt/Teachers' that got rid of some of the more shabby pieces of the transaction. Brian was starting to come back into the deal with his bigger vision and the wonderful prize of putting all the metallurgical mines together."

Stan remembers, "We saw another raise by Sherritt/Teachers'—they were still at $35 and a trust unit, but now they were going to allow for a lot more cash in the transaction." This revised offer would pay out as much as $965 million in cash (an increase from $850 million) and extend the guarantee for cash distribution to the end of 2004 instead of 2003. If all shareholders elected to take the $35-a-share cash option, they'd receive $20 a share (up from $17.63) and 0.429 of a right to a trust unit. There was no mention then of including Teck Cominco's assets in the deal.

I kept wondering if we could somehow put all the companies together and create a global force in the coal industry. As Stan says now, the turning point probably came "when each party thought that there was enough uncertainty that they might lose out on something—when we'd created the requisite tensions necessary to get everyone agreeing to a deal." Sherritt's much better bid now triggered serious talks during the second week of January in

Toronto, where Ian and Brian were based. They were in the meetings along with David Thompson, Jim Gardiner, Allen Hagerman, me, and Michael Korenberg, Jimmy Pattison's right-hand man, representing Westshore's interests.

Backing the negotiators was the usual armada of legal and financial advisors that such a merger requires. Sherritt/Teachers' had five key lawyers from the prestigious Torys firm in Toronto (and, the *National Post* added, "a cast that exceeds *The Ten Commandments*, the Cecil B. DeMille version"). Teck Cominco had five main counsel from equally prominent Lang Michener as well as their in-house lawyer. We had mergers-and-acquisitions expert Frank Turner, a partner in the Calgary office of the highly respected Osler, leading a group that included Stan Magidson on corporate and M&A matters, Chris Murray on income trusts, and Don Watkins and Jack Silverson on tax. Not to mention all those investment advisors: Goldman Sachs and BMO Nesbitt Burns for Sherritt, CIBC World Markets for Tech Cominco, and RBC Dominion Securities for us.

After long days and nights fuelled by fast food at Osler's office, I was getting tired and stretched tight along with the others who were trying to put the finishing touches on a restructured income trust. Finally, with everyone compromising a little, it looked like we'd reached an all-party agreement. Allen remembers being in the boardroom of the Sherritt headquarters with David, who was a pivotal player in shaping the transaction. They'd been sitting around since early afternoon to talk about the deal with Ian—who had a comfortable suite upstairs where he often retreated, sipping wine and catching naps.

I was with the negotiating group at about 2:00 a.m. the next morning when Ian called me up to his office for what I thought would be a last-minute bit of bargaining.

Instead, he said, "Dick, I have to tell you: The deal is off, we're not going forward."

Thunderstruck, I just lost it, waving my finger at him and exploding: "Ian, this is bullshit! We've cobbled this deal together, and I'm telling you that what you're doing now is dishonest. And I'll tell you, we'll let the world know how you guys are reacting."

When Ian announced his decision to the others, David Thompson joined me in lecturing him about the merits of the deal.

To this day, I don't quite know why Ian was backing off. Maybe he'd got cold feet because of the magnitude and all the ramifications of the merger. When I came downstairs, obviously enraged and ready to walk out, Stan said, "Dick, you'd better cool off down here. Are you prepared to go to the mat on that and give up a triple play?"

"I don't care. I'm not going to put up with that bullshit."

At that point, Brian Gibson stepped up to the plate. I've always got on well with the highly responsible head of Teachers'. Calming me down, he said the deal was *not* off and asked for another immediate meeting—and that's where cooler heads prevailed and Ian agreed to do the deal, after all.

Jim Gardiner was so concerned for me, worrying about my physical condition and the stress I'd been under, that he quietly used his American Express card to book a flight that would get me back to Calgary early that morning. The terms of the deal were made public on January 13.

A long time later, on a panel discussion about mergers and acquisitions with Stan and Harry at the University of Calgary, I said, "In every deal I've ever been involved in, personal relationships either make them happen or tear them apart. Keep these relationships at a high level. It's one thing to beat one another like hell in a corporate scene, but don't get into personal animosities.... If you don't have a good personal chemistry, or you don't respect the other person, the deals won't work or will fall apart at the worst time." In the end, the respect that Ian and I held for one another had carried us through that last-minute crisis.

A couple of years later, while contacting him about some human resources committee matters involving EnCana, I remarked, "Jesus, Delaney, I read in the paper this morning that you're trying to take over Stelco. You're trying to do the same thing you did to us."

"Oh yeah, we are," he said, "but it's much easier this time— for two reasons. Number one: We don't have to deal with you. And number two: They're broke and you weren't."

We continue to be good friends. Not long ago, he invited me to join him on a trip to visit some of Sherritt's properties in Cuba. There's an old Cuban saying that, translated, means that you can show courtesy and courage at the same time. I like to think that, despite our differences in the Fording merger, we've both demonstrated those qualities during our long business and personal relationship.

If I drew any lesson from the Fording affair, it would be that in any takeover attempt, it's wiser to go in friendly first and try to make a deal. There's nothing to lose—you can always turn hostile later, if you must. But if you don't have to, you've saved yourself an enormous amount of time, money, and hard feelings. A good recent example of what can go wrong is the breakdown of the proposed $17.8-billion "made-in-Canada" merger between Teck Cominco and the mammoth silver miner Inco Ltd. Industry observers say the chemistry between Teck's new CEO, Don Lindsay, and Inco's Scott Hand was sour from the start of Teck's unfriendly takeover bid. Not surprisingly, Inco (where David O'Brien was on the board) sought another suitor, which turned out to be the American mining giant Phelps Dodge Corp. And, as a result, Canadian industry lost two important senior Tigers.

OUR SHAREHOLDERS LOVED the creation of the Fording Canadian Coal Trust, approving the now-friendly deal by more than 99 percent at a special meeting in Calgary. I joked to them about the overheated language of our press-release war by describing the proposal as "the improved/enhanced/superior/alternative plan." It was a $1.8-billion agreement that gave Fording shareholders the options of $35 cash per share, to a maximum of $1.05 billion; or one unit of the Fording Trust per share, to a maximum of about 21.4 million units; or a combination of cash and units to those ceilings. Unitholders would also be entitled to a special distribution of $1.48 per unit in the following two quarterly distributions.

It was a convoluted deal, even for someone who'd been involved from the beginning, as I was. Harry Schaefer says I'm the big-picture man and he's the detail guy, as he was while keeping watch on Fording's interests. And, in the final analysis, we did all right on the transaction. The ownership breakdown had Teck contributing its metallurgical coal assets and $125 million in return for a 35 percent stake in what was called the Elk Valley Coal Partnership. The other 65 percent was Fording Trust's, in which Fording investors held 38.8 percent; the Sherritt Coal Partnership II (Sherritt and Teachers') contributed $375 million and held 22.7 percent, in which Teachers' itself held 6.7 percent; Teck Cominco contributed $150 million for 9.1 percent; Westshore contributed its coal terminal and $150 million for 9.1 percent; and two Sherritt subsidiaries—Luscar and CONSOL of Canada—contributed their joint-venture coal assets for 6.8 percent. (CONSOL, with its parent company in Pittsburgh, had proved to be a frustrating nitpicker during the negotiations, and in Mike Grandin's words, this "caused us a huge amount of agony—they wanted the deal done precisely their way.") Oh, and the Sherritt partnership bought Fording's thermal-coal assets for $225 million.

The collective cost of doing all this deal-making—from mailing out all ninety thousand shareholders' circulars at one time to paying the pricey fees of the lawyers and investment advisors—was about $100 million. Fording swallowed the expenses of Teck Cominco and Westshore as well as its own.

The media hailed the merger as "a victory for all parties," which would establish "one of the world's most formidable mining firms." And with the approval of the shareholders and then the Competition Bureau, my work was done. It was time to move on after seventeen years on the board, to step down from yet another chairmanship, and to step away from its pressures of time and emotional and physical energy. Time to have travel adventures and to relax more with Lois and our friends. And to give myself space to think and talk about, and perhaps even act upon, the three themes that seemed to have been looming so large in my life and career: private philanthropy, business integrity, and Northern Tigers.

But who to replace me as chair of the Fording Canadian Coal Trust and ensure its future as a thriving Tiger? Mike Grandin hadn't been actively involved in the negotiations, but as a conscientious and informed director, he had kept a watching brief on their progress. And the chairmanship somehow seemed a fitting follow-up for the man who, as Canadian Pacific's CFO, had helped create the conditions that let Fording fly out on its own from the CP nest.

During the last days of the bargaining with Teck and Sherritt, Mike had been off on a month-long holiday in New Zealand with his wife, Elaine. He was just enjoying his second week there when our board members made a conference call to him in his hotel room. "I'm stepping down," I told him. "We need to have a new chairman, and Michael, by the way, we've discussed it—and we think you are it." Because we were about to send out a press release announcing the new board, we had to name the chair. When Mike put the phone down, he turned to his wife and said, "Well, you'll never guess what they asked me to do."

He accepted and took over a mixed bag of consolidated companies. At first, the different corporate cultures led to conflicts at the senior levels, especially since Teck Cominco was now considered to be the managing partner of the trust. In 2004, a year after the merger, Jim Gardiner retired and Jim Popowich succeeded him as president, with Mike as CEO as well as chairman. When China went from exporting eight to ten million tonnes of coal a year to having to import about half that amount, Fording's profits soared as coal prices more than doubled—to $122 (U.S.) per tonne. In 2006, as the Chinese demand ebbed, the average selling price was forecast at $107.

Today, Jim Gardiner looks back on the dramatic change in the companies that were hived off from Canadian Pacific Ltd. and says, "I give David O'Brien a lot of credit for letting the companies get out there on their own and spread their wings." David looks at Fording and says that while its market capitalization is a seventh of EnCana's, it has been hugely successful. If it's not yet a Northern Tiger according to his definition—"powerhouses that are sufficiently large and diversified that they can compete around the world"—it's a big and strong player in its particular niche. He prefers to call Fording "a Canadian-based global champion."

borrowed a local horse to play in the Paris Open. And they know that when marrying Tara, a lawyer, he imported an elderly monsignor from Calgary to perform the church service in romantic Rome (after my wife Lois kept urging them to get hitched, for heaven's sake).

I'm one of his much-older friends. In fact, I knew his father before knowing him, when Ken Mathison and I grew up across the back lane from each other in Gleichen. His dad worked in our butcher shop and then became a manger in Burns packing plants. Ron occasionally swept the floor of our meat market long after I'd left home. Later, when he was deciding what to do at the University of Manitoba, Ken told him I'd done all right with my chartered accountant's training, so that's what Ron studied instead of taking law. He says I'm kind of a proxy father when his own isn't around, and over the years, we've become so close that he sometimes visits to ask personal advice. He did that in 2002, on the day the Scripps Clinic called him in Calgary to report that an aortic aneurysm was threatening his life and he had to consult a local cardiologist immediately (I got him in to see my specialist, and he recovered nicely from an operation in Houston to replace the aorta in his heart). It's not just a one-way street: For instance, when I needed help with evaluating land I was donating to the U of C, Ron had his in-house expert appraise it and suggest how I should structure the deal. And, most important of all, as someone who never had a son, I value my close relationship with a smart and caring man who's a couple of decades younger than me

What few people know about Ron Mathison is that he was a key silent partner in one of the more extraordinary success stories in the Oil Patch: Canadian Natural Resources, our second-largest gas producer. Ron was among a small group of investors who, in 1988, saw the possibilities in a bankrupt oil and mining company, operating only in Alberta with nine employees and a measly market capitalization of about $1 million. Among Canadian Natural's major financiers were Murray Edwards, a Regina chartered accountant's son and commerce grad who wound up doing deals at Peters & Co. in Calgary; fellow lawyer Jim Grenon, also at

Peters; and engineer Allan Markin, who'd just left the presidency of Poco Petroleum after its stock collapsed. This was at a time when most of the smart money was saying the oil business was on the decline. But Al became chairman of the restructured company, which bought land from majors such as Texaco and turned into a stock market darling as Dome Petroleum had.

Unlike Dome, CNQ (as the market calls it) has survived and flourished, with Murray taking an active part in the operation. It went from a standing start to becoming today's giant—with 2,500 employees producing 530,000-plus barrels of oil equivalent per day from operations in North America, the North Sea, and West Africa. Part of its growth resulted from building on the very high multiples of its share price to issue more stock or to make more acquisitions. CNQ is valued at about $22 billion and seems fated to go nowhere but up since announcing in late 2005 that it would bet $25 billion on expanding its presence in the Alberta oil sands. If its ambitious plan succeeds, it could become one of the world's biggest independent producers. Ron retains a sizable investment in the company.

The point of all this is that Canada needs more Ron Mathisons and Murray Edwards and more homegrown, domestically based Northern Tigers like CNQ, EnCana, and Fording.

Ron was all of forty-eight the day we were chin-wagging in his boardroom in the HSBC Building. Our conversation roamed across the range of Alberta and Canadian business, including the hot-house environment in Calgary that has created so many major companies, in and outside of the petroleum industry.

"Penn West is another one that was in Murray's sphere," Ron remarked. Murray Edwards chaired and was a prominent investor in what became Penn West Energy Trust, the major conventional oil and natural gas income trust in North America (ranked forty-sixth by profit, ahead of Enbridge, CP Rail, and Barrick Gold, in *Report on Business* magazine's most recent survey of Canadian companies). "It started from a market capitalization of about two or three million dollars, and it's now in the $6-billion range, you know."

"And that's not just due to today's high energy prices," I noted. "These companies have grown in a time when oil and gas prices were down and these guys were smart enough to capitalize on it."

Both of us agreed that such accomplishments haven't been limited to the petroleum industry. Murray, as an example, is chairman of Magellan Aerospace of Toronto (ranked nineteenth among Canada's largest tech companies), which makes aeroengine and aerostructure components as well as advanced products for military and space markets. "By most standards, Magellan is a dramatic success," Ron said, "and Murray also has a ceramics protection firm that makes armoured materials and has done extraordinarily well." Part owner of the Calgary Flames, he's also the major shareholder in Resorts of the Canadian Rockies, which owns the Lake Louise ski area and eight other ski resorts.

There are seven major railways in North America, and two of them—our biggest, CN and CP—are Northern Tigers. In 2005, CN's profits, which are higher than any of its North American competitors, rose by 24 percent to $1.6 billion as Canada's global trade exploded, especially with Asian customers. That was also CP's busiest and most successful year ever as its profits increased 32 percent to a record $543 million. The companies' share values have also hit all-time highs.

In the financial world, Manulife (as I've already explained) and at least the Big Five Banks are certainly Tigers. Collectively, they've posted better stock market performances than their counterparts in any other country.

We boast technological giants with a global reach. Our largest is the plane and train manufacturer Bombardier, which despite its struggles over the years, had a $249-million profit in '05, helped by higher sales of business jets, where it remains the world leader. Research In Motion (RIM), despite being sidetracked by its long patent fight over the BlackBerry handheld wireless device, held its grip on three-quarters of the U.S. market. SNC-Lavalin Group Inc., the engineering and construction multinational, has projects in more than one hundred countries. Our major telephone companies, Montreal-based Bell Canada and Vancouver-based Telus, have taken on Tiger proportions and remain strong despite the Harper government's decision to prevent them from becoming income trusts to avoid corporate taxes.

Mining? Alcan is the second-largest aluminum producer on the planet; the largest in food flexible, pharmaceutical, and cosmetics packaging; and a leading metal trader. Peter Munk's Barrick Gold recently took over Vancouver's Placer Dome and became the world's prime gold producer.

Even our food manufacturers stand tall beyond Canadian borders. The largest, Maple Leaf Foods, the Toronto-based meat processor and animal feed supplier, exports to nearly eighty nations and has operations in North America, Mexico, the United Kingdom, Europe, and southeast Asia. Chairman Wallace McCain's brother Harrison is co-founder of New Brunswick's McCain Foods, the next largest, one of our biggest private companies with $5.7 billion in annual sales and twenty-four thousand employees. It's the world's major producer of frozen French fries, which it sells along with other food products in 110-plus countries.

One of Canada's strengths has been our emergence as an energy superpower ever since the petroleum industry began recovering in the mid-1990s, a decade after Ottawa finally stopped influencing oil prices. Oil and gas companies now make up nearly 30 percent of the value of the TSX—and the effects are being seen from sea to sea to sea. Even those provinces without booming oil and gas fields share in the $27 billion the industry paid to governments in 2005. In Alberta, the oil sands—the world's second-largest deposit of crude—promise an economic impact of a $1.4-trillion bonanza in a province that is already debt-free and rolling in more money than the Klein administration seemed to know what to do with (I was disappointed when it distributed $400 in resource-rebate Ralphbucks to every Albertan).

The top Canadian-controlled energy companies (in order of recent market capitalization) are EnCana, Suncor Energy, Canadian Natural Resources, Petro-Canada, Talisman Energy,

Nexen, Canadian Oil Sands Trust, and Penn West Energy Trust. Two of them—PetroCan and Suncor—are among Canada's five biggest integrated oil companies, whose profits rose by more than a third in 2005 to $9.6 billion.

There's another brand of companies that—despite their lineage and the fact that each has a single major foreign shareholder— might be considered at least honorary Northern Tigers. In the Oil Patch, three of the most obvious giants in size and reputation are Imperial Oil, Shell Canada, and Husky Energy. The first two are wholly owned subsidiaries of Exxon in the U.S. and Royal Dutch Shell in Holland, respectively, while Husky's controlling shareholder is Li Ka-Shing of Hong Kong. But for all intents and purposes, they act like the best domestic corporations, maintaining their operational headquarters in Calgary with independently run boards of directors and social and cultural consciences that seem unmistakably Canadian in cast. Few people would dispute, for instance, that Imperial has been one of Canada's finest corporate citizens in its largesse to the communities in which it operates. This long-time resident (here since 1880) donates in disproportionately high volumes to the usual charitable causes. But it also has a history of fostering Canadian culture—everything from its no-strings financing of an early attempt to save one of the country's most esteemed print publications, *Saturday Night* magazine, to its recent $4-million gift to the Glenbow Museum, the largest in the Calgary institution's history.

And that's just a sampling of Canada's corporate champions, so many of whom have emerged in only the last ten and even five years.

I'VE LOOSELY DEFINED SUCH TIGERS as Canadian businesses with the strength and agility to withstand takeover attempts from foreigners. Two of their obvious attributes, of course, can be size and global reach—as David O'Brien, EnCana's chair, explains: "Northern Tigers are powerhouses that are sufficiently large and diversified that they can compete around the world." Or as his former CEO, Gwyn Morgan, describes them, "Canadian-headquartered companies that can play offence against the best in the world."

Despite those definitions, EnCana itself has stepped back from operating around the globe to concentrate on its North American assets. Which leads to my qualification that Tigers don't necessarily have to rank among the biggest and most diversified performers on the world stage. They can simply be strong enough to flourish primarily in their own domestic markets. Though Mike Grandin chairs Fording, which thrives because of its international sales, he says, "I don't think this has to be true for every company. With a lot of companies—and there's all kinds of evidence of this for large and small companies—your ability to create value is more local than global. There are industries where, if you have a large share of a very large market, you may not generate the best margins because you may be number five or ten in a market that's supporting twenty or thirty competitors. But in a more localized market—and you can define 'market' in terms other than geography—maybe you have the largest market share, and therefore, you really do have a competitive advantage and generate much higher returns on invested capital. So I don't think every company has to be a global leader."

On the other hand, Talisman Energy is one of Canada's most international petroleum giants, with production operations in the U.S., the North Sea, Norway, Algeria, Trinidad and Tobago, Indonesia, Malaysia, and Vietnam (about 40 percent of its natural-gas reserves lie in Asia). In 2005, it paid $2.5 billion cash for London-based Paladin Resources PLC and its holdings in the North Sea while selling some of its own wells there and a parcel of non-core oil properties in Canada—where it remains an active natural-gas producer in Alberta and B.C. Throughout the 1990s, CEO Jim Buckee oversaw about $4 billion in acquisitions to turn BP Canada, the former British Petroleum branch plant, into Canada's largest oil producer by volume.

Jim has always had a global view of things. Born in England, graduating from the University of Western Australia with an honours science degree and then getting his PhD in astrophysics at Oxford University, he worked for Shell, Burmah Oil, and BP's parent company in Norway, Alaska, and London before coming to Canada. Dr. Jim Buckee is now a Canadian citizen.

When he arrived in Canada, onshore petroleum prospects in North America were considered to be mature, he reflects: "We used to say go deep, heavy, or ugly—into seawater, heavy oil, or nasty politics. To limit yourself to onshore North America, as EnCana has done, makes things unnecessarily tough for yourself. Suncor's different because it's got a particular line of business—and incidentally, I'd say one quite hard to replicate, too." In 1992, "the price of gas was $1 or $1.50 MCF and oil was at $17 or $18 a barrel. The basin here is very mature for conventional oil, and the price of gas was very low. So when we were left independent, given my experience and other people's in what's now called Talisman, the obvious thing to do was to get an international footing to get to less mature areas and have access to bigger prizes. We've hired people who like doing that and, over the period, developed a lot of in-house expertise, both commercial and technical. As for being Canadian—first of all, the flag is a good entree, and secondly, we have access to a lot of geologists, geophysicists, engineers, and so on who we can deploy around the world.

"The other Canadian idea that we exported was having large working interests [in other countries] and controlling everything. When we went to the North Sea, we did in most cases a series of deals until we got 100 percent or near enough in all our oil fields. And that's proved to be very successful."

Now he realizes that Talisman is a tempting target for foreign buyers, possibly even the hungry China National Offshore Oil Corp. Staying independent is important to Jim: "We have choice of where and how much to invest and the timing of it. If you're a branch office, you have to go and beg for capital. When Talisman goes to various countries, it's *us*—you have to talk to us because we call the shots. If we were owned by something else, that wouldn't be true. And we facilitate a lot of other people coming to Canada, too—like the Indian energy minister—and having the

World Petroleum Congress in Calgary. A lot of the reason they come here is because they want us to invest in their countries—us and other people who invest internationally. They come through here and want to make friends, want to be allies. The Chinese are big friends."

At this writing, while Talisman has been approached by a couple of foreign corporations about a possible takeover, none has ever made a concrete offer. "In 2005," Jim points out, "Talisman's share price nearly doubled so [shareholders would] have been silly to have accepted any premium at the beginning of that year. A 20 to 25 percent premium wouldn't have done it—we did much better going with the market."

In defining a Northern Tiger, it might be a surprise to learn that many of us diehard nationalistic business people don't necessarily believe that a domestically based corporate champ has to be owned by a majority of Canadians. The problem is that Canada doesn't offer a large enough pool of homegrown investors to support large enterprises. Gwyn Morgan again, speaking generally as well as specifically about EnCana, says, "You can't build a huge, publicly owned enterprise without a lot of support internationally. So our independence as a company depends upon multinational investors. Because otherwise, our stock will not be priced competitively versus the value of the assets—and we will disappear.... [But] there is nothing that any of those shareholders do that directs management of the operation or headquarters. What they do is provide capital for us to take advantage of the market." In other words, having a broadly based range of investors, foreign or domestic—and not being beholden to a single influential block of shares—can ensure a Canadian company's independence.

However, the big danger is when a company is taken over entirely by a controlling shareholder and its headquarters is exported from this country. Other nations have similar problems, including the United States. Here in Canada, with a climate of low interest rates and private equity firms hungry to spend an excess of cash, billions of dollars have been exchanged in hostile mergers and acquisitions of our domestic corporations. In recent years, we've lost icons such as Dofasco, Molson, CP Ships, Hudson's Bay Co., and newer ones such as the B.C. gas giant Terasen Inc., industry-leading winemaker Vincor International, Trimark Financial Corp. (Canada's sixth-largest mutual fund company), Zenon Environmental (a global pioneer in water and wastewater treatment), Geac Computer Corp. (our largest software venture), and ID Biomedical Corp. (a developer of vaccines, contracted by Ottawa to prepare for a possible flu pandemic). In too many cases, their fates as Canada-centred enterprises remain in doubt. But at least one story has had a happy ending: A Saudi prince had taken over Fairmont Hotels & Resorts, but in the autumn of 2006, Oxford Properties Corp.—the property wing of the Ontario Municipal Employees Retirement Fund—returned seven of Fairmont's prestige hotels (including Jasper Park Lodge and the Banff Springs Hotel) to Canadian ownership.

What does it really matter if we lose strong domestic companies to foreign buyers? The question was raised anew in mid-2006 when Phelps Dodge of Phoenix made its abortive double play for both Inco and Falconbridge. Teck's Norm Keevil, whose own bid for Inco had failed, said Inco's Scott Hand "sold out Canada for his own purposes." In my view, despite the debates on both sides, the most important factor is where the head office is located and management decisions are made. It's not just an issue of flag-waving patriotism. It's the possibility of losing the vital infrastructure and support systems surrounding corporate headquarters that make a community and a country thrive. You become a branch-office nation. (How much can a headquarters matter to an individual community? My friend Jim Shaw of Shaw Cable pointed out to me that following the 1995 move of the corporate HQ from Edmonton, Calgary has gained about 1,800 jobs related specifically to running the relocated head office.)

As the details of the proposed Phelps Dodge deal surfaced, I was pleasantly surprised to read an editorial in the *Globe and Mail* that criticized Finance Minister James Flaherty for his offhand comment defending the merger: "I haven't heard any suggestions they are going to move the mines." It's true that, as Canadians, we own our natural resources and benefit through royalties on their extraction—whether by foreign or domestic companies—and we should be most concerned with having them developed efficiently and with the biggest payback to the nation. Both the current Conservative government and its Liberal predecessor have encouraged such investment as being crucial to overall growth and more jobs. And sometimes even Canadian subsidiaries of foreign companies have developed indigenous expertise that's exported to other countries, profiting our home economy.

Yet in its editorial, the newspaper—which is not exactly a fan of government involvement in free enterprise—urged Ottawa to use the *Investment Canada Act* to review the Phelps Dodge takeover for its long-term net benefits to Canada:

> The head offices for Inco and Falconbridge will move to Phoenix, Ariz. The new company will be traded in Canada but its primary listing will be in New York. The two mining giants will no longer be included in the benchmark S&P/TSX composite index. As a TD Newcrest report observed this week, the loss to a U.S. buyer "is a severe blow to the relevance of Canada's equity markets."

There's another factor—a financial one of great import to Canadian taxpayers—that needs to be considered in any discussion about losing our corporations to non-Canadian acquisitors. Many foreign companies burden their branch plants in other countries with debt. The payment of this debt then becomes tax-deductible—in other words, national governments stand to lose considerable amounts of corporate taxes when this ploy is practised.

As it turned out, Phelps Dodge was trumped by another foreign corporation, Companhia Vale do Rio Doce SA of Brazil—the world's largest iron-ore miner—which acquired Inco. And Falconbridge went to Xstrata PLC of Switzerland, which paid an astonishing $18 billion in cash. Peter Foster in the *National Post* scoffed at the loss of these Canadian companies, arguing,

Economic nationalism amounts to a form of primitivism that still sees the nation as a tribal unit engaged in a trading "battle." This requires it to promote domestic "champions," and exercise discretionary violence on private companies/tribesmen in the name of the public good.

On the other hand, Peter Munk, chairman of Barrick Gold Corp. of Toronto, the world's largest gold producer, said putting Inco, Falconbridge, and Teck together was a once-in-a-lifetime opportunity. Addressing Canadian mining executives, he said, "This opportunity will never arise again in your generation and not in your children's generation to put together a group like that. That's when you've got to have the determination and the balls and the courage."

In conversation, the thoughtful David O'Brien underlines and expands on those concerns, which I share: "Having Canadian-based, strong international companies is a critical element in this country's own identity and its future. If you have the head office of a major international company here, it enables your best and brightest to work in Canada rather than having to go somewhere else for the top jobs. It supports all kinds of other services that involve these best and brightest—from the lawyers to the marketers to the actuaries to the accountants. It supports other industries around it and actually helps small businesses get started, in many cases, as service to the big company. This is also where the research then occurs, the innovation.

"So to have a number of Canadian global champions is the lynchpin to economic success. It's not sufficient in and of itself because you need entrepreneurial businesses as well, among other things, but you've got to have a reasonable number of Canadian-based, globally competitive, or at least internationally competitive, companies.

"And having them is also very important in terms of supporting the universities, the cultural events, the social needs—all that. You know, the communities that get the philanthropic support are the ones where the heads of companies and the head offices are located. And you just watch an oil company taken over by an American company: Within two years, you've lost nine-tenths of that community support because the heads of that company live elsewhere and that's where they're focused. They don't have a stake in the community here, nor are they aware of it—they don't meet local people on a regular basis.

"As someone in charge, you find yourself in that conundrum: You have a responsibility to your shareholders and a responsibility to the larger community, and [you] try to find a route where you can marry the two. That's what we try to do in EnCana, by saying one plus one will make two and a half when we put them together. The stock price will go up, and before you know it, everyone will be better off. We had to find a way where it worked for the country *and* for the shareholders."

LIKE MANY OF MY FRIENDS and colleagues, I've been paying attention to the ideas raised in two bestselling business books—and wondering what they mean for Canadian corporations confronting the global economy. In *Good to Great*, while discussing the best corporate leaders being ambitious for their companies rather than themselves, Jim Collins mentions Colman Mackie, the late, great CEO of Gillette. I was intrigued by the two hostile takeover attempts, and a proxy fight he faced, and how he led the counter-attacks to save this legendary American enterprise that invented the safety razor in 1901. Instead of pocketing the windfall Mackie would have gained by capitulating to the investment group leading the proxy battle for control of his board, he and his senior people fought back by contacting thousands of investors individually, one telephone call at a time. Long-term shareholders were happy that management won, because secret projects then under way to develop new kinds of razors led to a decade of high stock values. The lesson: At a time when foreign raiders are eyeing Canada's most valued assets, such dedication to a company and its vision of greatness should be an inspiring tale for Canadian executives.

The other book is Thomas Friedman's *The World Is Flat*, in which he describes how the planet's economy has been transformed by the advent of the Internet and email, Web browsers, and search-engine software like Google's, all linked to a global telecommunications network through such technology as cheap, powerful computers and high-speed fibre optic cable and broadband connections. For the first time, any individual as well as any company located anywhere around the globe now have the potential to compete and propel development internationally—in effect, levelling the economic playing field and flattening the world. Friedman quotes the CEO of India's Infosys Technologies Limited as saying that all these wonders brought together at the start of this century "created a platform where intellectual work, intellectual capital, could be delivered from anywhere. It could be disaggregated, delivered, distributed, produced, and put back together again—and this gave a whole new degree of freedom to the way we do work, especially work of an intellectual nature."

These technologies form the basis of the burgeoning offshore-outsourcing movement in which a local company contracts with an overseas company to provide services that could be done in-house. An excellent homegrown example of this practice is Sun Life Financial's decision to become our first major insurer to outsource some of its domestic life insurance underwriting jobs to accountants and other university graduates in low-cost, high-productivity India. The company, Canada's second largest after Manulife, sells insurance there and in China and other Asian countries. "For Sun Life," CEO Don Stewart says, "the future lies beyond Canadian borders."

How can Canada create more of these Northern Tigers? Corporations themselves have to decide whether the goal is worthwhile and achievable. And if it is, they have to weigh the options for getting there—and all the challenges involved.

Go global: Globalization can be both beneficial and bad for Canadian corporations. The good might be obvious: Our companies grow in size and strength when they begin operating around the world. But they can also profit by reacting positively to the competition they face in leaving their own small ponds and leaping into deeper, wider waters.

Editorial writers seized on a Statistics Canada study in 2005 that showed foreign-based manufacturers operating in our country were generally much more productive than Canadian-controlled ones. But in fact, the study made a good case for our domestic producers to expand beyond their borders. It turned out in a careful reading of the statistics that the plants of Canadian companies with foreign operations were just as productive as foreign-owned plants operating in Canada—and even performed somewhat better in the areas of innovation and research and development. A major factor in their achievements seems to be the honing of the products and skills they have to do when competing with rivals in a larger arena.

For all the benefits of going global, there can also be a dark side, as I learned at Home Oil when we were drilling for oil in Guyana: You have to deal with foreign governments and unrest in developing nations. In another example, Talisman Energy was charged with complicity in the horrors being perpetrated in Sudan, where a consortium of international petroleum firms was drilling for oil in that war-torn African nation. Amid criticism from activists and even shareholders, the company sold its stake there in 2003. "The situation became intolerable," Jim Buckee says. And SNC-Lavalin has been embroiled in a dispute raging between the socialist government and its Marxist opposition in India's Kerala State. The company was accused of "cheating" and "treachery" over a contract to renovate and expand hydro-electric dams—while at the same time it had agreed to donate $27 million to build a community cancer centre.

Gerry Maier, who represented Conoco in many nations—including troubled Chad—views globalism at its best as a unifying force in the world, as I do: "In the long run, after working internationally and integrating North American and European ideas and the cultures of other countries, I can see it as being nothing but positive in terms of reducing strife between nations and even within nations themselves."

Or create a powerful niche: Suncor Energy drew the first commercial barrel of synthetic crude from the Alberta oil sands and, since 1967, has produced more than a billion barrels in its core business. It also has conventional natural-gas production in western Canada and refining, marketing, and retail operations in Ontario and Colorado. With more than five thousand employees and $10.5 billion in annual revenues, it places fifth among oil and gas producers in Canada. It has achieved that ranking without either going global or getting into the mergers and acquisitions game. As CEO Rick George explains, Suncor's secret has been to identify its strength and to excel in it: "If you think about it, we sit as the pioneer and the largest single investor in the oil-sands business—that is what we do—in the second-largest oil basin in the world. And in a great country next to the biggest market, I mean, we're fully occupied, working day and night, trying to continue to grow that business, I just cannot see why you would split off and go outside the country at this point. . . .

"For at least the fourteen years we've been a public company, there have always been rumours, and most people would put us on the list of potential takeover targets. And what I tell employees and our management team is, 'Listen, your only defence on this issue is a good offence. So if you want to stay independent, then what you have to do is deliver environmentally, socially, and financially. Suncor today has a cash flow multiple higher than our international competitors, and the reason is because of good strategy, good execution. You have to do that to earn the right to be independent. It is our only protective armour—and it's also one of the things that drives a lot of us to work: How do we continue that performance so that we can stay an independent company?'"

Rick was raised in small-town Brush, Colorado, the son of the local electrician and TV-shop owner. With engineering and law degrees, he went to work for Sun Oil, spending a decade in Britain before coming to its Canadian subsidiary, Suncor, where he and his family are now proud Canadian citizens: "I haven't forgotten my roots, and I'm still proud to be an American, but I've been fifteen years in this country and I would say I'm more emotionally tied to

Canada." He turned what was once called "the unluckiest company in Canada" into a thriving corporation that had a market capitalization of $1 billion on going public in 1992 and is at $40 billion today. "We moved this business from being one of the high-cost oil producers worldwide to what we believe is the lowest-cost one in North America," he says with well-earned satisfaction.

Contrast Suncor's accomplishments with the fates of MacMillan Bloedel, which pursued too many niches where it had little expertise, and NOVA Corp., which was torn between its quite disparate pipeline and chemicals niches. In both cases, the companies couldn't present a comprehensible explanation of themselves to analysts and investors. The idea is to focus on a sphere of operations that makes both business and story-telling sense.

But grow bigger: Whether a company goes global or confines itself to a narrow specialty within Canada, sheer size does matter if it wants to ward off takeover artists. In *Northern Edge*, Tom d'Aquino and David Stewart-Patterson write, "As the global evolution of the financial services industry is making clear...size is becoming increasingly important even for niche players." They quote Charles Baillie who, at the time, was the TD Bank's chair and CEO:

> We have seen a tremendous pick-up in technology spending by our competitors around the world and with the Internet and the advantages it gives to those who move first—settling for second is not good enough.... We have to get to be one of the top three or four names across North America. If we don't spend and get the brand known, others will pass us by. We have to do things on a much bigger scale than we really dreamed of before, and even if we're really good, it's incredibly uphill in this new world.

To go big, you must first dream big and then make sure your vision can become a viable reality. Al Markin, Murray Edwards, and their people at Canadian Natural Resources did that in preparing for a $6.8-billion launch of the Horizon Oil Sands Project in the forest and muskeg north of Fort McMurray. It's only the first stage in what's expected to be a gigantic mine and plant, producing five hundred thousand barrels of crude a day. But before going ahead in 2005, they spent four years and more than $400 million to plan their dream, incorporating everything from a private landing strip for 737s to an on-site Tim Hortons to entice six thousand or more workers to the plushest camp amid the sands. Again, good growth strategy, great execution. (And a long-term strategy built from within. As McGill University management professor Henry Mintzberg says, "Strategy is a continuous process. Any CEO that hires a consultant to give him or her a strategy should be fired.")

Another, more direct way of growing is to merge, as Fording, EnCana, and TransCanada Corporation did. Mergers fashioned to create companies strong enough to withstand hostile takeovers can be good things. But I'd like to add a caveat here, one I've only mentioned before: Studies show that the large majority of such alliances don't achieve their desired goals. Too many take place for all the wrong reasons. If I can quote myself from a speech I gave to the Canadian Club in 1998 just after one of the good mergers, between NOVA and TransCanada:

> Management egos have played a large role in many unsuccessful transactions and, unfortunately, that human trait has not disappeared. I will not exempt boards of directors from their responsibility in this area because they are there to ensure that shareholders don't get hurt by ego-driven deals.
>
> The revenue and income of investment bankers are driven by the fees earned from these mega-transactions, and accordingly, it is natural for them to propose mergers to managements who often fall in love with the idea without exercising enough of their own judgment.
>
> Financial institutions have often aided and abetted mergers by facilitating the financing of unsound deals. There are lots of examples close to home, with one of

the largest being the Dome takeover of Hudson's Bay Oil
and Gas.

Sometimes governments unwittingly create policies
and regulations that encourage fundamentally unwise
transactions. The Canadianization effect of the National
Energy Program is a good example.

Another quick caveat about reshaping companies to become
less vulnerable to predators: Though I approved the decision to
turn Fording Coal into an investment trust, I realized the problems
these financial vehicles can create. Investment bankers increasingly
want to turn viable companies into trusts—with the result that
there's a quick payback for investors and the companies might
have little motivation to grow by making foreign or domestic
acquisitions or investing in R&D to compete in a global market.

Precision Drilling of Calgary is one Canadian company that
should have taken this caveat to heart. Hank Swartout founded
Precision in 1951 and turned it into our biggest contract driller
and oil field–services provider, earning $424 million in profits dur-
ing 2004. But a year later, he decided to convert it into an income
trust that would trade at a higher-value multiple than a conventional company. The problem was that unlike Fording, which has
all of its assets contained within Canada, Precision had substantial
holdings in the U.S. And now they would be a big drag on the proposed financial vehicle because, under domestic regulations, the
income they produced couldn't easily be absorbed into a tax-free
trust. So the company sold its international contract drilling and
energy-service divisions to an American competitor for roughly
$2.3 billion. That left Precision a wholly Canadian operator rather
than an international one, no longer bragging about its bold
global direction (though it did inch back into the U.S. in 2006 by
providing a drilling rig to one customer, and it had plans for ten
more rigs there within two years).

Precision used to pride itself on its R&D, which was surely
sharpened by competing in the wider world—now severely
shrunk. This unhappy side effect of trusts seems true for some

other industries too, such as the high-tech field: Bob McWhirter, president of Toronto's Selective Asset Management, says, "Huge research and development expenditures usually can't co-exist with dividend payouts." Even Hank Swartout himself has said the trend to trusts is "not the best thing for Canada." And when Stephen Harper's government surprised the investment community in the fall of 2006 by deciding to tax income trusts, my friend Gwyn Morgan wrote: "The shareholders and employees of Canadian businesses provide the funds needed to run government programs and services. Therefore, research, reinvestment and growth are crucial to the future living standards of all Canadians. To the extent that trusts may have limited these things, the government had reason to be concerned."

Above all, be courageous: Canadian corporations can be much less aggressive than their foreign counterparts. The hostile takeover of Dofasco by a European steel superpower demonstrated that in spades. In the most recent wave of mergers and acquisitions washing over Canada—a trend that shot up by 22 percent in 2005 over the previous year and was expected to continue climbing throughout '06—our companies have mostly been the fall guys. Ken Smith, a managing partner at Toronto's Secor Consulting, watches such deals and concludes, "I think we've been conservative to a fault in M&A.... We are timid." And less ambitious about putting on ample weight by expanding to hold off pillagers. That was the sin we committed at Hudson's Bay Oil and Gas all those years ago in dealing with the sharks of Dome Petroleum. Today, among companies that have learned this lesson is Canfor Corp., the second-largest Canadian lumber producer, which in early 2006 bought the profitable timber producer New South Companies Inc. of South Carolina. As well as fattening Canfor up, the deal gave it access to operations down south that would not be affected by any future U.S. softwood-lumber trade duties or a rising Canadian dollar.

Of course, there's a possibility that in expanding, you might make some mistakes. If you do, there's comforting counsel from Sir Wilfred Grenfell, the brave missionary doctor who ministered to the

THE COMPANIES THAT DID 261

people of Newfoundland and Labrador: "It is courage the world needs, not infallibility.... Courage is always the surest wisdom."

WHAT ROLES SHOULD GOVERNMENTS take in creating the conditions to breed corporate champions of Tiger proportions? Plenty of them, as it happens. I created a little stir a few years ago in arguing that the federal government should keep its 18.8 percent stake in Petro-Canada. "PetroCan is a different animal than it was in earlier times. It used to be an energy-policy instrument, as opposed to a business," the *Globe* quoted me as saying in a column devoted to my apparent turnaround about Ottawa's involvement in the Oil Patch. Now, I said, having the feds keep a significant piece of the former Crown corporation is palatable to the West and gives the senior government a useful window on the industry.

For an old capitalist, I do have some contrarian views about government intervention in the Canadian economy. For instance, I've already stated my hesitation about having the big banks merge. The *Bank Act* states that large banks (with equity in excess of $5 billion) must remain "widely held," and I approve of its stipulation that no party can own more than 20 percent of any class of voting shares of a widely held bank and 30 percent of any non-voting shares. In effect, the legislation prohibits control of a large financial institution by any single shareholder or group of shareholders. We have a very good banking system, and any attempt to reduce competition could harm consumers.

There's obviously a part for governments to play in overseeing utilities, as well. By their very nature, power and water utilities are monopolies that need regulation. They're better being publicly owned and operated, just as police forces and prisons are. Water resources are a particular challenge: Canadians have to make damn sure we have enough fresh water before shipping it out of the country—and if we have, we can and should supply them with our excess in a deal that protects our interests. Peter Lougheed, Alberta's respected former premier, predicted a while ago that the U.S. will be aggressively seeking our fresh water within three to five years. "We must prepare, to ensure we aren't trapped in an ill-advised response," he wrote. "It would be a major mistake for Canada to handle this issue badly. With climate change and growing needs, Canadians will need all the fresh water we can conserve, particularly in the western provinces." If I can quote Professor Mintzberg again, "We all value private goods, but they are worthless without public goods—such as policing and economic policies—to protect them."

Letting my capitalistic tendencies kick in once more, I have to argue that most things run far more efficiently under free enterprise. Two of our biggest transportation companies, which went private, make my case. CN, as a government-backed railroad, was poorly run and bleeding cash, and today, it's an aggressive competitor throughout the continent, with a share price that jumped by 1,000 percent in the past decade. Air Canada, for most of its history, was a ward of the government that Ottawa had to keep baling out, and now it seems on its way to becoming one of the most successful airlines in the world, co-existing more peaceably with the upstart WestJet.

Where Ottawa *can* help enormously is in the realm of taxation. Like my friend Dominic D'Alessandro of Manulife, I believe that people in a privileged position have even more of an obligation to pay our fair share of personal taxes (and Canada has the highest level of income tax among G-8 nations). But like my friend Gwyn Morgan of EnCana, I know that so many Canadian corporations today have to compete unfairly with the rest of the planet. "If we pay higher taxes here than our competitors in Houston, then they are going to have an equity advantage. They are going to be more highly valued," he points out. "As long as Canada fosters a level playing field in terms of its domestically domiciled companies, there's no reason why we shouldn't be able to compete." His point is that the field is not always as flat as it could be: In a world of rivals paying their workers shockingly low wages, there's a case to be made for some tax relief for Canadian manufacturers in areas like the deduction for capital cost allowance on machinery and equipment. And the C.D. Howe Institute reports that Canada's business investment taxes are the third highest in the world—only China and Germany have higher effective tax rates than Canada—and Canadian businesses are at a significant disadvantage, particularly within North America.

Some observers believe governments can properly practise more direct kinds of intervention with business and industry to save Canadian head offices from the foreign interlopers. The *Globe and Mail*'s well-informed and opinionated Eric Reguly was writing not long ago about the proposed Phelps Dodge foray into the Canadian mining jungle. He pointed out that it was clear three years earlier that we needed a consolidation of the corporate tribes to prevent a grab by the likes of BHP Billiton or Rio Tinto (who had even considered Phelps Dodge then as a possible buyer?). The columnist asked,

> Why didn't the federal finance and industry ministers and the premier of Ontario lock the CEOs of Inco, Falconbridge and Vancouver's Teck Cominco into a room and bash their heads together? The message: Whatever it takes, guys, we'll help you make it happen.... Imagine if the mergers had been encouraged in the steel industry?

Though the wording of his suggestion might seem a little over the top, I admired his sentiments and wondered if he was correct in his conclusion: "With Dofasco gone and Stelco and Algoma essentially open for offers, the Canadian steel industry is pretty much finished."

If we don't want this to happen to the petroleum industry, governments must create the climate to nourish champion oil and gas companies. Pierre Alvarez, president of the Canadian Association of Petroleum Producers, points out strongly that the domestic industry is part of a highly integrated global energy-delivery network. "Maintaining internationally competitive fiscal and regulatory regimes in Canada is critical when this is one of the highest-cost places in the world to find and develop oil and gas. Attracting global investment to capital projects in the oil sands or offshore and developing technology here at home are key to the health of the sector and to sustaining Canada's strong growth prospects."

Is the government listening? Well, in the fall of 2006, Prime Minister Stephen Harper had a private session with Calgary business leaders at which I was pleased to hear that one of the priorities of his government was to provide the environment to develop more Canadian corporate champions. I hope I don't sound cynical in quoting the late Scottish-born businessman and philanthropist Andrew Carnegie, who said, "As I grow older, I pay less attention to what men say. I just watch what they do."

NOT ONLY IS CANADA BETTER off for having companies strongly competitive beyond our borders, but so too is the world. Canadians *can* do it, and in the doing, they bring a distinctive mindset and a wealth of attributes to their business dealings around the globe. Tom d'Aquino and David Stewart-Patterson, who are as passionate about Canada as I am, spell out some of what gives us our northern edge:

> Canadians are well positioned to triumph in the global economy. We have an ideal geographic location, with three oceans on our coasts and a common border with the most dynamic market in the world. We have a diverse, multicultural, and multilingual population. We have one of the most effective federations in the world, with an honest legal and regulatory environment. We invest heavily in human capital. We welcome large numbers of new immigrants every year. We have vast open spaces, a beautiful landscape, and massive resources, including a large percentage of the world's water supply. We have relatively secure borders.

As far back as 1981, I was telling the story about meeting the chief economist of a large Swiss bank who was on a global tour. When he asked me to describe our current situation in Canada, I listed a litany of problems, from the National Energy Program to ridiculously high interest rates. That sage old guy looked at me and said, "You Canadians are very funny people."

How in the world could you say that? I wondered.

"In Switzerland, we view Canada in quite a different light. You're blessed with a very large and beautiful country—situated next to the United States, your largest trading partner, across an undefended border. Your natural resources are enormous: water, oil, gas, minerals, coal, agriculture, forestry, and fishing. You're successful in manufacturing, as evidenced by the Auto Pact. You have high-tech capabilities with companies such as Northern Telecom. First-class infrastructure: Consider your roads, water and sewer systems, electricity, hospitals, schools, airports. You have developed capital markets and sound financial institutions. And an educated workforce. Canada is a very young country of only twenty-five million people, yet it's a member of the G-7 and recognized as one of the more powerful countries in the world.

"Mr. Haskayne," he summed up, "you seem to be a country in search of a problem!" It became obvious to me that all the issues I identified as negative were all within our control, whereas all the attributes he cited were part of our natural heritage built by our forefathers.

Rick George of Suncor brings the state of his adopted country up to date when he says, "I know it's a bit of a cliché, but the next couple of decades are ours to mess up. We have a very good strong democratic process; we have good fiscal balance and responsibility. Do we need to invest more in our universities and our infrastructure; do we need to continue to have a track record of improving environmentalism? Absolutely. But we've got great trade balances, a set of young people coming up who hopefully will again change society, the resources in a resource-scarce world. If we manage things really well, this [era] should be ours."

Nowhere do our strengths seem more apparent than in my hometown of Calgary, which brims with opportunity. You don't have to spring from a certain privileged class to succeed here. Ron Southern of the ATCO Group was a fireman's son. Harley

Hotchkiss, the former oilman and now chair of the NHL board of governors, grew up on a Depression-era farm in Ontario. Al Markin of Canadian Natural Resources was raised in one of Calgary's poorest neighborhoods. Ron Mathison is a classic example of what you can accomplish in this city—this country—if you're prepared to educate yourself, work hard and well, and have a little luck, too.

When young Ron Mathison and I sat and talked about all this not long ago, he told a story that typified the possibilities existing here today: "There's a fellow four years older than me who recently left a very large international company that was so enamoured of his skill set that they wanted to move him to their international headquarters, and he said, 'It's a great promotion, one of the top jobs in the Oil Patch, probably in the world, but I think I'd rather stay in Calgary.' He's one of the many Saskatchewan farm boys who wandered into engineering school, and thirty years later, he looks up and wonders if he should hop back into one of the other large companies here—the EnCanas or PetroCans—or does he do something on his own. 'His own' is a strategy to consolidate a number of companies in the oil and gas business who would function much better with larger-scale operations.

"So he comes in to see me and says, 'Do you think that this is a pipe dream?' This particular consolidation strategy involves $5 billion and is well formulated and would play well on an international stage. And he's able to come to any one of a number of offices around town and say, 'I think I need $10–$50 million of startup capital, and do you think it's a dream?' 'Well, it's not a pipe dream,' I said, 'and in fact, if we can come to terms, why don't we just do the deal right now?'"

Along with a growing breed of damn fine entrepreneurs, we have a whole lot else going for us in Canada. We lead the world in having the highest percentage of university degrees and college diplomas of any major industrialized nation. We have (according to the magazine *Foreign Direct Investment*) the fewest hurdles to overcome in launching a business, and (predicts the *Economist*'s

Intelligence Unit) we'll be the second-best country in which to do business over the next five years. That's based on our business, political, and institutional environments and our macro-economic stability, market opportunities, policies towards private enterprise and foreign investment, foreign-trade and exchange regime, tax system, financing, labour market, and infrastructure.

We also have that Canadian mindset, which is generally caring and insistent on integrity. Canadian Oil Sands' Allen Hagerman, of a younger generation, says, "We can do anything here. We have a well-educated population, we have resources, we have good infrastructure. Canada is the luckiest country in the world. We sit right on the doorstep of the largest consuming nation on earth, a democracy and a friend. But Canadians have a compassionate and a nurturing nature, which is different from Americans, and we should be out there on the global stage. We have something different to contribute."

"I think Allen is absolutely right," agrees Enbridge's Pat Daniel. "And this is one of the advantages that Canadian companies like ours have in operating internationally. Enbridge has operations in Colombia and Spain, but we don't bring any real political axe to bear when we go into another country. No baggage, and we go in as very technically confident, every bit as confident as our American peers. We are very conservative, very considerate of other people and other cultures, and therefore we work very well internationally. That's a real competitive advantage Canadians have got—and we just need to leverage it a little bit more. Because we are good, and we don't really tell enough people how good we are."

Chapter Fourteen

DOING THE RIGHT THING
The Ethics of Business

MY FRATERNITY BROTHERS SHOULD have known what was coming. I'd been speaking publicly and getting quoted in the media about touchy topics for more than a decade. In 1994, when I was receiving a Canadian Business Leader Award from the University of Alberta, I'd given a talk titled (a little provocatively) "Confessions of a Corporate Director." Some of it dealt with the roles various self-interested groups play in pushing mergers and acquisitions that are often indefensible: ego-driven executives and directors, fee-grabbing investment bankers, loose-pursed lenders, and the governments whose policies foster such transactions. Now, half a century after joining Kappa Sigma at the U of A, I was invited to speak to a gathering of frat members and others at the University of Calgary, supposedly on the theme of "Success in Business." My speech that September evening in 2005 soon turned to my pet subject: the declining ethical standards of business leaders in Canada and the U.S.

I mentioned a similar address I'd given at the university eight years earlier, when scandals had surfaced around Calgary's crooked Bre-X Minerals (false claims of Indonesian gold) and Toronto's troubled Livent Entertainment Corporation (accusations of financial irregularities). "They were undermining the confidence of Canadian financial markets in the eyes of foreign investors, and we were being heavily criticized for weak regulatory controls," I recalled. "And even then, people had forgotten the Dome disaster of the 1980s."

Today, I pointed out, there were even more and messier corporate transgressions and outright corruption—among them the American fraud and conspiracy cases of founding chairman Ken Lay and his colleagues at the infamous Enron Corp., and CEO Dennis Kozlowski and CFO Mark Swartz at Tyco International (convicted of looting $600 million from their own multinational). Contemporary Canada was not exempt from such shows of corporate greed: The topical example then was Quebec advertising executive Paul Coffin in the Adscam scandal investigated by the Gomery Inquiry ("It's ironic that he will be sentenced to a period of two years of house arrest and court-ordered to lecture to business students about ethics.") John Roth of Ottawa's Nortel Networks was another offender of note after the telecommunications giant cooked its books, causing the loss of thousands of jobs and many billions of dollars. In 2000, Roth had been named "Canadian Business Leader of the Year," and in '02, he stepped down as president and CEO. The scandal "has tainted that award."

I suggested, however, that the saga of Conrad Black was particularly embarrassing for Canada, the nation he'd disowned to become an English lord. The head of Hollinger International of Chicago was about to be indicted on eight counts involving $83.8 million (U.S.), which could bring forty years in prison for what the prosecution described as lining his pockets at the expense of investors (he later faced a total of twelve charges, including racketeering, money laundering, wire fraud, and obstruction of justice). Even if half the charges are true, it was still an embarrassing situation for Canada as well as for Conrad himself.

"I have personally known Conrad for many years as a fellow director of CIBC," I told my audience, "and for the life of me, I can't understand how he came off the rail so badly." He had all the trappings of success: a global newspaper empire; a high-profile and beautiful wife, the journalist Barbara Amiel; numerous prominent friends and business and political associates, including Hollinger board advisors Margaret Thatcher and Henry Kissinger; directorships in several companies, such as Canada's Brascan and CanWest Global Communications; respect as a biographer of

Maurice Duplessis and Franklin Roosevelt; and an Order of Canada. Yet soon after I spoke, he was to face the possibility of jail while helplessly watching his net worth being dramatically diminished—"He may end up broke," I predicted in my speech— and his reputation shredded. Meanwhile, his right-hand man, David Radler, would plead guilty to similar charges and quickly see his name stripped from a wing of the Queen's University business school, which also returned his $1-million donation.

Why, I wondered, why would Conrad allegedly risk all of this? John Jacob Astor, the multimillionaire New York real-estate investor, once comforted a failed associate by saying, "A man who has a million dollars is as well off as if he were rich." I like to paraphrase that by saying, "For all practical purposes, a person with $2 million is as well off as a person with $200 million." Conrad Black, on the other hand, once said of his and his brother's involvement in their Argus Corp. conglomerate, "The only charge that anyone can level against us is one of insufficient generosity to ourselves." In a survival-of-the-fittest business climate where success is measured only in dollars and cents or job titles, where even business schools are accused of promoting such materialistic criteria, an over-reaching quest for great wealth is often inevitable—and can topple even the toughest corporate titans.

Within my own profession, chartered accountancy, Arthur Andersen LLP has bitten the dust in the wake of its Enron involvement, and KPMG LLP has admitted setting up fraudulent shelters for wealthy clients to conceal billions of dollars in taxes and capital gains. These occurrences of "Enronitis" have become so frequent that many people believe the words "business" and "ethics" can't co-exist. They can, of course, and should. The scandals have had one salutary effect: the passing of the *Sarbanes-Oxley Act* in the U.S. to improve corporate governance and financial-reporting rules and the Multilateral Instrument 42-111 in Canada to harmonize our regulations with the Americans'.

During my talk, I mentioned that I'd recently spent a day with one of the most honest businessmen I know: petroleum entrepreneur Harley Hotchkiss, who happens to be the chairman of the

National Hockey League and who, at seventy-eight, was still displaying sound judgment. As Harley says, "You can have all the legislation and rules in the world, but you cannot legislate integrity. If people are going to serve on a board of directors, *sure*, they should have some experience and ability they can contribute, but they better have that basic integrity."

YOU MAY NOT BE ABLE to legislate it, but you *can* set standards for ethical behaviour in the business environment—yardsticks to measure up to—and do your damnedest to make sure the people around you and those running companies that affect our society hold true to them. I've been particularly interested in corporate governance ever since serving as one of eight members of the Macdonald Commission in the late 1980s when I was CEO of Interprovincial Pipe Line and a director of Home Oil, Manufacturers Life, and other companies. The Canadian Institute of Chartered Accountants created the commission in the wake of the 1985 failures of the Canadian Commercial Bank and Northland Bank. It was chaired by lawyer William Macdonald, a senior partner of MacMillan Binch in Toronto and a director of several companies.

Set up to study the public's expectations of audits, the commission urged a strengthening of the professional standards and independence of auditors and recommended "swift and tough actions" in certain areas. One of them was to amend auditing standards or provincial codes of conduct so auditors accept an audit only if they have the right to review and comment on financial disclosure outside a financial statement. This was obviously designed to prevent companies from concealing negative results from shareholders. Other recommendations were to require that auditing committees be made up of outside directors and to require auditors to point out in their reports any serious risk of business failure. And in the years since, an auditor's responsibility has been expanded to ensure reasonable assurance that financial statements are not materially misstated (to use their jargon)—that they're *honest*.

The truth is, though, that audit failures continued at companies such as Livent and Philip Services Corp., a Hamilton waste-recovery company that went bankrupt after a public offering in 1997. Part of the problem was that Canada's generally accepted accounting principles remained too flexible. And that's only one reason why I've never liked being on audit committees myself—even though with my chartered accountant's background and long experience as a CEO, I'm probably one of the more suitable candidates. ("Join no audit committee unless you can satisfy yourself that you are fully and truly financially literate," says the directors' director Bill Dimma. "And accept no audit committee chairmanship unless you can convince yourself that you are indeed an expert.")

One company that exemplifies good auditing practices and overall superior corporate governance is Nexen Inc., that extraordinary success story in Alberta's Oil Patch. Canada's fourth-largest independent petroleum company is led by Charlie Fischer (he's never called anything but Charlie). It's involved in several mega-projects, from the Long Lake extraction process in the Alberta oil sands due to come on stream in 2007 to the Knotty Head exploration wells in the Gulf of Mexico, which may produce as many as 500 million barrels of oil for Nexen. There are other operations in the North Sea, Yemen, and offshore West Africa. And, more to my point, it enjoys a reputation for transparency in its board dealings. In mid-2006, its senior VP, general counsel, and secretary, John McWilliams, won the Governance Gavel Award for excellence in director disclosure from the Canadian Coalition for Good Governance—forty-five of the country's leading institutional investors, whose assets under management total some $810 billion. (The coalition was launched by the Ontario Teachers' Pension Plan and shareholder advocate Stephen Jarislowsy, who co-founded Canada's first privately owned money-management firm, Jarislowsky, Fraser & Co. Ltd., in 1955. I met Steve during my HBOG years, and he remains a friend four decades later.)

In 1997, when Nexen was starting to operate in Nigeria, John McWilliams helped compose the International Code of Ethics for Canadian Business, which was later adapted by the United

Nations Global Compact, the world's largest voluntary organization to promote cooperation among corporations, not-for-profits, labour, UN agencies, and society in general in the area of corporate responsibility.

Nexen has an audit and conduct review committee of seven independent members (including chairman Tom O'Neill, former CEO of PricewaterhouseCoopers Canada, and Barry Jackson, chair of TransCanada Corporation and former CEO of Crestar Energy). Their task is to act for the board in overseeing such concerns as the integrity of financial statements, compliance with accounting and finance-based legal and regulatory requirements, and the independent auditor's qualifications and independence. And in dealing within and outside the company, Nexen has a website and an Integrity Hotline (with toll-free numbers in nine nations) for anyone to anonymously and confidentially report ethical issues through a third party.

EnCana is another oil and gas company with an Integrity Hotline. As a safety check to make sure the company and its people are acting openly and honestly, it allows shareholders, employees, and suppliers as well as outsiders—governments, nongovernmental organizations, and community members—to call, email, or write with questions and concerns.

EnCana's corporate constitution, as I've noted before, presents a solid vision for the company and mandates that employees be people of strong character who operate on the bases of trust, integrity, and respect. One of its many tenets is that "EnCanans do not tolerate unlawful or unethical behaviour, intimidation or harassment, environmental, health or safety negligence, workplace discrimination, or deceptive communication. At the end of the day, the most important thing is our reputation"—which is a line I've been repeating for a long time.

For Gwyn Morgan, that vision went hand in hand with his desire to create a Northern Tiger. "If you start off with an ethical base and ask what's the point of having a great Canadian-headquartered company," he says, "well, you want that company—its behavior and ethics and values and how it acts internally and in the world—to be as good as it can be. To create jobs for people, to create wealth for the country, to create great communities where it operates, to have people fulfill their career objectives, their potential, for themselves and their families. To have that foundational behaviour—and have everybody understand what it is that's expected of them in your organization. If you can do that, and you have great people, great assets, you've got the ethical cornerstone. And without that, you may have great fuel propelling you forward, great opportunities to act on, but if you don't have a steering wheel that keeps you on course, who knows where you'll end up? The best definition of the word 'culture' that I've heard is that it's how people behave when nobody is watching. The reason I think the corporate constitution is so important is that we have people doing all kinds of things, every day, everywhere, and I want to know that they know how they should act in any given situation."

A study of 365 enterprises in thirty countries found that 89 percent have corporate-values statements and more of the most financially successful companies singled out the qualities of honesty, openness, and commitment to employees. But while such statements are all well and good, it's useful to know that Enron had its own code of ethics, sixty-two pages long, with a foreword by Ken Lay as chairman, who wrote, "Enron's reputation finally depends on its people, on you and me. Let's keep that reputation high." Another classic example to illustrate that strategy is one thing, execution another.

Given the gap there can be between the written promise and the actual acts of ethical behaviour, has EnCana been carrying out the intent of its constitution? Well, maybe that's why it was ranked third by its peers from other prominent companies in the honour roll of Canada's most respected corporations and placed second for corporate social responsibility.

THROUGHOUT MY CAREER, I've had my own issues to weigh while serving on various corporate and not-for-profit boards. One is whether to even accept an invitation to join a board, a question more people should ask themselves. For example, what was former U.S. president Gerald Ford—a decent man with a great title but no business experience—doing on the board of Fidelity Trust Co. of Edmonton? After entrepreneur Peter Pocklington took control of Fidelity in the early 1980s, Ford attended a total of three board meetings before the company went insolvent. In my own case, I don't know anything about technology or the automobile business, and so I turned down offers to be a director of companies in those industries. For a couple of years in the mid-1980s, I was on the board of Royal LePage when Canada's largest real estate brokerage company was controlled by the Reichmanns. My friend Bill Dimma was CEO, and Gordon Gray, a respected forty-year veteran with LePage, was chairman. But realizing I neither knew much about nor was even interested in the real estate game, I stepped off as soon as decently possible. In his book *Tougher Boards for Tougher Times*, Bill offers another reason for either refusing a director's seat in the first place or resigning from one:

> [T]he director with character should sniff out the culture carefully before accepting a directorship in a company where management holds all the cards of empowerment. And, even if tentatively satisfied, that director should join with some conditional, if private, reservations. And should resign if it becomes clear sooner or later that the founders and/or majority shareholders and/or control block management are habitually insensitive to the rights of the minority and to the board's obligation to all shareholders.

Sometimes my concerns as a director were about potential conflicts of interest. In 1997, I was chairman of both NOVA and TransAlta, which were discussing the possibility of joint ventures. Wanting to avoid any conflicts because of my dual directorships, I felt duty-bound to consult with Bennett Jones Verchere in Calgary about my legal position. They said I would have four options if I felt there was any conflict: resigning from one of the boards, withdrawing from any discussions of a joint venture, acting as a mediator or facilitator in such a venture on behalf of both companies (and receiving pertinent information in confidence), or acting only for NOVA (where I'd been on the board longer) with the consent of TransAlta. The law firm cautioned, "It is not always enough in order for directors to avoid liability to simply declare the conflict and abstain from participating further in the matter. Directors have a positive duty to act in certain circumstances, to make disclosure of knowledge and information beneficial to the corporation and to counsel the corporation."

In the end, my loyalties never became an issue between the companies. But two years after taking the chair of TransAlta, I had to resign in all conscience to become chairman of the newly combined NOVA and TransCanada Pipelines—which were head-on competitors in the power business. TransAlta, however, asked me to stay on the board. I agreed with some reservations, but after two meetings, I realized it was a silly situation, rife with lurking conflicts, and left the board entirely.

Another instance of possible contention involved the Reichmanns when I was president and CEO of Interhome Energy. They had five representatives on the board and Imperial Oil had three (there were seven independents). The brothers wanted to have one of their people sit in on Interhome's management meetings, as they'd arranged to do at Gulf Canada, where they had majority ownership. They argued that such an arrangement would help them get up to speed on the company. I said, "Look, we've got Imperial as a shareholder and you as a shareholder. If you want any information, we'll give it to you, but we're not going to give you anything more than any other shareholder—period. If you're not happy with the way we're doing things, it's your responsibility to change management." That was the end of that.

More recently, I was watching the progress of Westshore Terminals, the coal-handling facility on the West Coast that had turned itself into a trust. Its shares vacillated as Jimmy Pattison kept investing and increasing his holdings. Every time he bought some stock, I did too. All this was well before Westshore got involved in the deal to take over Fording Coal while I was Fording's chairman and an investor. When the merger talks started, I decided it didn't seem right for me to be holding shares in both companies. "Look," I told the Fording directors, "I own a bunch of Westshore stock, and I want to disclose that, so no matter what happens, I'm not accused of being an insider." After seeking a legal opinion, they came back to tell me that legally I didn't even have to reveal my holdings. But I felt more comfortable selling the stock. It wasn't until after the deal was done and I had left Fording's board that I bought another batch of Westshore shares (which have performed well since, I'm happy to say).

The last board I've served on was Weyerhaeuser's, which is made up of intelligent and influential business leaders. Yet, as impressive as it and they are, the company and I haven't always seen eye to eye on some corporate governance matters. For example, the issue of "staggered boards," in which a portion of the directors have different lengths of terms. Sometimes these are referred to as "classified boards," in which directors serve various terms according to their classification. Most often, there are three different classes of board members, with each one serving a different length of time, and elections usually occur annually. Among the problems with the staggered system is that it can make directors complacent, and then they tend to develop too cozy a relationship with management. The biggest concern, according to a major study by three Harvard Law School professors, is that this kind of board harms shareholders by letting managers ward off value-enhancing offers from hostile bidders—even when most of the directors are independents—and don't even seem to benefit the shareholders of targets acquired in friendly deals.

Not only that, 73 percent of Weyeraeuser's own shareholders have said they don't agree with the makeup of such a board.

Well, I tried to argue my case with the others at Weyerhaeuser and even one of its New York legal consultants, who pointed out that a majority of public companies in his country have staggered boards. "You show me one example in the United States where this has been effective," I challenged him. And even though he backed off, our board remained staggered.

I guess Richard Francis Haskayne became a bit of a burr under Weyerhaeuser's saddle. Another time recently, I became very upset that the company refused shareholders' questions from the floor at its annual meeting. The management even evicted some people from the room and, as a result, we got a terrible write-up in the *New York Times*. Fortunately, that policy was reversed at the next meeting when a questioner from Seattle asked, "Shareholder proxies from many civic groups, including Amnesty International, Jobs with Justice, United Steelworkers of America, the Haida Nation, and Rainforest Action Network are here to respectfully present serious concerns. Will you let us speak?"

The company's response was that it had intended at the previous AGM "to efficiently address the maximum scope and breadth of questions in the limited time available. In retrospect, however, we sincerely regret this decision. To listen to our shareholders, we were reminded that there is no substitute for hearing from them directly, in their own words."

I've found other crucial differences in the makeup and procedures of American and Canadian boards. An important one is the issue I mentioned when discussing the Canadian Imperial Bank of Commerce: the benefits of having non-executive chairs, who oversee boards without being part of management. Weyerhaeuser was one of those that had a chairman who was also the chief executive. Steve Jarislowsky makes my point forcefully: "The chair[person], as well as the entire board, should be regarded by the CEO and any other management people as mentors of the company.... The board is the final authority, and there should be no doubt in anyone's mind."

Bill Dimma also has some good points to make about the usefulness of a lead director, or "independent board leader," as the position was called by the Saucier Committee, a creation of the Canadian Institute of Chartered Accountants, the Toronto Stock Exchange (TSX), and what's now the TSX Venture Exchange. Whatever it's called, the idea is to deepen the independence of a board and respect the rights and responsibilities of minority shareholders. From their perspective, Bill writes, "the appointment of any independent board leader who is not a truly independent director is potentially dysfunctional. In fact, use of the term 'independent' for a director who is a member of the management of a controlling shareholder is more Orwellian than the Saucier Committee intended." Amen.

The issue of ethics goes well beyond the boardroom into day-to-day operations. The single most common criticism these days is just how lavishly many CEOs and other senior managers are compensated in salaries, bonuses, and options. When I was at Home Oil and determining incentive bonuses for senior people, we gave them a range of performance targets, from production volumes to cash flows, that we asked them to shoot for—without telling them exactly how we would measure them at year's end. That way, they couldn't focus on one specific target as opposed to another just to ensure they got their bonus. Too many companies set up a goal that is simply a measure of financial performance without judging contributing factors. These factors might be out of an executive's control—a sudden rise in world oil prices, for instance— and yet he or she takes credit for achieving the earnings target. In other words, you have to look beyond the numbers. I've tried to create the same system of fair compensation in any company where I was the boss and to sell it, with less success, to those companies where I was a chairman or director.

EnCana has had a system that measured itself against sixteen other American and Canadian energy companies to determine bonuses. A good idea, but in one recent year, the oil producers in that list performed far better than EnCana, which is primarily a natural-gas producer, even though its operating results were spectacular. As a result, the targets it had set to trigger bonuses weren't achieved, the bonuses weren't given, and the company lost forty or so engineers, geologists, and geophysicists because they couldn't see hitting the mark over a three-year period. So the targets had to be lowered a bit.

In discussing the issue of executive compensation—and *over-compensation*—David O'Brien points out, "The trouble is, as long as you've got the U.S., which pays even that much more, and if you don't have a reasonable competitiveness, you lose your top people. It's the same old problem, whether it's in medicine, research, or in hockey—you lose your best."

As he reflects on his career, especially as head of Canadian Pacific Ltd., David acknowledges that "it's a very ticklish issue now, because over a period of time, the compensation of executives moved disproportionately to the rest of society, partly because we had a twenty-year bull market in the stocks and partly because of the use of stock options, beginning in the early '80s— all of which resulted in executives making a lot more money. You take the example of the typical head of a Canadian chartered bank, who today makes $8–$10 million a year, if you look at the value of the options and everything else. Twenty years ago, it was probably something under $1 million. I mean, it's just a huge, huge increase. And *I* was a beneficiary of this. I'm just saying that things have probably swung too far, relative to the average person."

True—and of course as a CEO, I also benefited from some decent salaries and generous stock options. Yet any largesse that came my way pales in comparison to what some contemporary executives have walked away with. Sour grapes on my part? Not at all: This butcher's son has always been far more financially comfortable in life than he could ever have imagined. But some of the corporate payouts today astonish me. After CIBC had to settle with Enron investors, John Hunkin received no bonus but left with $25.7 million in a retirement special-incentive program as well as $3 million in new share units. And the bank had one investment banker who made about $100 million in one deal. Robert Gratton, president and CEO of Power Financial Corp., which controls Great-West Lifeco, London Life, and Canada Life, has earned more than $173 million in a single year, almost all of it from options. Bernard Isautier, chair and CEO of PetroKazakhstan Inc., the Calgary-based petroleum producer, got $500,000 in salary and options worth $92.6 million in 2004—and a year later, the company was sold to China National Petroleum Corp. for $4.2 billion.

Frankly, all this is crazy. The new emphasis on making executives exceedingly wealthy, often at the expense of investors, is a trend that has gone wildly out of hand. And directors are often to blame for this outrageous state of affairs. Adam Zimmerman, the still-controversial ex-CEO of Noranda Forest Inc., has told financial analysts "it's a real false belief there's only one guy who can run any one of these big companies. There are a lot of good people out there." I'll leave the last comment on this subject—though I'm sure it won't be the *final* word—to John C. Bogle, founder of the Vanguard Group, the world's second-largest mutual-fund organization. *Time* magazine has called him one of the one hundred most powerful and influential people on the planet. So I'm impressed when he remarks on executive compensation, as he did in his book *The Battle for the Soul of Capitalism*:

> Over the past century, a gradual move from owners' capitalism—providing the lion's share of the rewards of investment to those who put up the money and risk their own capital—has culminated in an extreme version of managers' capitalism—providing vastly disproportionate rewards to those whom we have trusted to manage our enterprises in the interest of their owners.

Nobody has ever accused me of being an ardent environmentalist, but any thinking person today has to weigh the consequences of human activity on the natural environment. This is an area where ethical judgments must be made—not only out of concern for the health of the planet but also for the bottom-line reason that a company's economic fortunes might be affected by black marks against its environmental record.

Canada's big energy companies in particular are natural targets for activists, as MacMillan Bloedel was in the forest industry where protesters successfully ran international boycott campaigns against companies that clear-cut. And, at a time when climate change through global warming is front and centre, ethical investment funds often find it tricky to include energy companies in their

portfolios. A typical manager offering "socially responsible investing" is The Ethical Funds Company of Vancouver, which judges a
company on whether it has an effective environmental management system and how committed it is to disclosing environmental
practices, including its record of compliance. Perhaps surprisingly,
the three top holdings in its major Ethical Growth Fund are
Suncor, EnCana, and Petro-Canada. (Suncor was recently named
for the second time as one of three Canadian companies among
sixty major corporations considered to be world-beaters on a climate leadership index. Compiling the rankings is the Carbon
Disclosure Project, a global coalition of institutional investors
with $21 trillion [U.S.] in assets.)

In recent years, I've been involved in three major enterprises—Fording, TransAlta, and EnCana—that are right in the
thick of the debate over three different energy sources. There's no
question that Fording has to deal with the criticism that coal can
be one of the dirtiest fuels around. But clean-coal technology
already exists on a small scale, and the Alberta government
recently announced it will make an investment to investigate how
practical clean coal could be to pursue within the province. Such
technology is among the best and cheapest ways to prevent pol-
lution from carbon dioxide from more than doubling by 2050,
according to the International Energy Agency, a Paris-based consultant to twenty-six oil-importing nations. And a top-drawer
Canadian advisory panel, the National Round Table on the
Environment and the Economy, has recommended converting to
clean-coal technology to produce electricity, stressing the need for
those coal-fired co-generation plants that recycle steam to use for
both power and heat.

The fourteen round-table members are labour representatives,
environmentalists, municipal officials, Aboriginal leaders, and
business and industry heavyweights, including Falconbridge chair
David Kerr, GE Canada CEO Elyse Allan, and Suncor oil-sands
executive VP Steve Williams. They've said the Conservative government is at least heading in the right direction with its
recommendations to help reduce our greenhouse gas emissions by

60 percent by 2050 through current and emerging technologies—without harming the economy. Among other proposals, they urged Ontario to expand its generation of electricity through nuclear power by more than 50 percent during the next four decades. TransCanada has invested in a relaunch of Ontario's Bruce nuclear power plant, the largest of its kind in North America, and CEO Hal Kvisle has long argued that this shouldn't be seen as a scary proposition.

"All of the waste that's ever been generated at Bruce—*ever*—is floating in a swimming pool that is not as big as an Olympic pool," Hal says. "It's submerged under the water, and I have stood right beside that water on-site at Bruce. It's not harmful to anyone. The water absorbs all the radiation that this weak fuel puts out, and you could take all of that spent fuel, drill one deep hole into the Ontario Canadian Shield, and put it all down there." Hal has some surprising allies in making his case for nuclear power. Among them are the coalition government of liberal and social democrats in Finland, where a safe, state-of-the-art nuclear facility is under construction, and Saskatchewan's NDP government, which is trying to attract a large-scale uranium refining plant to the province that would use local yellowcake, the powder that's processed into nuclear fuel. (TransAlta, meanwhile, spent $30.2 million on various environmental projects in 2005 and is hoping to eliminate its greenhouse gas emissions entirely by 2024.)

That round-table panel also called for the capture and underground storage of carbon dioxide emissions from petroleum production, including the oil sands, with a target of 30 percent by 2030 and double that by 2050. EnCana is a global leader in this experimental technology, attracting international visitors to its project near Weyburn, Saskatchewan. Since 2000, more than seven million tonnes of CO_2, the worst of the greenhouse gases, have been injected through drill holes into pipes below farm fields. Another twenty-three million tonnes are expected to be stored there safely forever. The company's experts call it "a big, simple process." And it has a nice financial spin-off: The gas is liquefied before injection and, like a solvent, it frees oil in the underlying rock—which has extended the producing life of EnCana's reservoir in the area by decades.

The global warming issue won't be going away, in Canada or the U.S. For example, Weyerhaeuser—which has forestry operations in both countries—plans to spend $344 million (U.S.) to reduce its greenhouse gases by 40 percent by 2020. Here at home, Peter Lougheed, the prime political architect behind the birth of Syncrude, shocked Albertans a while back when he urged a moratorium on any new oil-sands development until public hearings could reflect citizens' views on the environmental and social costs. That's a stunning suggestion, with all sorts of economic fallout. My real hope is that the climate-change challenges raised by the oil sands and our other energy sources can be met by made-in-Canada ingenuity of the kind that EnCana is pioneering.

DR. GREGORY DANEKE, the University of Calgary's first chair of business ethics, says, "In the aftermath of major corporate scandals, such as Enron and Hollinger, it is high time that ethics and economics become reacquainted. This is especially vital in light of mounting resource and technological challenges, such as global climate change. Such challenges will not only call into question our core values, they will greatly tax our capabilities for coordination and cooperation, which is the real test of our humanity as well as our economic institutions."

Enron and Hollinger weren't mere flashes in the frying pan of bad business. They are symbolic of deeper problems that have become increasingly obvious in the worlds of commerce and industry. Corporate leaders themselves have the primary responsibility to raise the ethical bar in all their dealings. But our educational institutions have a big job to do as well—even though Dr. Daneke acknowledges the general belief that if students haven't absorbed ethics at home, it may be too late to learn them in business schools. Yet he's said, "I firmly believe students *can* learn to think differently in university. In fact, it should be incumbent on them to think differently and more broadly about their own values—the ones they've acquired from their families and the ones they'd like to adapt and change to new environments."

Before coming to Calgary in 2005, he was a professor of technology and resource management at Arizona State University, teaching business ethics and public policy as well as strategy and entrepreneurship, and has been a consultant to multinationals and the U.S. and Canadian governments. His chair at the U of C links ethical issues with specific industry and community issues, especially energy and the environment. It was funded by some pretty responsible corporations in the field—Nexen, Suncor, Shell Canada, TransAlta, and Enbridge—as well as Deloitte & Touche, Fraser Milner Casgrain, and the Institute for Chartered Accountants of Alberta. Dr. Greg Daneke's services are shared between the philosophy department and the Haskayne School of Business.

Yes, the school bears my name. How that came to pass—well, that's another story.

Chapter Fifteen

HOMECOMING
The Case for Private Philanthropy

THERE IT WAS IN THE FALL OF 2005, on the front page of the *Globe and Mail*'s business section, a colour photograph of my rough-hewn mug, and on the inside, an older colour picture of me embracing Lois at the official opening of the Haskayne School of Business at the University of Calgary. The day before, the *Calgary Herald* had quoted me on the front page about Gwyn Morgan's surprising announcement that he was retiring from EnCana. That evening, I'd felt honoured by a gala evening attended by eight hundred—colleagues, friends, family—as I was inducted into the Junior Achievement's Calgary Business Hall of Fame. And that morning, illuminated photos of my larger-than-life face and those of the two other inductees, Harley Hotchkiss and the late Fred Mannix, began to greet people in the busy corridor of Bankers Hall, where I have my office in the heart of downtown.

So I sure didn't need the publicity of the column in the *Globe* that talked about my philanthropic contributions. But I was grateful that the columnist did go on to discuss a pet thesis of mine: the vital need for more of us who've done well in our business careers to volunteer our time and pragmatic experience as well as our money to not-for-profit organizations. To act as individuals—not just through the companies that employ us or through the ones we own. To give back—but wisely. I knew the late Francis Winspear, another Alberta-bred accountant who was president of more companies than me—nineteen of them—was a pro bono director of the University of Alberta's School of Commerce, founding president of the Edmonton United Appeal, and a co-founder of the Edmonton Symphony and the Edmonton Opera. He once said something that rings true with me today: "Giving money requires even more prescience, more imagination, more executive skill, than making it." You have to consider carefully where you devote your energy as well as donate your cash. Education is my main philanthropy of choice, and the U of C has been high on my list of involvements.

My most absorbing relationship with the university began in Toronto one day in early 1990. I was back east as head of Interhome Energy—working feverishly with Price Waterhouse to mount a defence against the Reichmann brothers' attempt to take control of our company—when I learned the name of the new chairman of the University of Calgary: Richard Francis Haskayne. I'd received a forwarded fax of a press release from Alberta's advanced education minister announcing that Robert Wilson's successor as chair of the board of governors was me.

To my great surprise.

The last contact I'd had with the university was with Murray Fraser, the relatively new president and a kind and ethical human being. He'd taken me to lunch one day late the previous year and said, "Dick, I really need you. Bob is at the end of his term, and your name has been submitted as chairman, and we're having trouble finding the right person."

"Jeez, Murray, I'm dealing with the Reichmanns right now. I don't understand university governance. I don't know what the hell your senate does, or the difference between the general faculties council and the board of governors."

"I just want to convince you that it's the right thing to do," he replied.

Important as I knew the U of C loomed in the city and the province, I was not convinced the chairmanship of this very public institution was any role for me. I'd been actively engaged with the university as president of Home Oil during the 1980s when we held meetings in our fancy dining room to raise funds for what's now Scurfield Hall in the original business school. That, for the time being, was as far as I wanted to be involved. And now this.

I was mad as hell. I didn't even know who the minister of advanced education was (it turned out to be John Gogo, with whom I was to have a positive relationship in the years ahead). Premier Don Getty, the retired oilman and Edmonton Eskimos quarterback whom I knew well, was as embarrassed as I was about the premature announcement. But because my name had been made public, it appeared to be too late to do anything about the screw-up.

As it turned out, my six years in the job were some of the most satisfying of my career. Unlike corporate boards, which meet behind carefully closed doors, half of the university's sessions were wide open to anyone, including the press—which I sometimes forgot about in the heat of discussion. Some of the governors, among all the business, academic, and community types you'd expect, were even students. I once got into a debate with Nick Devlin, the student-council president on the board, about the number of local people the overcrowded U of C was turning away. Politely but firmly, he was pushing for the government to provide more money to reduce the waiting list, which was probably topping a thousand then. No other governors were responding, but, a little atypically as a chairman, I did: "Listen, I don't know how you can say they're not going to get an education. There's a big university up the road that has been around longer than us, and they seem to have room there. Some of the rest of us attended there years ago, and it's not all bad."

Nick argued that students were already having trouble earning enough money to stay in Calgary, much less to attend the University of Alberta in Edmonton. During a break in our meeting, reporters crowded around as he said, "When we're dealing with the board, we deal with people who have made it and are successful and are a little bit removed from the difficulties of life as a student.... I don't think any of the board members have eaten Kraft Dinner in a long time." Although I apologized to my fellow governors for challenging Nick, his quote made the papers the next day.

At the end of that year, we had a dinner at the president's house where I handed out plaques to retiring members. One of them was this little bugger, Nick, who walked up with a brown paper bag in hand and, after receiving his plaque, asked for the floor. He made a speech about how we'd had our debate and I'd gotten flak for it in the media, and so he wanted to give me a memento in return. Out of the bag, he pulled a trophy made of a Kraft Dinner carton with the wording, "The Kraft for Best Board Chair/Dick Haskayne/In appreciation of your Leadership and Friendship (In case of cutbacks, open box)." I still have the trophy and cherish it—and Nick, who later received the Order of the University of Calgary and became a crown prosecutor with the federal Department of Justice in Toronto.

The board faced more serious problems during my tenure. Shortly after I became chairman, some governors threatened to resign over a provincial government proposal that would have let the advanced education minister veto any changes in the university's program of study. (Ultimately, the province added a qualifying phrase: "without derogating from the general powers of a board...to manage and control a university.") A year later, I was incensed when a controversial professor accused several departments of not pulling their weight in scholarly research and claimed that the university's leadership lacked integrity and credibility. As well as defending Murray Fraser and his people, I responded with a practical businessman's approach: "This university is here to do a hell of a lot more than just research." And in my final year at the helm, I was warning of a fiscal crisis as the board approved a bare-bones budget—the toughest in the U of C's history—that spurred faculty to warn of job action if no pay raises were forthcoming.

The most poignant personal situation I had to deal with on the board was the resignation of my boyhood friend Vern Hoff. Because he'd been a schoolteacher, farmer, municipal councillor, and active volunteer in Gleichen, I recommended him as a governor because of his rural perspective and his general wisdom. He was serving well on a board with nine other non-academic members, including Charlie Fischer of Nexen and corporate lawyer

Brian Felesky. But Vern was on the personnel committee when it considered the issue of extending benefits to partners in same-sex relationships. He was old school through and through, a rock-ribbed conservative and a strong Christian, and though the issue didn't offend my morality, it did his. Our full board voted in favour of extending the benefits. After wrestling with his conscience for six weeks, Vern resigned just one year into his term. I regretted his leaving.

Operating a university is a big business—ours was the fourth-largest employer in town—so I tried to run the board like a public company's, confining the debate to the issues without being autocratic about it. Fortunately, I had the counsel of Murray Fraser and a superb board secretary named Rhonda Williams, a leader in corporate governance in Canada (who jabbed me in the ribs when I was being too outspoken in front of the press). And some great colleagues, including Ann McCaig, who was a long-term governor before becoming chancellor in 1995. The wife of the late Trimac Corp. founder, Bud McCaig, was born in Tisdale, Saskatchewan, the daughter of an implement and car dealer and a Russian-immigrant mother who worked as a maid before struggling to become a nurse.

Ann, a former Miss Saskatchewan Roughrider, earned a bachelor of education. She is as smart as she is beautiful—serving as a director of Suncor Energy and a trustee of the Killam scholarships for students and professors and convincing others to also invest time and money in causes such as helping sick kids and addicted teenagers. We have a mutual-admiration society based in part on our shared rural roots but mostly on our similar way of viewing the world. In a speech she made a couple of years ago to The Canadian Club about volunteerism, she said, "Dick will often refer to himself as 'the butcher's son from Gleichen.' It's because he has never forgotten where he came from." And nor has wonderful Ann. I was thrilled when, in the same speech, she mentioned the influence my folks had on me: "Dick has never forgotten the values and principles that were instilled in him by his parents. They made sacrifices and worked hard to take care of their family while at the same time they cared about others around them."

While Lee was ill, the minister of education pressed me to stay on as board chair, which I did for another three-year term because it was at least something I could do close to home. We'd had a $40-million fundraising campaign in my first term, ably headed by Ann and former chancellor Jim Palmer, but funding continued to be a challenge. And this in wealthy Alberta where only 43 percent of high school students were moving on to post-secondary education—the lowest rate in Canada—and a province that even into the new century would rank second last, after Nova Scotia, in supporting post-secondary education. In 2003, a TD Bank Financial Group report on the Calgary-Edmonton corridor (subtitled "Take Action Now to Ensure Tiger's Roar Doesn't Fade") pointed out that "a long period of government cutbacks" meant that "student debts have skyrocketed" to an average on graduation of $18,000. No wonder some of my corporate friends and I felt compelled to fund scholarships for deserving young people wanting to attend universities and colleges. Fortunately, things have since improved somewhat as an embarrassed provincial government began making advanced education a priority. Not a moment too soon.

One of the benefits of being involved in community and charitable activities is the relationships you develop in those endeavours. A prime instance in my life was my years chairing the university's board. It's a non-paying position, yet I spent as much time on it as any one of the corporate chairs I've held. In retrospect, I felt I made a contribution during a difficult era in its history because of the 25 budget cuts it had to face. But on the plus side for me were the associations that continue to this day—for example, Murray Fraser became one of my best friends, and I'm still close to his wife, Anne, and their sons. My friendship with Ann McCaig continues to be as strong as it ever was when we had the university in common. Another example of the payback from this sort of community involvement is my ongoing role as a trustee with the Alberta Heritage Foundation for Medical Research, where I serve with people of the quality of Harvey Weingarten, the current president of the U of C, and Indira Samarasekera, the distinguished new president of the University of Alberta.

When I retired as chair in 1996, after two three-year terms, my NOVA Chemicals compatriot Ted Newall took over from me and then Brian MacNeill succeeded him. Brian, ex-Enbridge and current chair of Petro-Canada, has nicely summed up the difference between corporate and academic boards: "The problem with a university board is you get so many factions, and they don't always realize what their role is. There are grad students and union reps and teachers who view themselves as just representing their constituencies, and I say, 'Well, remember, if we get sued, we all get sued.'"

BY THIS TIME, I HAD A NEW WIFE and soulmate. In January 1994, I'd still been depressed after Lee's death, had lost twenty pounds, and was having problems with my waterworks. It seemed like a good idea to visit the Scripps Clinic in San Diego for a physical and take along Don Campbell, who was having some heart trouble, and Marlene, who just wanted a checkup. After getting some counsel and a clean bill of health, we stayed down south to play a little golf. And it was there, on the links, that I encountered Lois Heard.

She tells friends now that she knew within three days she was going to marry me someday: "The chemistry was right, the ethics were right, the whole package was perfect for me." All I knew was that she was a poised, pretty woman (a magazine writer has described her as "strikingly beautiful"), athletic, and all of five feet, who was down there to refurbish a house she'd decorated for friends. She was a self-employed professional interior designer in Calgary, and she was single. The confidence I saw in her probably came from the fact that she'd been solo for eighteen years, mostly running her own business as well as raising her five now-adult children. I happened to know her friends the Bennetts, and it was they who'd invited me to golf and dinner with a group of people, including Lois. It turned out she had met Lee and me socially a couple of times, just long enough to say hello. Greeting her now on the golf course, I gave her a big hug. Over dinner, we seemed to click immediately as friends. A Calgary couple asked us to a party the following evening, and then I invited Lois to a restaurant dinner with the Campbells the next night.

Don and I were staying around to attend a golf school. "Will you call me when I get back to Calgary?" I asked Lois as she left to fly home.

"Pardon?" she said, a little shocked. "Why in the heck would I do that? You know my name, my company name. I'm in the phone book."

Lois had just walked in the door of her house when the phone rang. It was me, inquiring whether she'd made it back safely—and if she would be free to go out with me one evening when I returned. Though not a social butterfly, she just happened to be attending a concert with a girlfriend on that date. But she did suggest I could perhaps call her to schedule another night. Which, when I got back, I did. Whatever happened to the written warning I'd given myself after Lee's death to watch my own behaviour and be "CAREFUL and CAUTIOUS"?

Letting my guard down launched a courtship of two years. I was to discover that her background and mine (and even Lee's) had many striking parallels—as well as some significant differences. Her great-grandfather had come from Youghal, the same little medieval village in country Cork, Ireland, as Lee's birth father had. Lois was one of two daughters and a son of Reece and Paula Kenney, both born in the U.S. but raised not far from where I grew up. Reece's father had left Utah to run southern Alberta's enormous McIntyre Ranch (which still operates more than a century later). He then brought the family to Calgary, where he helped found Ranchmen's Gas and Oil and leased cattle ranching land from the CPR in Redland, just northwest of Gleichen. Like my dad, Reece was a butcher, briefly running one of his family's retail shops. And, like me, he later became an accountant, doing the books for the Burns packing plant. After moving to the ranch, he was playing cribbage in a nearby town when he met Paula, the daughter of a lumber company manager from Minnesota. They married in the village of Rockyford, where she was a secretary in the municipal office.

Lois, their middle child, was born the same year as me. She was a tomboy, playing baseball and winning gun competitions but never feeling like a true country girl. "You love to go back to Gleichen," she told me, "but I could not care less if I ever went back to a rural setting. It was a wonderful upbringing, but I never, ever belonged there. There weren't enough books for me, not enough art for me. I went to Drumheller, thirty miles away, once a week for my piano lessons. And I loved school; it was a passion of mine. I just felt so stifled and told my mother I had to go to university. My dad was Victorian, born in the 1800s, and he was saying all I could take there was nursing or teaching. What I did do was major in phys. ed. and minor in English—but my parents never knew that."

Both Lois and I were extroverted, learning-mad country kids determined to get a higher education. In another coincidence, we attended the University of Alberta at the same time—and though never meeting one another there, I knew her best girlfriend and sometimes drove her back home to the town of Rosebud. Lois tells me now that she and I were perfect for one another in our later years but not when we were young—"You probably would have spoiled and ruined my children totally. You're always trying to help."

Instead, Lois met Sandy Heard at university, married him, and then moved to Ontario where he taught at Trinity College School, the independent boys' high school in Port Hope. She put her own teaching on hold while having their first four children: Pam, Janice, Cynthia, and Mark. She then briefly taught at Port Hope Junior High part-time until getting pregnant with Rod. By that time, realizing she wanted a different career, she took psychological testing that confirmed her interest in interior design, which she'd been doing informally for friends for over a dozen years.

Lois didn't practise design professionally until she and her husband moved back to Alberta, where he became headmaster of Strathcona-Tweedsmuir, a country day school in Okotoks. By then, their marriage was shaky, and it ended in 1977 when she moved back to Calgary with her children. Working first for two local designers, she eventually branched out with her own free-lance business, surviving as a single mom and putting the kids through school.

When I met her, Lois was a great-looking grandmother. She wouldn't even introduce me to her family for the first five months, and when I did get to meet nine of the grandkids at a birthday party, she warned me to curb my congenitally cursing tongue. Luckily, the little ones seemed to like me as much as I fell for them, and even though I kept slipping up, they never seemed to notice my casual swearing. And as time went on, I felt a bit like a surrogate father to the grown children and a granddad to their kids, who still come to me for career advice. The Heards would become a branch of my extended family. I formed a special bond with plain-talking Pam, the eldest daughter, even following up on her request to have me show her around the Gleichen of my boyhood.

In the spring of 1995, I asked Lois—Lo, as I was now calling her—to help me buy a suit. As we passed Birks, I directed her into the jewellery store and introduced her to a saleswoman who took us into a back room and presented her with a tray bearing six engagement rings. Lo started to cry and said she'd left her glasses in her purse back at my office. I went to fetch them, leaving her dangling there for half an hour as I kept meeting friends in the mall. When I finally returned, she said, "Dick, that is the most unromantic way to ask me to marry you"—while the saleslady was killing herself laughing.

If my proposal took an accountant's overly practical approach, so did my suggestion for a pre-nuptial agreement. I asked her to meet my financial advisor, Bill Tynkaluk. He left the impression that the marriage contract would be for her protection because I was bringing the major assets to the relationship and Lois wasn't. And she said, "What do you mean, Dick's got all the assets? I have five kids and eleven grandchildren, and he doesn't have any! It's me with the assets—he only has money."

We got married anyway that fall, with her whole family on hand and Don Campbell and my nieces Leslie and Laurie standing up for me. Our so-called honeymoon was a trip to Japan with twenty-two people from MacMillan Bloedel, where I was a director, as the lumber company held a board meeting and visited some of its customers there. Lo was right: We've been ideal partners in our second childhoods, travelling the world, collecting Canadian art, and buying and having her redesign beautiful houses on the brow overlooking Calgary's downtown, on Bearspaw land north of the city, and in Palm Desert.

There've been some sobering stretches in the time we've had together. She contracted cancer and had to have one lung removed by Dr. Gary Gelfand, and only two years later, she underwent a bowel reconstruction. These were scary times for both of us. If courage is grace under pressure, then Lois was the most graceful of patients. She continues to have bouts of coughing and has to pace herself to the best of her ability, conserving her still-astonishing energy. Meanwhile, Lois has always looked after me as much as she could—trying to make sure I eat sensibly and don't press the pedal to the metal too hard—and, in spite of her best efforts, having to take care of me after my bypass surgery.

BEING CHAIRMAN OF THE BOARD of governors was far from being my final link with the University of Calgary. The most public involvement, well after I'd left the position, was the renaming of its Faculty of Management as the Haskayne School of Business in 2002. The dean of the faculty then was David Saunders, the former associate dean of the masters' programs in business at McGill University. He was ambitious for Calgary's business program as well as for himself—he'd later become dean of the much-lauded Queen's School of Business in Kingston—and was looking for ways to turn our faculty into a full-fledged school. One idea came from consultant Peter Ufford, who'd earned a reputation as being a champion fundraiser as external-affairs VP at the University of British Columbia. Naming schools for their benefactors was an increasing trend: The University of Toronto had the Joseph L. Rotman School of Management, Western Ontario had the Richard

Ivey School of Business, and the University of British Columbia was soon to have the Sauder School of Business.

Independent consultant Peter Ufford had confidentially polled several dozen friends of the university in Calgary, me among them, to recommend prospects whose names would carry enough weight and credibility to be associated with a local business school. Of course, there was a catch: The people approached would have to be well fixed enough to make a sizable donation for the privilege of having it named for them.

I told David that I wasn't even comfortable with having the school bear any name, whomever's it was. Look what happened with the Houston Astros' baseball home, the Enron Stadium, or the various auditoriums and galleries christened for the disgraced accounting firm Arthur Andersen—they all had to be renamed.

Despite knowing my doubts about the idea, at some point David told me my own moniker had been suggested as a possibility (apparently one of the two highest-ranked in acceptability). Would I be interested? Well, first of all, I said, I didn't have the kind of money to make a significant enough contribution to the cause. I knew that Joe Rotman, who'd been involved in real estate and resource financing, oil trading and merchant banking, had given the U of T $15 million over fifteen years. I was certainly well off, but he was Wealthy. Besides, since 1996, I'd been awarding ten $4,000 bursaries a year to first-year students at the U of C in honour of my wife Lee (as well as similar awards to those at the University of Alberta in Edmonton and Calgary's Mount Royal College and the Southern Institute of Technology, in Lois's and my name). And I'd recently given the management faculty the major donation that established a $3-million chair in accounting, along with generous support from the Chartered Accountants' Education Foundation. And then they named the chair for me. Enough was enough.

That's when I really got to know the remarkable Dr. Harvey Weingarten, the university's recently appointed president (succeeding my friends Terry White and the late Murray Fraser in the position). Harvey had been a distinguished scholar and researcher in psychology and medicine before becoming provost (academic vice-president) at McMaster University in Hamilton, where he was the chief architect of an ambitious five-year academic plan. With his full beard and unruly thatch of hair, he may have looked like a mad scientist, but the man had damn good insights into the psychology of business people and a gift for both organization and the building of relationships. And he was pragmatic as hell: "Our job is to get the job done," he'd say.

Harvey was soon to discover that, in his own academic realm, Alberta's post-secondary institutions were not producing enough skilled people in the most obvious of fields: "I didn't have to be a rocket scientist to figure out our universities should be the world leaders in energy and environmental research." One of his first clever moves in the new job was to meet with business leaders downtown—the Morgans, MacNeills, O'Briens, and Fischers who make Calgary such a "can-do" town. "These people understand institutional culture and change and the issues of leadership," he recalls. "I learned a ton from those guys." He has since taken to dropping in to my downtown office occasionally just to talk (he likes to seat himself at the round table in the meeting room where he can view a starkly beautiful, snow-white rural scene by the Native artist Allen Sapp).

Early on, he approached Ralph Klein. Harvey's opening salvo was not to bemoan a lack of funds but to ask a man who'd never attended university and wasn't known as an unswerving supporter of post-secondary education, "What can our universities do for the province? What's going well? What can we do that we're not doing?" At that point, observers say, the populist premier unfolded his arms and talked, asked questions, and listened. In a later meeting with him, Harvey and Jack Davis, the CEO of the Calgary Health Region, took the tack that "everything the government has done for the province has brought a level of growth and prosperity that is wonderful—but just understand that we cannot keep up on both the educational and health sides of things."

Harvey Weingarten now brought the same charm and shrewd psychology to bear on both Lois, who was having similar doubts about seeing my surname on a business school, and me. Somehow the idea seemed presumptuous and glory-seeking. But there were a few rationales that convinced us, after all. One was that publicizing the donation might encourage others to make similar gestures. It's a compelling argument, based on research, and one that I would later use to encourage friends and associates to have their generous donations publicly acknowledged. Another reason was that having a name on a business school is good marketing, a form of branding: The public considers the school to be something of a stand-alone entity, strong enough to compete against all those other christened schools fighting to attract the same pool of MBA candidates and top undergraduates. And finally, giving publicly rather than anonymously is usually seen as a sign of confidence in a university's leadership—and Harvey was just about a year into the job and was frankly looking for such support.

So Lois and I capitulated. As for the donation itself, the university and I came up with an innovative solution. Real estate consultants working for the U of C were looking for rural land on which to build a new health-sciences facility to house research animals. The provincial government had agreed to give the university $8 million to replace the existing facility near property I owned along the Bow River in the Bearspaw area just west of Calgary. When the realtors came across my 310 acres, the university suggested I donate them as part of any gift to the business school. We agreed to give 220 acres, which were valued at $8.7 million. At the time, I thought that was too high an amount—but in fact, Peter Ufford assured me that in his experience as a chief fundraiser at UBC, any land gift always appreciated dramatically. Which is what's been happening with this parcel ever since—as I'll explain later.

There was a public ceremony launching the Haskayne Endowment for Achieving Excellence, which would expand the business school's research capabilities by financing professorships, scholarships, bursaries, and capital projects. Not surprisingly, I used the event to talk about the shameful state of business ethics.

The Haskayne School of Business has taken on an independent life of its own ever since, in ads to recruit students and media reports that mention its name in the same breath as the Rotman's and the Ivey's. I've had a few amusing encounters because of the profile my name now has in the wider world. Once, I took some of my grandkids to the Cowboys bar in Ron Mathison's Penny Lane mall and was greeted by a big bouncer, obviously a student in his off-hours, who was wearing a button with the Haskayne School's name. Another time, I was paying for a piece of jewellery with a credit card and the female owner asked, "Are you related to the Haskayne School of Business?" Assured I was, she said someone in her family had been a student there, and she insisted on giving me a discount.

Academically, the school is earning accolades, including its recent ranking as second overall for the social and environmental impact of its BComm and MBA programs in the annual Knight School Ranking sponsored by *Corporate Knights* magazine. The MBA program also placed second in the category of institutional support—which measures such factors as faculty research, new-student orientation, and endowed faculty chairs—and in the relevance of its courses to sustainable education. Not long ago, the school's BComm students, coached by Dr. Bob Schulz and competing against twenty-eight universities, came first in six events at the national Inter-Collegiate Business Competition at Queen's University—extending their winning streak to twenty-eight years. And a team of four undergraduates, filling in for New York University at the last minute, placed third at "the Olympics" of business-case competitions hosted by the Marshall School of Business at the University of Southern California.

When Harvey Weingarten talks about my endowment and others from private philanthropists, he says, "The most important thing the community gets from us is six thousand graduates a year. I feel an incredible obligation to serve our public at the level of quality that they merit. We are living in an extraordinary fast-growing community with very high expectations. And very simply, there is not enough money the government can give us so that we can supply everything the students need. So what do we need? We need some tangible financial help from the community. I have

never asked anyone to put money to things that we were not prepared to put our own into.

"But we need something else. I don't think the public university system is well structured or responsive enough to the
community or to students. And one of the things that philanthropy
does is to move the university much more quickly in directions we
have to go and to set up different structures and programs. I use
the big donors to drive the university forward so that, five years
from now, we are doing things differently."

WHY AM I GOING ON SO LONG about my relationship with the
University of Calgary? Because this real-world, concrete example
out of my own experience might help to underline my message
that all of Canada needs more private philanthropists who contribute not only their money but also their talent and time to
community causes.

There are a lot of like-minded people in my circle of friends.
Charlie Fischer of Nexen, for one. Six-foot-three and sporting a
trademark handlebar mustache, Charlie is a graduate in both
chemical engineering and business administration from the U of C
and a thirty-four-year veteran in the petroleum industry. In 2005,
Maclean's listed his company as one of Canada's one hundred best
employers, and *Alberta Venture* magazine named him the
province's "Business Person of the Year." He was being honoured
in part for the astonishing year Nexen had—to be capped by the
record $2.9 billion in capital spending it planned in 2006 to
develop massive new projects in the oil sands and the North Sea.
But what the business publication also pointed out is his highly
personal commitment to the corporate philosophy of giving back
to the communities in which Nexen operates. It's not just a corporation that's contributing, it's the CEO, on his own time and dime.

Charlie long ago worked for Gerry Maier and me at Hudson's
Bay Oil and Gas and for Gerry and Doc Seaman at Bow Valley
Industries. He still calls on all three of us whenever he needs some
crucial counsel. I don't know if he's complaining or what when he

tells people, as he did the magazine, "Haskayne has probably made me work harder in the community than anybody."

The guy does work hellishly hard outside the office. This father of two daughters was co-chair, with the splendid Ann McCaig, of a $50-million fundraising campaign for the stunning new $253-million Alberta Children's Hospital on the University of Calgary campus—for which he won the Association of Fundraising Professionals' Generosity of Spirit Award. (As a life member of the hospital foundation, I'd dragooned him to serve.) He's been deeply involved with the university itself—on its management advisory council as well as on the board of governors in many roles, from vice-chairman to audit-committee chair. He now sits on the dean's advisory council for the medical faculty. And he's chair of the foundation for the Hull Child and Family Services Foundation and has chaired the organization it supports, a residential and community centre offering intensive and comprehensive treatment for emotionally disturbed kids and their families. In previous years, this volunteer-to-all-causes has also been on the board of the Canadian Olympic Development Authority and the McMahon Stadium Society and has presided over the Calgary Petroleum Club. He's married to Joanne Cuthbertson, the next chancellor of the U of C, where she has been chair of Education Matters, a new public trust for Calgary education, and a supporter and advisor to the education faculty.

Not surprisingly, a couple of years ago, Charlie received the Haskayne School of Business Distinguished Leader Award as well as an honorary degree from the university. The man is a classic example of the old saying that if you want something done, ask a busy person. And he epitomizes another adage, this one from the writer and philosopher Henry David Thoreau: "It is not enough to be busy...the question is: What are we busy about?"

Another mindfully busy fellow is Harley Norman Hotchkiss, the Calgary Flames' co-founder and chair of the NHL's board of governors who oversaw the drama of the players' strike and then the healing as hockey's rules changed for the better. At the same time, Harley has also remained deeply involved in his great charitable work. Over the years, he's headed the Foothills Hospital's board of management and the Alberta Heritage Foundation for Medical Research (endowed from provincial petroleum royalties) and co-chaired the $50-million Partners in Health project to support the city's health services. But his most personal cause is the Hotchkiss Brain Institute, named for Harley and his wife, Becky, who gave $10 million in 2004 and a further $5 million in 2006 to help fund a new centre of excellence in brain research and clinical care on the U of C campus. It's built on the foundation of the Calgary Brain Institute, a collaborative venture between the universities in Calgary and Lethbridge and some community health groups. The institute should benefit all Canadians with leading-edge investigations into the neurosciences and educational programs explaining conditions that affect the brain.

Harley hoped that the family's contribution would also kick-start donations to an even bigger cause: REACH, a $300-million effort in community fundraising. Headed by the Hotchkiss's daughter Brenda Mackie, Calgary Flames president Ken King, and RBC investment banker Bill Sembo, the campaign is now under way by the U of C, the Calgary Health Region, the Calgary Health Trust, and four newer centres: the Brain Institute, the McCaig Alberta Bone and Joint Institute (founded by Bud and Ann McCaig), the Libin Cardiovascular Institute (Alvin and Mona Libin), and the Markin Institute for Public Health (Al Markin). In Harley's case, there was a private reason for supporting such medical research: He has a small brain aneurism that he gets checked every year, and a brother died of an aortic aneurism, conditions that prompted the Hotchkisses to make a significant donation to a neurological unit at Foothills Hospital.

For his contributions to the community, Harley has been given the Woodrow Wilson Award for Corporate Citizenship (the same honour I received from the Woodrow Wilson International Center for Scholars at the Smithsonian Institution) and was named to the Hockey Hall of Fame.

"I've just got a fundamental belief that as you move through life, you have some responsibility to share with others, particularly with those who are not as fortunate as you've been," he says. "And I see what medical research will do. By doing things in the private sector, committing resources and some time and energy, I think we're catalysts for making things happen that maybe wouldn't otherwise. We also bring the understanding that we care, we want to see things better, and are appreciative of the opportunities we've had, particularly in this city, in this province. I feel very strongly about this because there are people I know and respect who don't feel that way. They say, 'Look, why do you want to support health care? That should be all government.'"

Texas billionaire Boone Pickens—a friend of Harley's, who used to do business in Calgary—recently donated $2 million (U.S.) to the Hotchkiss institute for a Centre for Neurological Science and Advanced Technologies. Harley took the opportunity to challenge younger people to get involved in philanthropy: "I believe you should, even when it hurts a bit, commit some time and some resources." And Pickens added, "We've got to start bringing leaders up from the next generation." Dick Wilson, whose own retirement as a VP of EnCana sparked a Dick and Nancy Wilson Fund at the Calgary Foundation, told the media, "Over the last ten years, it seems it's just the same faces actively engaged. Right now, there's a mini army of community leaders, but they're not being replaced one-for-one."

While I know many executives and entrepreneurs in their forties and fifties who *are* engaged—people such as TransAlta's Steve Snyder and the high-profile Murray Edwards—the point needs making time and time again. Steve came from the east and has since chaired the local United Way campaign, the Calgary Zoological Society, and the Calgary Stampede Foundation. "These institutions need business and strategic advice and financial support," he argues. "Calgary is a very involved community. And it was clear to me that you just can't buy your way in by giving a lot of money to get on a board—with many of them you actually have to volunteer."

Meanwhile, family foundations play a prominent role in Calgary, in Canada, and in the world. For example, the Mannix family has funded the low-key Carthy Foundation, launched in

1965, which originally directed its philanthropy to arts and culture, social services, health, environment, and education. At the family's one hundredth anniversary celebration in 1999, they announced a $100-million contribution, half to endow the foundation and the rest for charities across the country. Since then, the Carthy has focused on a new mission to create opportunity with and provide education for young people. The Kahanoff Foundation was established in 1979 from the estate of Calgary oilman Sydney Kahanoff. One of our largest, it has given $60-million-plus in Canada and nearly $50 million in Israel in the areas of health, education, culture, social services, philanthropy, community development, and research. Other families have contributed by setting up funds within the Calgary Foundation—among them, investment manager David Bissett and his wife, Leslie, who donated $8.2 million in 2000 and their friend, oilman J.C. Anderson, who a year later gave the foundation its largest-ever single contribution, $11 million in shares of Anderson Exploration.

In the summer of 2006, four grandchildren of the late Alberta philanthropist Eric Harvie surprised Albertans by endowing the province with 3,246 acres of historic ranchland along the Bow River between Calgary and the town of Cochrane. The government paid $40 million for property that is likely now valued at twice that figure. In the past, their grandfather's generous donations—nearly half a billion dollars' worth in today's values—founded Calgary's Glenbow Museum and funded numerous major community projects, including the Calgary Zoo and the Banff Centre for the Performing Arts. A lawyer and petroleum entrepreneur, he bought the original ranch in the Cochrane area in 1933, and a son, the late Neil Harvie, acquired and expanded it twenty years later with neighbouring land near Calgary. Now it will become the Glenbow Ranch Provincial Park, a stunning sweep of grasslands, wetlands, and large wooded tracts that open up the waterway to the public for day use. As Alberta Community Development Minister Denis Ducharme said, "It is one of the most visually spectacular and environmentally important pieces of land in Alberta—its environmental impact is huge."

Lois and I were delighted to be able to do our part in linking downtown Calgary with what will be a park stretching the fourteen unbroken kilometres beside the Bow to Cochrane. We've sold the city two key parcels of land we owned on the northern riverfront near our Bearspaw property. The ninety-one acres went for $10.3 million—well below market value—half of that as a charitable receipt. It's an ecologically sensitive stretch of native foothills fescue grass, which once lost, could never be grown again. And, in a wonderful feat of urban planning, the city of Calgary has linked this acreage with the new provincial park by buying the 220 adjoining acres we'd already donated to the university. It paid $20 million for the land to establish this new city parkland, linked to urban trails, and the funds will directly benefit the Haskayne School of Business. The whole package of land will be called Haskayne Park.

As well as making donations, Lois and I have become something of a tag team in local charitable circles. We're honorary chairs of a new $40-million capital campaign for Heritage Park, Canada's largest historical village, where actors portray pre-1914 life in western Canada. I've been honorary chair of the Alberta Mentor Foundation for Youth, and she's served on its committees. She's on the Hotchkiss Brain Institute council, and I'm on their policy board as well as the boards of the Bone and Joint Institute and the Heritage Foundation for Medical Research. She has helped raise funds (a chore she hates) for the Calgary Counselling Service and the Cantos Music Foundation, which is dedicated to organ music with a museum, a festival, and concerts throughout the year. And we open our home every year to welcome the first-year students who've earned the bursaries we've endowed—a wonderful time to recharge ourselves with the enthusiasm and idealism of youth.

Lois has her own favourite philanthropies, including AARC—the Alberta Adolescent Recovery Centre for drug and alcohol rehabilitation—and cultural organizations such as opera, ballet, and the symphony. And one day, she surprised me with a phone call: "How's everything? Guess what I just did? I've just given Rosebud Theatre $100,000."

"You did what?"

Rosebud, Alberta, is not far from where she grew up, and today, one of the few things remaining there is the province's only professional rural theatre company and the Rosebud School of the Arts. "A society without the arts," my dear wife says in her defence, "is a crude, almost barbaric society."

Lois also makes the case, as I do, for the sheer necessity of any kind of private philanthropy: "Isn't it a miracle, such a blessing, that we have enough money to do this? But people don't have to give money—they can volunteer, too. There's an onus on society to give as much of your money and time as possible, particularly your time. That's what makes the world go around."

I'VE COME A LONG WAY in telling my story. Now it's time to go back to where it all began—the hamlet of Gleichen—and where I returned a while back on a sweet late-summer day. This time, my visit home was inspired by more than mere nostalgia. I was there to announce a project that, with any luck, might help the local communities a little. The occasion was the Gleichen-Cluny fall fair and the special Homecoming events for Alberta's centennial cele-brations in 2005. I spent this Saturday morning showing off the community to a friend. As we drove down streets punctuated with "For Sale" signs, I pointed out how so much of my past has been erased. Gone are Doc Farquharson's pharmacy and his competitor kitty-corner across the street, the two druggists always vying to stay open later than the other. The pool hall, where Native kids were some of the deadliest shots, is a vacant lot. And there's a trailer parked on the corner where publisher/undertaker George Evans long ago put out the *Gleichen Call* and prepared the dead to be put into the ground.

Some people and places have survived. We stopped in to see an old chum, Peggy Menard, still pretty at seventy-nine and working in the morning sun on her impeccable garden in a pleasant residen-tial neighbourhood. She reminisced about how her mother and brothers had milked the cows that supplied their dairy in the days before my "Dick's Milk" tokens. A short drive away—there are no long drives in Gleichen—the little white clapboard United Church, where Lee and I were married, still stands with its steepled bell tower at the foot of the newly renamed Haskayne Avenue. But during the week, it's now also an outreach school for disadvantaged students from the Siksika Nation.

We headed back towards Highway 1 and the Homecoming grounds. I wanted to make a couple of stops along the way, the first at the small local cemetery. Bob and Bertha Haskaye, the honest butcher and the community caregiver, are buried here beside one another. Looking around the graveyard—here was the headstone of the wife of the Canadian Pacific roadmaster, there was the village blacksmith's—I could have told a story about every one of those people, most of them friends of my mom and dad. Then I drove for a couple of minutes to visit Mike and Sherrie Yule, who'd bought the neighbouring farmhouse where Lee's parents once lived. It had begun life in 1926 as the Salvation Army's Eventide Home for elderly men. I'd acquired it more than four decades ago and, after my in-laws moved out, sold it to the nice young Yules, who raise grain on my surrounding leased land. Mike is boyish-looking and quiet, Sherrie more exuberant. Talking with her hands, she tells the story of how Lois met her eighty-four-year-old mom at a wedding and found out she'd had nine children. "Oh my God," Lois said, "I had five. So you never found out how it happened, either."

The Yules were just a hop, skip, and a jump from the scene of the Homecoming: the Gleichen and District Arena and Curling Club and its Gunners Restaurant, named for the local hockey team. The brilliant blue Alberta sky was painted with clouds as white as exploding milkweed—a great afternoon for a fair. Kids were taking horse-drawn wagon rides and cavorting with farm animals at a petting zoo, homemakers and gardeners displayed their choicest jams and vegetables, cowboys competed at the nearby rodeo, and folks relaxed at the beer garden. I met up by the yellow registration tents with my niece Laurie and my partners, Shauna and Nancy, and their husbands, Murray and Randy. We all mingled with the locals. Walter Hayes, whose dad had dammed up a creek and cut ice in the winter with a big handsaw to cool my father's meat all summer. Cec Crowfoot—the great-grandson of Crowfoot, the Siksika chief who signed the historic Treaty 7 with the British crown in 1877—whose own son Strater has an MBA and is chief of his tribe. Bud McKay, the son of the local hardware-store operator in the '30s, who told me, "I remember your dad in the butcher shop. We'd go in to see you all in the back with a pot-bellied stove, and he'd give me a wiener."

And Vern Hoff, my friend who'd resigned on principle from the University of Calgary board of governors while I was chair-man. Vern was retired now from teaching and farming, but his community involvements included chairing the Homecoming com-mittee. He was behind the idea of christening Sixth Avenue with our family name and honouring me this evening as a favourite son. First, there were a whole lot of others being celebrated. The arena, packed with people, was buzzing as Vern stood at a mike, against a painted backdrop of cowboys rounding up cattle, and said, "I used to be a school teacher, so I expect silence here. A great big Gleichen welcome to all you people who came to be here today. It may not be the same town, but the spirit is the same as when you were here. Communities like ours just don't happen."

Gleichen was paying homage to dozens of old-timers, one of them aged 101, who'd lived eighty or more years in Alberta or forty or more in the hamlet. Men and women "who coached a team, laced up kids' skates... who made squares, sandwiches, and potluck dinners... who worked and supported businesses here... who helped their neighbours in any way." All of them came up to the front, sometimes with help, to receive their Centennial Builders' Awards.

Then it was my turn. I wasn't surprised to find that good old Larry Plante, fellow prankster and hockey player, was introducing me. After doing his schoolboy trick of stumbling as he strode up on stage, Larry was his irreverent self. He brimmed with stories from our past, like the one about how we'd train together by run-ning along the tracks to my dad's slaughterhouse "and then have breakfast at the Haskaynes—bacon and eggs and four pork chops." At the end, he said, "The only thing I wish is that your mom and your dad were here—they'd be very proud."

The community gave me a plaque that read, "You're proud of your roots, and we're proud of you." Going up on stage, I said, "I've faced a lot of audiences, but I've never faced one as critical to live up to—with all my friends here." Choked up, I began with some one-liners: "When I tell people I'm a butcher's son from Gleichen, they say, 'Where the hell is Gleichen?' And I quote my friend Dave Powell, who said, 'It's the only place where the water is stronger than the whisky.'" Getting serious, I said, "I learned as much as I know about business right here in Gleichen."

And then I made the announcement I'd come home to make: Lois and I were launching the Haskayne Gleichen Cluny Bassano Community Fund—$1 million over ten years to support local projects and student awards. I'd been raised in Gleichen, gone to high school in Cluny, and played hockey in Bassano, where my brother Stan had his butcher shop and my niece Laurie is a school librarian. I owed all three places big-time, and now I was trying to repay the debt. Some of the money will go (and has gone) to supporting the community in general: assistance for seniors, health and recreation, the arts, or civic beautification such as restoring the historic water tower at the entrance to town. The rest of the money is financing at least five entrance-award scholarships each year, worth $4,000 apiece, for students from one of the three communities who will be attending a post-secondary institution.

These were the hamlet, village, and town that bred me and taught me about life and business and, most important of all, about ethics. Someday, I hope, some of those students will work for—or even run—ethical Canadian companies and help to transform them into true Northern Tigers.

"It's a small appreciation for what you've done for us," I told my friends that evening. After everybody had lined up for an Albertan beef dinner, a piper and some red-coated Mounties marched into the arena as we all sang "O Canada." And then the bands came on and the dancing began.

INDEX